†

Books by Alvin Schwartz

FOR FAMILIES

Hobbies
Going Camping
The Rainy Day Book
To Be a Father
America's Exciting Cities
How to Fly a Kite, Catch a Fish, Grow a Flower
A Parent's Guide to Children's Play and Recreation

FOR YOUNG PEOPLE

The Unions
University
Old Cities and New Towns
Museum
The People's Choice
The City and Its People
What Do You Think?
The Night Workers

HOBBIES

AN INTRODUCTION TO CRAFTS, COLLECTIONS,
NATURE STUDY AND OTHER LIFE-LONG PURSUITS

BY Alvin Schwartz

DRAWINGS BY BARBARA CARMER SCHWARTZ

SIMON AND SCHUSTER · NEW YORK

AN ACKNOWLEDGMENT

The individuals and organizations listed below shared their knowledge with me and thereby made this book possible. I am grateful to each.

Frank Akstena, Alphaeus H. Albert, Joel E. Arem, Donald Baird, Edward Benfield, Florence Boles, Elizabeth Boyd, Diane L. Brian, Virginia Brizendine, Philip Budine, V. Clain-Stefanelli, James Cornell, John Counts, Howard Cross, Herman M. Darvick, William H. de Neui, Bill Dunkerly, Robert K. Francis, Bruce Gimelson, Rita Goodheart, Arnold E. Grummer, Theodore J. H. Gusten, A. Hogle, Matthew Horvath, Hugh J. Kelly, William M. Klein, Mr. and Mrs. Carl Krotki, Norman Lacey, Winn LePage, H. L. Lingquist, David M. Ludlum, Moe Luff, and William L. Macmillan, Jr.

Also, Patricia Marchiando, Kneeland McNulty, Mr. and Mrs. John Mercer, Jesse Merida, James E. Neeson, Kenneth Negus, Mr. and Mrs. Sam Nocella, Jr., Reidar Norby, Richard Olssen, Lillian Opatashu, Janet Pollak, Donald T. Perdue, Lee Pierson, Felix Pogliano, Jr., Beatrice E. Reeve, Joseph L. Richey, Joseph Rosewater, Mrs. Robert Salkin, Carl Scheele, Michael C. Shannon, Helen Silver, Calvin B. Simmons, T. R. Soderstrom, Mr. and Mrs. Thomas C. Southerland, Jr., Kenneth C. Spengler, Clark Stevens, Carol Stoddard, Michael D. Sullivan, G. S. Switzer, Charles G. Thomas, Peggy Tuttle, M. Vukovich, Jr., Eleanor Wear, Raymond J. Watts, William O. West, Adna G. Wilde, Jr., Lila Wilshire, Robert Zakaluk.

American Craftsmen's Council, American Federation of Mineralogical Societies, American Malacological Union, American Meteorological Society, American Numismatic Association, American Paper Institute, American Radio Relay League, Aquarium Club of America, Arts Workshop of the Newark, N.J., Museum, Chandler & Price Co., Eastman Kodak Co., Edmund Scientific Co., The Edward Orton Jr. Ceramic Foundation, Federal Communications Commission (Amateur Radio Service), Franklin Institute, General Biological Supply House, Charles Hamilton Autographs, Inc., Honeywell, Inc., and the Institute of Paper Chemistry.

Also, International Paper Company, Lord & Burnham, National Audubon Society, National Ceramic Manufacturers Association, National Federation of Stamp Clubs, New Jersey State Museum, Norwood Loom Co., National Oceanic and Atmospheric Administration, Postmark Collectors Club, Postal Slogan, Cancel & Meter Society, Princeton, N.J., Public Library, Princeton University Natural History Museum, Print Council of America, School Products Co., Science Associates, *Scientific American*, and Scott Publications, Inc.

The Smithsonian Institution's Astrophysical Observatory, Museum of Natural History, and Museum of History and Technology; The Stanley Works; United Postal Stationery Society; United States Mint (Philadelphia); United States Post Office (Philatelic Sales Unit); Unitron Instrument Company; U.S. Cancellation Club; Ward's Natural Science Establishment; West Virginia Pulp and Paper Co.

I also am grateful to Julie Houston, who, as this book's editor, helped in many ways, and to my wife, Barbara Carmer Schwartz, who prepared the drawings for this book and made countless other contributions.

ALVIN SCHWARTZ

Princeton, New Jersey

CONTENTS

An Acknowledgment   5

An Introduction   13

part i: CRAFTS

1. Ceramics   17
Types of clay. Digging and preparing natural clay. Basic equipment. A potter's wheel and a kiln. Techniques: wedging, modeling, coil, slab, pinch pot, sculpture. Drying with, without a kiln. Glazes. Firing. Organizations and instruction. Bibliography.

2. Making Paper   26
A simple paper: equipment, methods. Making pulp from rags and vegetable fibers: equipment; preparing pulp; making sheets of paper; adding a watermark, a leaf, a blade of grass. How to find other papermakers. Bibliography.

3. Making Prints   35
Equipment and supplies. Relief prints: transfer prints, stampings, monoprints; cardboard prints; potato prints; linoleum prints; woodcuts. Incised printing: etching, engraving, drypoint; experiments with acetate, plexiglass or clay. Serigraphy: equipment, techniques. Instruction. Bibliography.

4. Printing by Press   46
Establishing a printery. Equipment: presses, type. Setting type. Pulling a proof. Locking up. Ink, paper. Printing techniques. Other amateurs. Bibliography.

7

5. PHOTOGRAPHY 57
Types of cameras. Buying a camera. Camera care. Accessories. Film. Using a camera. Developing and printing pictures: equipment, techniques. Instruction. Organizations. Bibliography.

6. PUPPETRY 73
Hand puppets. Rod puppets. Theaters for hand and rod puppets, including scenery, props, stage lighting, plays, sound effects. Shadow puppets: shadow theaters, related equipment. Marionettes: construction, costumes, controls, storage, theaters. Plays. Bibliography.

7. WEAVING 92
Getting started. Looms and other equipment. Projects. Yarn. Dyeing yarns. Using a loom. Organizations. Sources of supply. Bibliography.

8. WHITTLING AND WOODCARVING 102
Whittling for the fun of it. Knives and other tools: purchasing, sharpening, storage. Lumber: types, sources. Projects, techniques. Bibliography.

9. WOODWORKING 109
A place to work. A workbench. Basic hand tools. Lumber: quality, recommended types, sizes. Projects, plans. Using hand tools. Power tools. Safety. Organizations. Bibliography.

PART II: COLLECTIONS

10. AUTOGRAPHS 125
Signatures, documents, other opportunities for collectors. Terminology. Specialization. Organizations. Dealers and other sources of materials. Values. Pitfalls. Display and storage. Bibliography.

11. COINS 134
Possibilities for collections. Sources of coins and other currency. Determining value. United States currency. Currency of Canada and other

countries. Medieval and ancient coins. Care and storage of specimens. Organizations. Museums. Bibliography.

12. POSTAGE STAMPS   148
Starting a stamp collection. Types of collections. Sources of stamps. Value, condition, other considerations. Storage, care. Bibliography.

13. PRINTS AND REPRODUCTIONS   161
The pleasures of collecting. Reproductions, prints and their sources. Prices. Misrepresentations. Display, storage, care. Exhibits, lectures, clinics. Organizations. Bibliography.

14. OTHER COLLECTIONS   168
Two score other collections to consider.

PART III: NATURE STUDY

15. BIRDS   173
Getting started: field guides, equipment. Where and when to find birds, including techniques of attracting birds. Identifying birds. Counting birds, banding birds, nest research. Organizations. Bibliography.

16. FISHES   183
Creating an environment for fish: equipment, water, plants, setting up a tank. Buying fishes. Feeding. Treating illness. Goldfish. Tropical fish. Other marine life and the use of salt water aquariums. Native fish and amphibians. Organizations. Bibliography.

17. FOSSILS   201
Countless forms of ancient life. Origin of fossils. Types. Getting started: books and equipment. Hunting fossils. Preparing specimens. Storage and display. Bibliography.

18. INSECTS   213
Some misconceptions. Where and when to find insects. Common species: collection and care of live insects; techniques for attracting, killing and mounting specimens. Assisting museums. Organizations. Bibliography.

19. PLANTS   226
The many possibilities for hobbies. Basic equipment. Major organizations. Trees. Wild flowers. Grasses. Non-flowering plants: algae, horsetails, mosses, ferns. Lichens. Molds, mushrooms and other fungi. Collecting techniques, equipment, crafts, advice on storage and display.
Bibliography.

20. ROCKS, MINERALS, AND GEM STONES   250
The possibilities. Getting started: books, museums, clubs. Types of
rocks. Types of minerals. Where to find minerals. Clothing and equipment. Collecting techniques. Cleaning, storage and display. Gem stones:
cabochons, facets, lapidary techniques and equipment. Bibliography.

21. SEA SHELLS   261
An extraordinary diversity. Techniques and equipment for collecting.
Identifying shells. Packing, transporting and cleaning. Exchanging
specimens with other collectors. Buying shells. Storage. Bibliography.

PART IV: SCIENCE AND COMMUNICATION

22. ARCHAEOLOGY   279
The right way and the wrong way to begin. Finding sites. Excavating a
site. Organizations. Bibliography.

23. ASTRONOMY   285
Getting started: books, organizations. Equipment: using a telescope.
Exploring the sky, including solar observation and photography. Mak-
ing a telescope. Opportunities for research. Bibliography.

24. RADIO   295
A brief history of "ham" radio. Basic equipment. Obtaining a license.
Additional equipment. Organizations. On the air, including opportuni-
ties for public service. Bibliography.

25. WEATHER FORECASTING   305
Predicting weather through periodic observations: clouds, temperature,
humidity, barometric pressure, wind direction and speed, including the

equipment needed. Measured precipitation. Using weather maps. Preparing a forecast. Organizations. Bibliography.

ILLUSTRATION CREDITS   325

INDEX   327

An Introduction

THIS BOOK is concerned with activities for after hours. They include crafts, collections, nature study, and other pursuits to which one might devote a lifetime. Each chapter provides an introduction to one such interest. It describes the opportunities and the equipment needed, tries to explain the techniques involved, and suggests what to read next.

What I personally find most pleasant about long-term activities is the exploration involved. I know of nothing more enjoyable than the opportunity to examine at my leisure what fascinates me and to acquire new knowledge and new skills with only pleasure as my goal. It also is satisfying to introduce members of my family and other friends to my interests. Frequently I make converts or acquire helping hands or at least gain a patient audience.

This book took far longer to write than most I have written. One of the problems was the extensive subject matter. But the other had nothing to do with work. Some activities so ensnared me it simply was difficult to leave them behind and move on to other things. I hope your experience is the same.

PART I

CRAFTS

CERAMICS
MAKING PAPER
MAKING PRINTS
PRINTING BY PRESS
PHOTOGRAPHY
PUPPETRY
WEAVING
WHITTLING AND WOODCARVING
WOODWORKING

1·CERAMICS

THERE IS NO MATERIAL more pleasant to handle or more relaxing to work with or more responsive to the human will than clay. Using only your fingers, you may quickly turn a shapeless lump into a pot, a dish, a mask, a head, a figure, or whatever else you wish. If you are not satisfied with the result, you need only mash it up and try again. When at last you create something that pleases you, it may endure for thousands of years just as the work of ancient potters before you.

At the outset all you need is a place to work—such as a basement, a garage, or a kitchen—a quantity of clay, some modeling tools, a few decorative materials, and access to a kiln. Later you will want to learn to use a potter's wheel, since much of the fun of ceramics lies in what can be achieved with this device. Still later you may wish to buy a wheel and also a kiln.

CLAY

There are several types available. The following are *not* recommended: oil-based clay, which does not harden; clay formulas which harden with relative permanence without being fired in a kiln; clay formulas which harden after being heated in a kitchen oven. These products do not model as well as ordinary clay and are not as satisfying to handle. Nor do they achieve the strength and permanence of a clay that is fired at a high temperature in a kiln.

It is far better to work with natural clay. You might start with a simple red terra cotta variety which would yield earthenware, a porous product which does not vitrify, or become glasslike, in the kiln. It is easy to model and easy to fire. Even if you know nothing about using

17

a kiln, there is little you can do wrong in preparing terra cotta for firing. Another possibility is a clay called Jordan buff, which also is easy to work with. It is fired at somewhat higher temperatures than terra cotta and produces a non-porous "stoneware" which does vitrify. In its moist state Jordan buff is gray, but in firing it turns pink. There also are many specialized clays which differ in their strength, their adaptability for various purposes, the temperature at which they must be fired, and the color they yield, all of which is usually indicated on the package. Advanced potters frequently use special blends, mixing various clays according to established formulas or their own formulas to achieve particular results.

Clay is available either in moist form or in a powder which is mixed with water. Usually it is sold in 5-, 25-, 50-, and 100-pound quantities. Start with the five-pound packages of moist clay, which will cost about a dollar each in an art supply or hobby shop. If you find you enjoy pottering, buy a fifty-pound can. This may seem like a lot of clay, but it will be gone before you know it. After you have established your interest, it will pay to buy clay in even larger quantities. If you live in or near a large city, it would also be wise to do some shopping, since large ceramic supply houses often have lower prices than local outlets. Determining whether there are commercial refractories nearby that sell clay also might be worthwhile. Those that do often make it available for far less than retail cost.

You also can obtain clay free if you are willing to dig it yourself or if you can convince your family to help you. Your state geologist or state geological survey can tell you where clay beds are to be found. The best time to do your digging is in the summer or the early fall, when the clay is likely to be dry. Otherwise, digging clay is a messy process; moreover, wet clay is heavy. You will need a shovel and a garbage can. Fill about two-thirds of the can with clay. When you get home, break the clay into small pieces with a pounding tool. Then fill the can with water, stir vigorously, and let the contents stand until the clay dissolves, which should take several days.

At this point you will need another garbage can. Place a piece of window screening on top of the can and pour the dissolved clay through the screen. This will remove sticks, stones, and other impurities. Then let the clay settle to the bottom, which will take several days more, and pour off the water that accumulates on top. Repeat the process until no more water appears.

18

At this point the clay still will be too moist to use. To draw off the excess moisture you will need a number of plaster bats, which are described in the section on equipment. Place a bat on your work table. Then place a large gob of clay on top of it. Cover the clay with a second bat, then add more clay and another bat. If this is not enough clay for your short-term needs, add still another layer. In a few days the bats will have absorbed the excess moisture and the clay will be ready for use. Meanwhile, keep what is left in the garbage can tightly covered. Frequently clay obtained in this way is terra cotta. In any case, it will be necessary to test small slabs in a kiln to determine at what temperatures the clay can be fired.

To keep moist clay from drying out, it should be stored in a plastic bag which is closed by twisting the top and securing it with a wire. For large quantities use heavy duty garbage bags or the plastic bags peat moss comes in. The bag, in turn, should be kept in a container with a tightly fitting cover.

Grog. This is clay which has been fired and crushed. When grog is added to moist clay, it makes it easier to fire without breaking. Some clays already have grog mixed in. If not, it is easy enough to add some. Purchase a fifty-mesh grog and add a quantity equal to about 6 per cent of the clay.

Slip. This is a clay with the consistency of pancake batter. It serves as a kind of glue with which to fasten two or more elements of a work. Advanced amateurs also use slip in making casts from molds. Slip can be purchased inexpensively, but it is a simple matter to mix up whatever is needed. Take a quantity of ordinary clay and add water until the right consistency is obtained.

BASIC EQUIPMENT

Table. A large table covered with oilcloth.

Wedging Wire. A cutting device which is used to determine whether clay is free of air bubbles and therefore suitable for firing. To make a wedging wire, attach dowel sticks, as handles, to the ends of a one-foot length of 18-gauge wire.

Plaster Bat. This is a base on which clay is placed when it is to be modeled. It helps keep the clay moist and permits the work to be turned and carried without undue handling. Initially you will need three or four bats. To make them, mix a batch of plaster of Paris and pour it into aluminum pie pans or one-inch-deep paper plates.

Modeling Wheel. This is a kind of lazy Susan which makes it easier for the potter to turn his work in modeling or decorating.

Tools. The most important tools are your hands. In modeling, it also is useful to have a sharp knife, a pointed stick like an orange stick, a tongue depressor, and a small block of wood. For trimming excess clay, use one of the many wire loops that are available commercially. For cutting designs in the surface of a work, use an orange stick or a small finishing nail mounted in a dowel stick. For imprinting existing designs, use a fork, a comb, a bottle cap, or any other object that yields an interesting pattern. For finishing a surface, purchase an elephant ear sponge or use a rubber dish scraper.

ADVANCED EQUIPMENT

Potter's Wheel. This ancient device is used to "throw" perfectly concentric pots, vases, bowls, and similar objects. Initially you will use a wheel in an instructor's studio. Should you decide to install one at home, a new wheel would cost $150. A secondhand model, if one were available, would, of course, come to somewhat less. Some potters build their own wheels. A plan for a simple kick wheel is included in *Step-by-Step Ceramics,* a book listed in the Bibliography.

Kiln. Electric kilns also are expensive. A small test kiln can be purchased for under $50, but the firing space is only a six-inch cube. A kiln with an 11-inch firing space is available for around $100. But the larger sizes, which are a far better investment, require an expenditure of several hundred dollars. The more costly kilns include pyrometers, which register the interior temperature. With the less expensive models the potter relies for this information on peepholes and pyrometric cones which wilt at particular temperatures.

To reduce the expense of a kiln, some potters build their own. A plan for the construction of an electric kiln is available from the Engineering Station, University of New Hampshire, Durham, N.H. 03824. Ask for Publication #1, "Making an Electric Kiln." It also is practical to construct a less costly gas-, oil-, or wood-burning kiln. The possibilities are considered in *Ceramics: A Potter's Handbook,* a handbook listed in the Bibliography. At this writing plans also were available from Rosemary and Denise Wren, Potters Croft, Oakshade Road, Oxshott, Surrey, England.

20

TECHNIQUES

It would be useful at the outset to spend some time literally playing with a ball of clay to regain a sense of the possibilities. Then experiment with each of the methods described later in this section, creating pots, vases, heads, figures, anything that strikes your fancy.

Wedging. Before modeling an object that is to be fired in a kiln, it is important to "wedge" the clay. The process removes any air bubbles and thereby reduces the possibility of an explosion or simple breakage. Wedging also eliminates lumps from clay, which makes it easier to work with. Start with a quantity the size of a grapefruit and cut it in half with a wedging wire. Then knead each portion as you would bread dough. Some potters beat the clay with their hands as hard as they can, which not only removes bubbles but makes them feel better. Early potters also relied on their bare feet in wedging. They would fill a tub with clay, then walk in it. Five or ten minutes of wedging usually is all that is necessary. To test for bubbles, cut the clay in half once more with the wedging wire.

Modeling. It is best to start with the coil or slab technique, then experiment with the pinch pot method and with sculpture. In all cases avoid creating objects with sharp angles, since they are inclined to crack. Also avoid elongated protrusions, since they tend to fall off. If it becomes necessary to interrupt your work, carefully cover it with a plastic bag so that it doesn't dry out.

Coil Method. This involves rolling or squeezing a quantity of clay into snakelike lengths the thickness of a sausage. To make a small bowl, fashion several such "snakes." Then form the base of the bowl. With a rolling pin, roll out a quantity of clay to a depth of about a quarter inch and cut the shape needed with a knife. Place a coil of clay on top of the base, positioning it so that it follows the edge. To assure that the coil stays put, pinch it to the base. Place a second coil on top of the first and pinch these together. Add as many additional coils as needed in the same way.

To obtain a bowl with a pinched waist or a flaring lip, diminish, then increase the length of the coils. For a bowl with a large bulge, increase, then slowly decrease their size. If a pot begins to sag as you work, wait until the coils in place are partially dry before you add more. This should take about an hour. A head also can be constructed of coils, but close the top with a thin circular disc of clay. After 24 hours of drying,

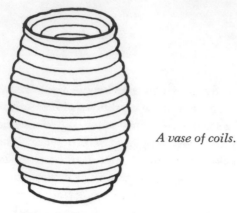

A vase of coils.

an object becomes "leather" hard. It is relatively firm, yet pliable enough so that changes still can be made. This is the time, if desired, to remove coil marks, improve the shape, and add designs to the surface through incising or stamping.

Slab Method. This technique involves fashioning objects with slabs of clay. To create slabs, you will need a rolling pin and two pieces of narrow wood a quarter-inch thick and at least a foot long. Yardsticks are good for this purpose. The width of the slabs needed will determine how far apart you place the sticks. Arrange the clay between the sticks, position the rolling pin on the sticks, and roll the clay into a slab. To give a slab an interesting texture, roll the clay on a piece of burlap.

Slabs can be used in many ways. A single slab might serve as a tile or might be cut into small pieces for a mosaic. It also might be used to make a cylindrical pot or vase. In this case, prepare a base and encircle it with a slab. Next join the ends of the slab and fasten the slab to the

Preparing a slab.

Creating a vase from a slab.

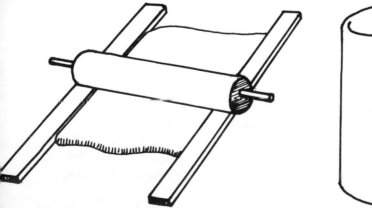

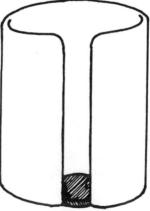

base. In joining two pieces, place a quantity of slip on the surfaces involved and press together. For added strength insert a thin coil of mushy clay inside where the sides meet the base. Some potters wrap slabs around cans or boxes to achieve particular shapes. Slabs also are used in creating masks, heads, and bird houses. Bear in mind that the slab and coil methods can be used in combination.

Pinch Pot Method. Place a small ball of clay in the palm of your hand. Push both thumbs into the center, then revolve the ball slowly, shaping it with a pinching motion as it turns. The effect is that of a rudimentary potter's wheel; the result is a vessel that might take the form of a bowl, a dish, or a small pitcher or might even serve as the basis of a head.

Sculpture. Heads and simple figures may be carved from a solid block of clay with small knives, trimming wires, and other cutting devices. When the piece is leather hard, use a spoon or knife to scoop out enough clay from the interior so that the walls are not more than an inch thick. Otherwise the sculpture will neither dry nor fire properly. It may be possible to remove the necessary clay by cutting a hole in the bottom or at the back. If not, cut the object in half, scoop it out, and rejoin the two pieces with slip. Be certain, however, to leave a small hole that opens into the cavity.

DRYING

There are three stages in the drying process. The first, as already noted, is leather hardness. After a day and a night of drying, the clay is firm but still moist enough to be worked. When the object fully dries, after a week or two, it is called "greenware." Although greenware seems durable, it tends to be brittle and should be handled with care. It only achieves permanence in the third stage, when it is fired and becomes "bisque."

DECORATING

All objects may be incised with patterns when they are leather hard. The process is called "sgraffito." Otherwise, the nature of the decoration depends on whether greenware or bisque is involved.

Greenware. If you do not have access to a kiln, your work may be decorated in one of several ways. It can be painted with a thick tempera paint, then waxed. It also can be covered with a non-firing glaze which resembles a glaze Indians used to decorate their sun-dried earthenware. Or it can be covered with an engobe, a colored clay with the consistency of slip, and then incised so that the original surface shows through. When the engobe is dry, it also may be waxed.

Bisque. Although bisqueware can be decorated as above, it is far more desirable to apply a glaze to such work. A glaze is a mineral coating that yields a waterproof glasslike surface. When it is fired, it literally becomes part of the clay. There are clear glazes which permit an incised design or an engobe to show through. There also are many richly colored and textured glazes. A number may be applied to green-ware and fired at the same time it is converted to bisque. Others can only be used with bisque, with the result that an object must undergo two separate firings. The latter method actually is preferable, since bisque is considerably stronger than greenware and a glaze can be applied with less chance of breaking the object in handling. A beginner might either pour glaze over his work or immerse it in a pot of glaze. An experienced potter also uses a paintbrush (a ¾-inch short-haired water-color brush) or a spray gun.

The kind of glaze one uses also depends on the kind of clay involved and the temperature at which it fires. The glazes a beginner uses ordinarily will fire at a relatively low temperature. These include a number made with a base of poisonous white lead. Of course, bowls and plates treated with such glazes should not be used with food. In addition, the potter should be certain he has no scratches the glaze can penetrate and that he doesn't put his fingers in his mouth after handling such a product.

FIRING

Since a kiln is costly, many amateur potters rely on those at schools, community art centers, and craftsmen's guilds, where for a set fee they may have their work fired. When this chapter was written, the firing costs in my area were a half-cent per cubic inch for bisque and one cent per cubic inch for glaze work. Varying with the kiln, a firing may take from four to twenty-four hours.

ORGANIZATIONS AND INSTRUCTION

It would be worthwhile to join a craftsmen's guild. Such an organization would enable you to meet experienced ceramicists and also might be a source of instruction, a kiln, and supplies at lower than standard prices. If you do not know of a guild nearby, write for information to the American Craftsmen's Council, 29 West 53rd Street, New York, N.Y. 10019. Instruction also is provided by museums, adult schools, and private art studios. Should you decide to become a professional potter, one of the best places to train is Alfred University, Alfred, New York, which is known throughout the world for its ceramics program.

BIBLIOGRAPHY

Books

Ceramic Sculpture, John B. Kenny, Greenberg Publishers, New York, 1963.

Ceramics: A Potter's Handbook, Glenn G. Nelson, Holt, Rinehart & Winston, New York, 1966.

Clay and Glaze for the Potter, Daniel Rhodes, Greenberg Publishers, New York, 1957.

How to Make Ceramic and Clay Sculpture, Julia Hamlin Duncan, Museum of Modern Art, New York, 1960.

Pottery: Materials and Techniques, David Green, Faber & Faber, London, 1967.

Step-by-Step Ceramics, Jolyon Jofsted, Golden Press, New York, 1967.

Stoneware and Porcelain: The Art of High-Fire Pottery, Chilton Co., Philadelphia, 1959.

Periodicals

Ceramics Monthly, 4175 N. High Street, Columbus, Ohio 43214.

Craft Horizons, 44 W. 53rd Street, New York, N.Y. 10019.

2·MAKING PAPER

THE INGREDIENTS depend on what is available. Rags, sawdust, and the fibers contained in rope are useful to the papermaker. So are facial tissues and old newspaper. So are grasses, stalks, corn husks, reeds, and the leaves of the cattail, the iris, and the cabbage. But these are only some of the possibilities.

The process is not at all complicated, but it takes time. The ingredients are thoroughly shredded, and to the extent possible beaten to a pulp. Then they are cooked, soaked, and strained and the resulting fibers are added to a tub of water. A screen is then immersed in the water. When it is removed it bears a bed of pulp. When the pulp is carefully pressed and dried, it becomes a sheet of paper. Both the color and the texture of such paper often are lovely. Moreover, the paper is a delight to use, particularly in making prints and in printing material that has been set in type.*

The first paper is said to have been created some 2000 years ago by a Chinese eunuch who used hemp and wood bark as his raw material. From that point until early in the nineteenth century all paper was made by hand. Since then machines have done this work. There are still papermakers who work by hand, but these largely are amateurs who create paper for the pleasure involved and are few in number. Yet making paper in this way requires no skill and no investment to speak of—only patience and care—and it offers unique rewards.

A SIMPLE PAPER

The paper described in this section is unusual in that it takes but a short time to create. The result is not beautiful, but I include it

* See Making Prints, Chapter 3; Printing by Press, Chapter 4.

here so that you may get a sense of what is involved in making paper. This paper can be made on a kitchen table covered with newsprint. With most papermaking, however, you will need a basement or a garage or some other place with a cement floor where you can slop water and also store things for long periods. For this project you will need the following equipment and materials:

A pan, baking dish, or tub 8″ × 10″ or larger and at least two inches deep
A piece of aluminum or copper screen with a fine mesh; the screen should be at least 6″ × 8″ but small enough to be placed inside the container
A large bowl
An egg beater
An iron
Thirty sheets of facial tissue, but not the "wet strength" variety; an equal amount of newsprint may be substituted
Two ounces of liquid starch
One dozen blotters 8″ × 10″

To make the necessary pulp, half fill the bowl with warm water. Then tear the tissues into small pieces and add them to the bowl. Beat with the egg beater until the tissues have dissolved. Then mix in the starch, which will strengthen the paper and make it practical to write on. Pour the pulp into the pan or baking dish; add enough water to fill the container almost to the brim, and stir vigorously. The mixture should yield four to six sheets of paper.

To make a sheet, slide the screen below the surface of the water; then with both hands lift the screen straight up. It will emerge carrying a bed of pulp. Gently shake the screen to distribute the pulp evenly. When the surface water has drained, cover the pulp with a blotter. Then carefully turn over, so that the screen is on top and the blotter is on the bottom, and place on the table. Replace the screen with a second blotter. To extract the remaining water gently apply the rolling pin. Then replace the wet blotters with dry ones and press with a warm iron until the paper inside is dry.*

The remainder of this chapter deals with more ambitious projects.

* A "machine" which produces paper of this type with still less effort was available at publication. For information write Tom Starke, 919 Taft Street, Kaukana, Wisconsin 54130.

EQUIPMENT

Most of what you need is available in the kitchen or a home workshop or can be made easily.

Cutting and Beating Instruments. This equipment is used to break down the raw materials prior to cooking. In working with cotton fibers from rags, you will need a scissors, an egg beater, and a potato masher or a mortar and pestle. With vegetable matter you will need a short piece of pipe or two-by-four and a hammer or a wooden mallet.

Kettle. For cooking, soaking, and mixing, use a soup kettle or a large pot. It should be rustproof and resistant to corrosives such as caustic acid that may be needed to speed disintegration of vegetable matter. Stainless steel is excellent; enamelware should be avoided. Once you commit a pot to papermaking, no longer use it for food.

Rubber Gloves. For use with corrosives.

Strainers. For use in washing flesh from vegetable fibers.

Storage Containers for Pulp. Use plastic, glass, or stoneware.

Dipping Vat. This is the container from which beds of pulp are removed. The vat should be several inches deep and large enough to accommodate the largest screen you will be using. (See below.) The possibilities include a large photographic developing tray, a rectangular dishpan, or a washtub. A homemade plywood box waterproofed with spar varnish also would serve.

Screens. As noted earlier, a copper or an aluminum screen is needed to lift the pulp from the vat. With heavy vegetable pulp, use a one-eighth-inch hardware mesh. If the pulp is thinner, as with rag pulp, use a finer mesh. The size of the sheet you want determines the size of the screen you need. Some papermakers prefer an 8″ × 12″ sheet. Others work with sheets as large as 16″ × 20″, using them as is or cutting them in half. However, large screens are heavy when laden with pulp and are hard to lift.

A screen is called a mold. It may be used as is or for convenience tacked to one side of a thin frame. In that event, the pulp is collected on the flat side. The sheet that results may be somewhat irregular, but it can be trimmed if desired. To obtain a sheet which does not require trimming, some papermakers use a deckle with a mold.

A deckle consists of two frames which have been fastened together, one on top of the other. The bottom frame has a slightly smaller opening than the one on top. This produces a ledge inside on which the

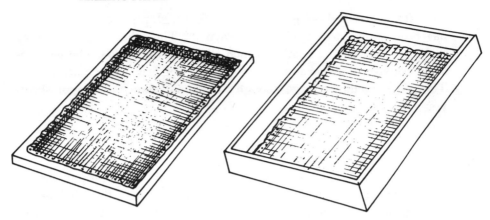

A dipping screen or mold.   *A mold inside a deckle.*

screen, or mold, is placed. When a mold and deckle are removed from a dipping vat, the pulp is shaped by the top part of the deckle. The experienced papermaker will have several screens or mold-deckle combinations in different sizes.

Drying Sheets. Sheets of highly absorbent material are needed to dry the beds of pulp. Blotters, heavy muslin, chipboard, and felt are practical. However, felt is a better investment for the prolific papermaker because it can be reused more often than the others. Each drying sheet should be at least two inches larger on all sides than the largest piece of paper you will be making. At the outset you probably will need a dozen drying sheets.

Drying Equipment. In making a small quantity of paper, use a rolling pin to remove the water from the pulp and an iron to dry and compress the fibers, as described earlier. If you have a photographic print dryer, use it first, then use the iron. When you become more experienced and make paper in larger quantities, you will need a drying press. A screw-type mounting press would be ideal, but it is likely to cost $100 or more. However, a homemade press will work almost as

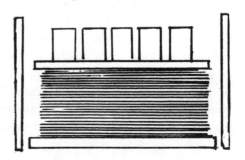

A drying press.

29

well. It consists of three parts. One is a foot-high plywood frame which has been waterproofed with spar varnish. The other two are heavy waterproofed "drying boards" which fit inside the frame. The paper is dried between the boards under the weight of bricks or cinder blocks. The press should be large enough to accommodate the largest sheets you will be making.

PREPARING PULP

After you have prepared the facial tissue pulp described earlier, experiment with rag pulp and rag paper. Then during the growing season create pulp and paper from plants, which you will find yield the most intriguing results of all.

Pulp from Rags. Use clean cotton or linen rags. However, do not use cloth made from synthetic fiber, since it is virtually impossible to break down. Sort the rags into piles by color and make separate quantities of pulp from each. By doing so, you will be able to produce paper in various colors and also achieve special effects.

Cut the rags into tiny squares with a scissors. Then cut each square into fluff by starting at one corner and making exceedingly fine diagonal cuts. If the fabric is loosely woven, you also might pull it apart thread by thread and cut the threads into the smallest pieces you can. You will need at least a cup of snippets to make the effort worthwhile. When you finally have your cupful, place it in a kettle, cover with several inches of water, bring to a boil, and simmer for at least an hour. Then pour the fibers and water into a bowl and beat vigorously with an egg beater until you become bored. At that point carefully drain off the water and place the fibers on a sturdy table. Either beat them for several minutes with a mallet or hammer or grind them with a mortar and pestle. Then store with water in a covered container. Label the container with the color and origin of the pulp and the date it was made, and wait at least a week before using it.

Pulp from Vegetable Fibers. Some 200 years ago a German clergyman named Jacob Christian Schaeffer made paper from reeds, cabbage, cattails, corn husks, potato plants, burdock, and the leaves of such trees as the walnut, tulip, and horse chestnut. In modern times an English artist named John Mason has made paper from nettles, cow parsley, flax, grasses, stalks, and the leaves of the iris and the gladiolus. He describes his experiences and methods, and includes samples of the results, in a wonderful book which is listed in the Bibliography.

To make a useful quantity of vegetable pulp, gather at least a sack of mature plants. If you are a patient sort, soak the plants for several weeks until they begin to rot. This will make it far easier to separate the fibers you need from the flesh. Place your plants in a plastic garbage pail filled with water or heap them on a cement floor or on the ground. Then keep them wet and bide your time.

If you are anxious to move ahead, skip this step and start with cutting and cooking. Cut the stems and the most fibrous leaves into small pieces. Place this material in a large kettle, fill the kettle with water, and add a small quantity of caustic soda. Bring the water to a boil and simmer for several hours until the ingredients are quite soft. Then pour them into a colander or a strainer and wash with a vigorous stream of water until the pulpy flesh is separated from the fibers. Store the fibers in a container with water for several days. Then drain and beat, using the implements listed in the section Equipment. When the fibers cannot be reduced further, wash them again, store in water, and label.

MAKING PAPER

This step should take place in a basement or a garage, as discussed earlier. Be certain to protect your work table with newspaper or oilcloth. Arrange the dipping vat and screen, or mold and deckle, at one end of the table. Also have your drying sheets and other drying equipment available.

Preparing the Vat. Fill the dipping vat with water. Add two cups of pulp solution and stir with a stick. Also consider the following additions.

Size: This is a substance which strengthens the paper and reduces its absorbency, making it easier to use with ink. Vegetable pulp contains a natural size, but other types of pulp will benefit from this ingredient. Some experienced papermakers prefer to do their sizing several weeks after the paper is made, but adding size to the pulp itself produces satisfactory results. For a soft pliable paper, add a quarter-cup of starch to the solution, plus an additional tablespoon with every second sheet. Powdered clear gelatin also yields a pliable paper. Add half the envelope initially, then small portions as you progress. For a hard finish use a powdered glue size available at art supply shops and carefully follow the directions.

31

Sawdust: A handful of sawdust will coarsen the texture of paper made from rag pulp. Add to the dipping vat and stir.

Dyes: The color of handmade paper is attractive in its own right, but interesting effects can be achieved by adding a small quantity of a dye to a vatful of pulp. By vigorously stirring the dye so that it is well distributed, you change the color of the pulp and the paper. By gently swirling the dye a few times, you produce a paper with a swirled or streaked effect. Commercial dyes, natural dyes derived from plants, and the colored rag pulp described earlier all may be used this way.

Making Sheets: The first step.

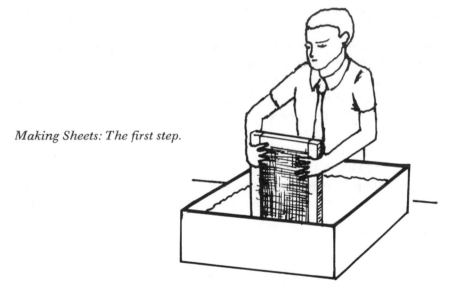

Making the Sheets. Position yourself in front of the dipping vat and stir the solution. Then hold the screen, or the mold and deckle, in a vertical position at arm's length at the far end of the vat. Insert it into the water to a depth of about three inches. Then move it toward you into a horizontal position. Next lift the screen straight up and out of the solution. So that the pulp it carries is evenly distributed, shake the screen gently in each direction. Then hold it over the vat until the water it carries runs off and dry the paper as discussed below. Each time you remove a bed of pulp, stir in another cupful. Also add more size as necessary.

Drying the Paper. If you are making a small quantity of paper, follow the drying directions in the section A Simple Paper. With a dozen sheets it is more efficient to use the drying press described in the section Equipment. Position it on the floor on top of a half-inch pile of newspapers. Place one of its two drying boards inside at the bottom. After the water has drained from a screen, cover the pulp with a drying sheet. Then turn the sheet, the pulp, and the screen over so that the sheet is underneath and the screen on top. Place the entire unit on the board, press down lightly, and remove the screen.* Repeat with each subsequent bed of pulp. When the last bed is in position, replace the screen with a drying sheet, cover with a drying board, and add cement blocks or bricks as weights. Leave the paper in the press for several days. Then spread the sheets on a table to dry separately. If the paper is wrinkled or curled after it dries, cover with a drying sheet and press with a warm iron. All new paper should be stored for two weeks before it is used.

DECORATIVE DEVICES

Watermarks: To create a watermark for your paper, form a design with a thin copper or brass wire. Then sew the design to the side of the screen that receives the pulp.

Double Sheets: Objects from nature such as blades of grass, flower petals, and even butterflies and other insects traditionally have been used to decorate handmade paper. The decoration is placed on a fresh bed of pulp. A thin second layer of pulp is then placed over the first layer. With the decoration between them, the two become one.

OTHER PAPERMAKERS

There is no organization of amateur papermakers. Should you wish to meet other papermakers to exchange ideas, you might learn of such persons through a variety of sources: an art supply dealer; an art teacher; the curator of prints at an art museum; a local crafts council; or a club of book collectors, bookbinders, or amateur printers.

* Since a bed of pulp tends to adhere to a drying sheet, some papermakers simply peel them off the screen together and stack them, but this is a tricky process.

33

BIBLIOGRAPHY

Papermaking as an Artistic Craft, John Mason, Twelve by Eight Press, 2 Ratcliffe Road, Leicester, England, 1963. A volume every paper-maker should own.

Papermaking: The History and Technique of an Ancient Craft, Dard Hunter, Alfred S. Knopf, New York, 1957.

3·MAKING PRINTS

THERE HAVE BEEN professional printmakers in our midst for hundreds of years. They work today essentially as they did in the past. First they create an original design which they transfer to wood, metal, stone, or some other substance. Then they ink the design and print a limited number of copies individually by hand.* However, one need not be an artist to create simple designs and make prints of his own. There are only three requirements: a knowledge of basic techniques, the appropriate equipment and materials, and a desire to experiment. The options are broad. They include potato and linoleum printing, woodcuts, drypoint, "paper lithography," and silk screen printing, or serigraphy, with each yielding a unique result.

A PLACE TO WORK

Use the corner of a kitchen, a spare room, or a well-lighted basement. If you have a back yard or a secluded porch or terrace, work there on nice days. If other persons in your family become interested in printmaking, it would be pleasant to have a family studio in your home where anyone could work when he wished.

EQUIPMENT AND SUPPLIES

A Large Table.
Printing Equipment. You will need a piece of heavy glass 8" × 10" on which to spread ink, a small brayer, or roller, with which

* Collecting the work of professional printmakers is discussed in Chapter 13.

to distribute it, and a rubbing implement such as the bowl of a wooden spoon for transferring an inked design to paper. The techniques described in this chapter do not require a press, although advanced methods such as etching and lithography do make use of such equipment.

Printing Ink. Ask for block printing ink. There are two types: water-based and oil-based. Both come in a variety of colors. However, cleaning up is easier with the water-based type. Special inks are available for printing on textiles.

Paper. For making proofs, use blank newsprint; for finished prints, use a 30-pound charcoal drawing paper, a good quality colored stock, or a handmade paper. See Chapter 2, Making Paper.

A particular printing technique may also require other equipment and materials. This is discussed separately.

A NOTE ON TRANSFERRING DESIGNS

Many of the printmaking methods described below require transferring a design to a printing plate. Ordinarily the following procedure is used. Sketch the design on tracing paper and darken the back of the paper with a soft lead pencil. Then place the paper on the printing surface and redraw the lines, exerting pressure as you do so. In the process you transfer the design to the plate.

Bear in mind, however, that the design that appears in a print is the *reverse* of the design on the printing plate. In most cases this makes no difference. It must be taken into account, however, when letters and numerals are involved or when part of a design must face in a particular direction. If a print is to be correct in such situations, the design on the plate must be the *reverse* of the original design. To reverse a design, draw it on tracing paper with soft lead; then place it face down on the printing surface and retrace it from the back.

RELIEF PRINTS

The prints described in this section are made from a raised surface. Typically the printmaker cuts away portions of a plate, such as a linoleum block or a wood block, and prints with the design that remains. However, other approaches also are discussed below.

Transfer Prints. Many persons had their first experience in printmaking as children when they covered a coin with a piece of paper, then rubbed the paper with a crayon or pencil. What emerged was a print, or a rubbing, of one side of the coin. Using a grease pencil, some adults make rubbings of the intricate patterns carved in low relief on old tombstones. As with the coin, the result is a transfer print of someone else's work.

Using a related technique, transfer prints can be made of a leaf, a feather, a fern, a weed, a blade of grass, or other objects from nature that are relatively flat. The imprint they yield can be used as a wall decoration or to enliven a fabric or the end papers of a book or some other object. Heavily grained wood, fabrics such as burlap, and other materials with a pronounced texture also lend themselves to transfer printing. Although decorative in their own right, they are particularly useful as backgrounds on which other designs are printed. In his print "Rowing Alone," for example, the artist Paul Shaub used the texture of wood planks to create the effect of water. He then overprinted an oarsman on the "water."

To make a transfer print, cover the table with newspaper, place a small quantity of ink on the glass, and spread it with the brayer. Position the object to be printed next to the glass and, using the brayer, cover it with ink. Then move it to a clean place on the table, cover it with a sheet of printing paper, and rub with the bowl of a wooden spoon. Move the spoon slowly with a rotating motion, exerting considerable pressure. Then carefully remove the print and set it aside to dry. To make a second print, reink the object.

Stampings: The stamp might be a button, a thread spool, a tongue depressor, a drinking straw, a wood block, or whatever else intrigues you. Apply ink or thick tempera paint to one end or one side of the object and press carefully against the printing paper. To produce an overall design arrange the impressions side by side or at random or overlap them. If you use ink for stamping, roll it out on the glass, then transfer it with a dauber or chamois or some other lint-free material. If you use paint, apply it with a brush.

Monoprints: This transfer technique requires a piece of acetate or a sheet of glass (other than the one used for ink). Create a design on the surface, using oil-based ink, a tusche crayon, or thick paint. Then cover with a sheet of paper, burnish with a spoon, and carefully remove your print.

Cardboard Prints. Using this type of relief print, it is necessary to build up a surface rather than cut it away, as with the techniques discussed later. Make several versions of the design you wish to print and work with the one that pleases you most. Transfer the design to a sheet of heavy cardboard and cut it out with a scissors or a sharp knife. Then mount it on another cardboard which will serve as the printing plate. If the design has separate elements, transfer the overall plan to the plate so that the pieces can be positioned accurately. If the design should not be reversed in printing, turn it over before pasting it in place. To obtain a print, ink only the raised portions, cover with a sheet of paper, and burnish.

It also is possible to prepare cardboard prints with an ink-impregnated paper. This eliminates the need for inking, but the other steps are the same. The paper yields up to two dozen prints.

A potato carved in relief.

Potato Prints. There is a tendency to regard the potato print with disdain, but this attitude is rooted in a misconception. In its proper context the potato print may match the results obtained with more formal techniques. Shortly before this was written, a shop in New York was asking $1100 for a pair of hand-woven draperies decorated with potato prints created by a celebrated printmaker. Since it is soft and expendable, the potato also is a useful aid in learning how to cut a design in relief.

Select a large firm potato. Keeping its size in mind, sketch a simple, bold design. Then cut the potato in half along its length or width and transfer your design to the printing surface. With a sharp paring knife cut away the sections not needed, making your cuts at a depth of about an eighth of an inch. Use the printing method described in the section Stampings.

Linoleum Prints. Linoleum printing is a more complicated process, but it is in no sense difficult.

38

Materials, Equipment: Purchase your first linoleum blocks in an art supply store. If you find you enjoy working with linoleum, buy it by the sheet at a floor covering outlet. The best type for your purposes is battleship linoleum. For under $10 you can obtain enough for two dozen blocks. Cut off what you need each time with a sharp knife, then glue it to a piece of wood planking the same size. You also will need cutting tools. To start, purchase a linoleum-woodblock kit. For a relatively small sum you acquire a number of gouges and a selection of knife blades with a universal handle. As you gain experience, you might acquire, or make, specialized tools. There are in all over 1500 kinds.

Techniques: The best size block for a beginner is $4'' \times 6''$. It provides sufficient space in which to work, yet not so much that it is intimidating. As you acquire experience, slowly increase the size of the block you use. Many amateurs work with a block $8'' \times 10''$ in size, but even one $12'' \times 18''$ is practical if you plan carefully.

In many respects the process is similar to that of making potato prints. You create your design, transfer it to the plate, and remove the unwanted surface. In cutting, hold the block steady with one hand positioned just behind the tool. Since linoleum is soft, it yields readily, but keep your cuts shallow. When you have removed all the linoleum you feel is necessary, ink the printing surface with the brayer, cover with a sheet of newsprint, burnish, and pull a proof. If you find there is still more to be done, wash off the ink and resume cutting.

The linoleum block yields clear bold illustrations which make lovely wall decorations. It also is useful in producing bookplates and birthday cards. Some beginners also envisage making Christmas cards with linoleum, but this is a tedious process unless only a few are needed. Serigraphy, which is discussed later, is better suited for this purpose.

Wood Cuts. Because wood is harder to cut, it is a more difficult medium than linoleum. The prints that result also are different. They seem softer, more subtle, more muted.

Materials, Equipment: Use spruce planking or any other wood that is clear of knots and has a consistent grain. Later you might turn to woods with more irregularities, such as pine, since the grain and the knots may be useful in a particular work, but such wood is also more of a challenge. Professional printmakers frequently use $3/8''$ plywood, which is warp-resistant, a desirable feature when you are making a large number of prints and must wash your plate periodically. Blocks of wood for printmaking also are available in art supply stores, but purchasing a plank at a time is cheaper. Use the same kind of tools as described in the discussion of linoleum prints. If you own a set of cabinet chisels, also use these.

Techniques: The cutting process is similar to that used with linoleum. However, it is necessary to cut *with* the grain. It also is important to be careful. The possibility of having a tool slip is greater with wood than with linoleum, since it is more resistant. Remove the unneeded surface at a depth of an eighth of an inch. Then pull off a proof and make any changes necessary.

INCISED PRINTING

This method is the reverse of relief printing. Instead of cutting away material, the printmaker cuts the design in the body of the plate. As a result, he prints from below the surface rather than from the surface itself. Incised printing also is called "intaglio," which in Italian means "to carve in." Intaglio prints differ markedly from others in their delicacy and great detail.

One of the basic techniques of producing an intaglio print is etching. It involves the use of wax-covered metal plates and an acid bath which bites into the plates where the design has been incised in the wax. It is a costly procedure that is best explored under the guidance of a teacher at an art studio. The other basic intaglio methods are engraving and drypoint, both of which involve incising copper or zinc plates with sharp instruments. Since such plates are several dollars each, these media also tend to be costly for one who is just exploring. As a substitute, however, a beginner might experiment with acetate or plexiglass or even a quantity of clay. With such materials he can learn a good deal about incising.

Materials, Equipment: Purchase acetate sheets at an art supply shop or a stationer's, then mount them on wooden blocks. Plexiglass may be bought in sheets from a supplier or possibly obtained free in scrap form from a sign maker. Consult the classified section of your telephone directory under "Plastics," "Plexiglass," or "Signs." Terra cotta and Jordan buff are the two kinds of clay that can be used in incising. You also will need a number of scratching tools. These may be purchased in various weights. However, your dentist's old scrapers also will serve and so will nails of various sizes if you sharpen their points.

For convenience, these might be set in dowel sticks. The intaglio process also requires a paper which has enough resiliency to pick up from below the surface of the plate. For proofs, use a soft, pulpy bogus paper. For finished prints, use a 60- to 80-pound printmaking paper. One of the best is Fabriano.

Techniques: Cut the design no deeper than one-sixteenth of an inch, or you will have difficulty in printing. Then ink the plate thoroughly, making certain there is sufficient ink in all the grooves, and wipe the surface clean. Cover the plate with a slightly moist sheet of paper and burnish with as much pressure as you can manage. To properly moisten the paper, soak it for fifteen minutes, then dry between blotters for a half-hour or until it feels barely moist when pressed against your cheek. A paper that is too damp or dry will be difficult to work with.

OIL AND WATER

The oldest of the techniques in this category is lithography, which provides the printmaker with great freedom of expression. However, it is impractical for the amateur in that it requires an expensive limestone or a specially prepared sheet of zinc as a plate and an elaborate press for printing. In recent years a satisfactory substitute called paper lithography has been developed. As with traditional lithography, the design is applied to the plate with an oil-based tusche crayon. Instead of stone or metal, however, one uses a special sensitized paper as a plate and a simple press.

Serigraphy. This is another term for silk screen printing. "Serigraphy" is used to describe the process when it has an artistic orientation. "Silk screen" is used when signs, posters, and other commercial efforts are involved. Under either name it is a relatively easy method for a beginner to master. The technique resembles that used in stenciling. In that process the letters or designs to be printed are cut or punched out of a piece of heavy stencil paper. The stencil is then positioned on a surface and the paint is brushed across its face, with the result that whatever is represented by the open spaces is imprinted.

In serigraphy a silk or nylon screen held rigid by a wooden frame serves as the stencil paper. Such screens contain thousands of tiny holes. With the method described later, those holes are blocked except for those that represent the design. When the screen has been prepared, it is positioned over a sheet of paper and paint is forced through the open

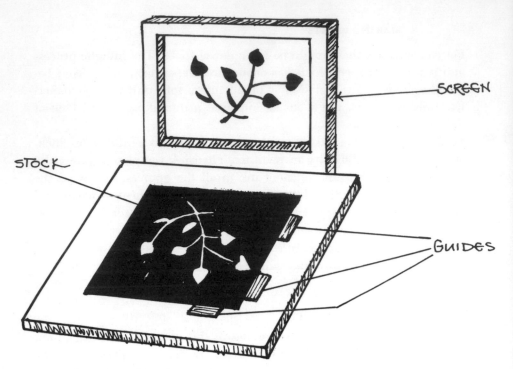

SCREEN

STOCK

GUIDES

Printing with a silk screen.

holes with a squeegee, a rubber strip attached to a handle. When the printing surface receives the paint, the design is imprinted.

Serigraphy is particularly effective in printing bold designs with solid blocks of ink. It also is relatively easy with this process to use two or more colors. The prints have a frank, direct quality, but unlike those produced by other methods they lack tonal contrast. Along with paper, serigraphy is used to print on wood, metal, fabric, leather, glass, and porcelain. It also offers an efficient means of producing Christmas cards; hundreds can be printed in a matter of hours.

Equipment, Materials: Basic equipment and materials may be purchased in a kit from an art supply store or hobby shop or separately from a silk screen supplier.

Screens: At the outset acquire a 16″ × 20″ screen with medium fine screening and a plywood base. Ultimately you would want a number of screens in different sizes and counts (fibers per inch). Once you become familiar with screen construction, it is not difficult to make your own.

Feeding Guides: When installed on the board below the screen, these assure that each print appears in the same position on every sheet of paper. You will need a set of three guides.

Squeegees: A separate squeegee is needed for each screen with a different width. It should be one inch narrower than the inside dimension. Squeegees cost between 20 and 30 cents an inch.

Paint: Use finger paint or a paint especially prepared for silk screen work. When surfaces other than paper are involved, consult your dealer.

Other equipment and materials required vary with the method and are described below.

TWO TECHNIQUES

Film: This approach involves cutting a design in plastic film, much as one would cut out a paper stencil, and positioning the film on a screen, closing all the holes except those occupied by the design. A removing liquid is used to clean the screen.

Tusche and Glue: After the design is prepared, it is placed under the screen as a guide. The printmaker then outlines the design on the screen with an oil-based tusche pencil and fills in the area with a tusche crayon or tusche liquid. Next the entire screen is coated with a water soluble glue which blocks the holes. The screen is then washed with turpentine which removes the oil-based tusche but not the water-based glue. When it is no longer needed, the glue is removed with water.

If two or more colors are to be applied, each is printed separately with a different screen which contains only the portion of the design involved. To make certain that the colors line up properly, use feeding guides.

INSTRUCTION

Courses in various aspects of printmaking frequently are offered in adult education programs at local high schools, YMCA's, and community art centers. More comprehensive programs may be available at an art workshop conducted at a museum or at a private studio.

43

BIBLIOGRAPHY
General

Introductory Surface Printing, Peter Green, Watson-Guptill Publications, New York, 1968.

New Creative Printmaking, Peter Green, Watson-Guptill Publications, New York, 1965.

Printmaking, Dona Z. Melisch, Pitman Publishing Corp., New York, 1965.

Printmaking Without a Press, J. Erickson, A. Sproul, Van Nostrand-Reinhold Co., New York, 1966.'

Prints and How to Make Them, Arthur Saidenberg, Harper & Row, New York, 1964.

Simple Printmaking, Cyril Kent, Mary Cooper, Watson-Guptill Publications, New York, 1967.

Linoleum, Woodblock Printing

Block Printing on Textiles, Janet Erickson, Watson-Guptill Publications, New York, 1961.

Craft of Woodcuts, John R. Biggs, Sterling Publishing Co., New York, 1963.

Frontiers of Printmaking: New Aspects of Relief Printing, Michael Rothenstein, Van Nostrand-Reinhold Co., New York, 1966.

Linocuts and Woodcuts, Michael Rothenstein, Watson-Guptill Publications, New York, 1964.

Linoleum Block Printing, Francis J. Kafka, Taplinger Publishing Co., New York, 1958.

Lithography

Craft of Etching and Lithography, Gerald Woods, Charles T. Branford Co., Boston, 1966.

Creative Lithography and How to Do It, Grant Arnold, Peter Smith, Magnolia, Mass.

Serigraphy

Complete Book of Silk Screen Printing Production, J. I. Biegeleisen, Dover Publications, New York, 1963.

Serigraphy: Silk Screen Techniques for the Artist, Prentice-Hall, Inc., Englewood Cliffs, N.J., 1965.

Silk Screen, Bernard Steffan, Pitman Publishing Corp., New York, 1963.

Silk Screen as a Fine Art, Clifford Chieffo, Van Nostrand-Reinhold Co., New York, 1967.

Books for Young People

Paper, Ink, and Roller, Harvey Weiss, Young Scott Books, New York, 1958.

Printing for Fun, Koshi Ota, McDowell, Obolensky, New York, 1960.

4·PRINTING BY PRESS

MANY OF THE EARLIEST PRINTERS in this country were among the finest craftsmen of their day. Some also were pamphleteers who used their presses to disseminate their ideas on current issues. All set type by hand, then printed their work on a hand-operated press. With a few notable exceptions, there no longer are commercial printers who work by hand or who use their presses as a means of personal expression. The development of automatic presses and machine-set type and the pressure of mass markets has seen to that.

Today it is the amateur printer who operates a small personal press. Although he may issue an occasional broadside, more frequently his output includes beautifully fashioned bookplates, letterheads, greeting cards, and similar material for his personal use. If he is ambitious he even may turn out pamphlets or short books which he sets and prints a page at a time, then painstakingly stitches and binds. Ordinarily the design, the paper, and the craftsmanship are of the highest quality, but none of what he prints is for sale.

If you are fascinated by words, type, and design, establishing a modest printery in a spare room or in the corner of a basement or a garage is an exciting way to express your individuality.

ESTABLISHING A PRINTERY

Amateur printing is one of the more expensive hobbies. Over the first few years one easily could spend $750 or more on a press, type, and other basic equipment, as much as it might cost to set up a complete woodworking shop or a radio shack. After this investment, however, a printer's expenses should be quite small unless, in a rash moment, he decides to purchase a still larger, fancier press. If he should lose interest in printing, his investment still will have value, for the market in secondhand equipment is a lively one.

Since the investment required is large, it is wise to approach amateur printing with caution. One important step is finding someone with whom to discuss the possibilities. The best person would be another amateur, but if there are none to be found, talk with a local job printer or with a teacher of printing or graphic arts at a vocational school. Another useful step would be to spend part of a day in a print shop looking and learning. If you should decide to go ahead, a printer or a teacher might serve as a good source of information on where to make purchases and how to handle any technical problems that arise.

Once you have acquired your equipment, you will want to give your press a name. Like all amateur printers, you also will be entitled to print a business card that carries the name of your press and your name followed by "propr.," a traditional printing term for proprietor.

ACQUIRING EQUIPMENT

You will need a press, a table with a hard surface, a composing stick, a chase in which to place type you have set, equipment to lock it in position, ink, paper, cleaning solvents, and also other equipment and supplies. A good deal of this may be purchased secondhand from a supplier or even a printer. In fact, a printer may even give you outdated equipment just to get rid of it. Since job printing is not the most stable business, auctions and classified ads may be still other sources of what you need.

PRESSES

Most amateurs use a letterpress, which is so named because it presses letters against a printing surface. Generally they work with a platen press which produces an impression by bringing together two flat surfaces: one with the type or illustration to be printed, the other with the paper. Such presses vary in size, speed, accessories, quality, and price. They are available in full-size floor models and also in bench models which must be fastened to a table. The bench model, or pilot-type press, is a wise choice for a beginner. The smallest practical size is a 5″ × 8″ press, which can be purchased new for under $200. The

47

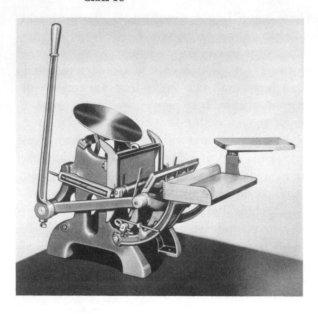

[ABOVE] *A pilot press.* [BELOW] *An 8″×12″ floor model.*

dimensions represent the maximum size of the block of type it can print. They also are the inside dimensions of the chase that holds the type. A more flexible size is 6½″ × 10″; such presses cost at publication from $300 to $500. Of course, secondhand models may be available for considerably less. Many amateurs eventually acquire a used full-size press. At times an amateur also may add an antique press to his shop, which can be a fascinating possession. However, these are scarce and very costly.

TYPE

There are thousands of type faces from which to choose, but initially select only one. Base your decision both on its appearance and its utility. It should be handsome and also flexible enough to meet all your immediate needs. In making a choice, bear in mind that every face has a distinctive personality. Even those that resemble others have many more differences than similarities. One of the basic differences relates to serifs, the tiny cross strokes sometimes found at the top and bottom of a letter. If a type face has serifs, it is known as a serif type; if it lacks serifs, it is called a sans-serif face.

Baskerville, Bodoni, Caslon, and Garamond are four faces that might be excellent choices. The type samples below give a sense of their appearance.

This is Baskerville.
This is Bodoni.
This is Caslon
This is Garamond.

All four were designed originally for use on a hand press. They also possess an elegance and delicacy many contemporary faces lack. Before reaching a decision, study several type catalogs to determine what is available. Also familiarize yourself with how type is used in books, magazines, pamphlets, and other media.

Almost every face is available in a standard vertical form called Roman type. Most also are available in lighter, darker, thicker, and thinner versions, and in italic. Each type face also comes in a wide range of sizes so that it may be used both in text and in headings. The sizes are based on a system of measurement in which one inch equals 72

49

points. A face typically is available in the following point sizes: 6, 8, 10, 12, 14, 18, 24, 30, 36, 48, 60, and 72. Some faces also have smaller and larger sizes.

For your first purchase acquire a type face in Roman in three sizes: 10-point, 14-point, for the text or body, and 18-point for headings and display. This would involve purchasing three sets, or fonts, of type, each of which would include about a thousand characters. A next step would be to acquire these sizes in italic. For a press larger than 6½" × 10" display type ranging up to a 36-point size would be appropriate.

Hand-set type is cast from lead, either in a foundry or with a monotype machine. The type cast in a foundry is far more durable and, as a result, a better buy. The cost for the smaller sizes can be estimated quite roughly at a dollar a point; for 30-point type and larger it would be less.

Since a font consists of over a thousand characters, it also is necessary to acquire one or more type cases. A new case costs about $9. To save money some amateurs use one case for two or three different sizes of type. Ideally type cases should be stored in a cabinet, but these also are quite expensive. If you are diligent, however, you may find a job printer who would be delighted to have you take his old wooden cases and cabinets in return for removing them. If you can't find a philanthropist, however, or even secondhand equipment, store the cases you have on a table with a cover to keep off the dust until you are able to acquire a cabinet.

Rules and Ornaments. Rules are lines used to divide columns, frame blocks of type, and serve other decorative purposes. Ornaments are small figures and designs also used to enhance the appearance of a project. You will need a quantity of each.

Word and Letter Spaces. The basic unit is called an "em quad," a square equivalent to the point size of the type involved. Thus, a 12-point em quad is a 12-point square. Wider spaces include a 2-em quad, which is twice as wide as the basic unit, and a 3-em quad, which is three times as wide, and various "em" spaces which are narrower still. The narrowest unit is a hair space, which looks the way it sounds. Ordinarily, a 3-em space is used to separate words and sentences. Letter spacing is used to fill out a line. It also is used to improve the appearance of a line through adjustments in spacing between words or letters.

Line Spaces. These are thin strips of metal called leads (and pronounced leds). A beginner will need a selection of 1-point, 2-point, and 6-point leads. The 6-point variety also are known as slugs. Between lines, use either a 1-point or a 2-point lead. The slugs serve various purposes. The best way to buy leads is in long strips sold by the pound. Initially purchase five pounds of 6-point leads and a five-pound mixture of the 1-point and 2-point kind. You also will need a slug clipper to cut the leads to the appropriate length.

Line Gauge. This is a kind of ruler used to measure the length and depth of lines of type. The units of measure are points and picas. As noted earlier, there are 72 points to an inch. There also are 12 points to the pica and 6 picas to the inch.

DESIGNING PROJECTS

Every effort should, of course, be designed in advance. What you arrive at depends on the project, its needs, and your conception of what is attractive. As a general rule, the goal should be as much open space, or white space, as possible.

SETTING TYPE

To set type by hand you will need an eight-inch composing stick. Adjust the stick to accept the length of the line required. Then hold the stick in your left hand; even if you are left-handed, you should learn to use it this way. Place a lead the length of the line in the bottom of the stick; then set the first line. The type is set upside down from left to right. If the nick on the base of a piece of type faces up when you add it to the line, it is facing in the right direction. Position your thumb so that when you add a character it holds it in place.

Setting type by hand.

One of the maddening experiences in learning to set type is making certain that each line occupies precisely the space available. At times a line will fit perfectly just as it is set. More often it will be necessary to increase or decrease the space between words and letters. The challenge is adjusting the spacing evenly so that it is not disconcerting to the reader. The process is called justifying. If justifying a line seems difficult, however, do not be discouraged. Setting type so that the lines are well spaced and also look well is an art that is acquired only with experience.

When you have filled the composing stick, place a lead on top of what you have set, then slide the type onto a metal tray called a galley. In doing so, position the stick on the tray, then place your thumbs behind the type and your forefingers in front and gently push. If there is still more to be set, arrange several pieces of furniture (see below) around the type already on the tray so that it doesn't fall apart. After everything has been set, remove the furniture, wrap a string around the type six or seven times and tuck the loose end into one of the corners. At this point the type becomes a "form."

ILLUSTRATIONS

If you also wish to print a photograph or a drawing, it first must be made into a plate. Photographs are converted to halftones, drawings to line engravings. A local job printer will be able to tell you where to send your material.

PULLING A PROOF

The next step involves pulling a proof to determine if there have been errors in setting and spacing the type. Some amateur printers have a proof press for this purpose, but it is not difficult to pull a proof directly from a galley. You will need ink, an inking platen, and a brayer. You also will need a planer and a mallet or quoin key (see below).

First ink the form. Then lightly moisten one side of a sheet of newsprint and place it moist side up on the form. Position the planer on top of the proof sheet and tap it gently at several points with the mallet or key. If the form is a large one, move the planer from section to section, tapping it as you progress. Then take the newsprint by one corner and peel it from the form. If you find errors, untie the form, place furniture around it, and make the changes. Before proceeding to the next step, remove the ink from the form with a rag and a type cleaner.

LOCKING UP

This involves positioning the type in a steel rectangle called a chase, then locking it in place so that it does not shift in printing. The following equipment is needed:

Chase. Ordinarily a chase is provided with a new press. However, it is useful to have two.

Imposing Stone. In a commercial printing shop, locking up usually is done on a marble slab or on the steel top of a table or a cabinet. However, a sturdy wooden table with a flat surface will serve as an imposing stone if you cover it with a sheet of metal or heavy glass.

Furniture, Reglets. The material needed to lock a form into a chase consists of small blocks of wood, metal, or plastic, called "furniture," and narrow strips called "reglets." They are used to fill the space between the form and the inside of the chase. Those made from wood are the least expensive, but even so are not cheap. However their cost can be reduced substantially by purchasing strips of hardwood of the appropriate width and height and cutting them to the required lengths. The dimensions are listed in standard equipment catalogs. Furniture and reglets usually are stored in a special cabinet, but initially shoe boxes will serve.

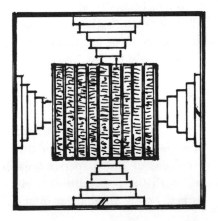

Locking up.

53

Quoins. These are small wedges which exert the pressure that holds the form and the furniture in place. You will need at least two pair and a key to lock and unlock the quoins.

Planer. This is a perfectly flat piece of hardwood that is moved across a form to make certain that the type is level.

Locking up is relatively simple. Place the galley with the tied form inside the chase. Then slide the form into position. Next, arrange the furniture and the reglets as shown in the diagram. This involves constructing four V's, once on each side of the form. The smallest pieces of furniture are positioned at the form, the largest at the inside of the chase. In the V's at the top and the right, use quoins rather than furniture in the space adjoining the chase. When all the furniture is in place, tighten the quoins with a quoin key. In the final step use a planer to make certain the type is level. In each position tap the planer gently with a mallet or a key. The form is now ready for the press.

INK

All you will need initially is a one-pound can of job black ink. It is likely to last several months and meet all of your needs. If at some point you decide to print in color, purchase tubes or cans of the primary colors. Also buy a supply of "mixing white," which will yield various tints when mixed with a primary color. Bear in mind that some kinds of paper require special inks. A glossy paper, for example, may require a gloss ink, and a bond paper a bond ink. If in doubt, ask your supplier. To keep ink from forming a scum after a can has been opened, press wax paper on the surface.

In addition, you will need a quantity of reducing varnish to thin the ink if it is too thick and a quantity of cornstarch to thicken it if it is too thin. To remove ink from type use benzene (turpentine leaves a scum) and a supply of lint-free rags.

STOCK

One of the distinguishing features of work from a private press is the high quality of the paper, or stock, that is used. There are hundreds of fine papers available commercially. To familiarize yourself with the possibilities, study the catalogs of a number of manufacturers. Some amateur printers also use handmade paper they either buy for a dollar or more a sheet or make themselves, as described in Chapter 2. The texture and color of such paper, when combined with a carefully selected type face, yield a remarkably handsome result. In selecting paper, take into account the following considerations.

Purpose. Varieties of book stock will be appropriate for much of your work, including broadsides, bookplates, and the contents of a booklet. Bond paper is suitable for letters. Cover stock is useful for covering booklets and also for greeting cards. When in doubt as to which paper would be appropriate, consult your supplier.

Durability. The more durable a paper the more costly it is likely to be. Expendable work, such as a broadside or a greeting card, clearly does not require paper that will last many years. On the other hand, such paper would be appropriate for a family history or a book of poems written by friends.

Finish. Finishes range from smooth and slick to heavily textured.

Weight. Standard papers range in weight from 30 pounds to 120 pounds. However, a 70-pound text stock will meet many of your needs.

Opacity. If a work is printed on both sides of a single sheet or consists of several consecutive pages, the stock must be sufficiently opaque so that the printing does not show through.

MAKEREADY AND PRINTING

Although each type of press operates somewhat differently, the sequence of steps in "making ready" and printing does not vary greatly.

Installing a Tympan. A tympan pack helps control the impression a form makes when it is brought in contact with a sheet of paper. The tympan is one part of the pack. It is a sheet of oiled manila paper. The other part is a backing placed under the tympan. It consists of a pressboard, which is a kind of hard cardboard, and as many sheets of paper as are needed to make the tympan smooth and tight. With a hand press a tympan usually is installed on the platen, the surface where the paper and the type come together.

Inking the Press. Many presses have a device that automatically distributes the amount of ink needed. However, most bench models must be inked by hand. In such cases, the ink is placed on a circular oscillating plate; it is then automatically spread on the type by rollers. A beginner often will find it difficult to estimate just how much ink is needed for a particular job. In such cases, the wisest procedure is to start with a small amount, then add more as necessary.

Testing the Impression. The next step is printing on the tympan to determine if the impression the type makes is clear and even. If particular sections are lighter than others, it will be necessary to add pieces of backing under the tympan in the areas involved. The impression also provides a guide in positioning gauge pins on the tympan. These pins hold the paper the printer feeds while the press is in operation. After they have been installed, several test sheets are printed. If no further adjustments are needed, the printer begins his run.

OTHER AMATEUR PRINTERS

In a few areas amateur printers have formed their own organizations. But usually there are too few for such a purpose. To learn of other amateurs, consult local printers and printing suppliers, art and printing teachers, and craftsmen's associations.

BIBLIOGRAPHY

Creative Bookbinding, Pauline Johnson, University of Washington Press, Seattle, 1963.

Graphic Arts Procedures, R. Randolph Karch, American Technical Society, Chicago, 1957. A high school textbook for printing students.

The Making of Books, Sean Jennett, Pantheon Books, New York, 1964.

Methods of Book Design, Hugh Williamson, Oxford University Press, London, 1956.

Printing as a Hobby, J. Ben Lieberman, Sterling Publishing Co., New York, 1963.

Printing for Pleasure, John Ryder, Charles T. Branford Co., Boston, 1955.

Types of Typefaces, J. Ben Lieberman, Sterling Publishing Co., New York, 1967.

5·PHOTOGRAPHY

THE FILM the photographer uses is a strip of clear plastic which has been treated with chemicals to make it sensitive to light. The camera he uses is, in effect, an eye, functioning much as a living eye does. With its lens it collects the light reflected by the object it "sees." The lens then focuses this light into a chamber at the back of the camera, where the photographer's film captures the image involved. What the camera sees and what it produces depends, of course, on how well the photographer sees. No matter how fine his equipment, it is his sensitivity and artistry that determine the result, for the camera is at best an extension of the photographer—his third eye, as Edward Steichen once wrote.

All the equipment a beginning photographer needs is an inexpensive camera and some film. Later he will want a more versatile, higher quality camera and possibly color correction filters, a flash unit, a tripod, additional lenses, and darkroom equipment. Ultimately some advanced amateurs acquire several cameras for different purposes. I know of one who has at least ten. Some also buy more gadgets than they can keep track of, but these give them infinite pleasure. At the outset, however, it is wise to concentrate on but one piece of equipment and on what is involved in taking pictures.

CAMERAS

With the many different cameras it sells, a well-stocked camera shop is a confusing place even for the experienced photographer. However, every camera on its shelves works essentially as described above. Moreover, all have three basic parts: a focusing device which takes into account the distance to the subject, a diaphragm which controls the size of the lens opening and thereby determines the amount of light that reaches the film, and the shutter which controls the length of time—how many seconds or what fraction of a second—light from the lens will strike the film.

One of the basic differences in cameras lies in whether they are "adjustable" or "non-adjustable." The non-adjustable model is a lineal descendant of the earlier box camera. Just like its ancestor's, its lens opening and shutter speed and the distance at which it can operate either are fixed at one point or function within a narrow range of possibilities. Despite such limitations, these cameras, like their ancestors, can produce remarkably fine photographs if the photographer knows what he is about. On the other hand, the more costly adjustable cameras provide great flexibility in dealing with lighting and related factors. The most widely used cameras in this group are the reflex and the 35-millimeter types.

Reflex cameras are vertically shaped instruments perhaps five or six inches high. There are two types: a single lens reflex camera with one large lens, and a double lens model with one lens above the other. In both, the lenses are linked to a ground-glass viewing device which shows precisely what will appear on the film when a picture is taken. The reflex is a highly versatile camera which may be used for carefully composed artistic work and also for action shots. The pictures it takes are relatively large, measuring $2\frac{1}{4}'' \times 2\frac{1}{4}''$. This makes it possible to use them without enlargement, a feature which is useful to amateurs who print their own work. An important drawback of all but the most expensive models is that the camera does not accept additional lenses such as a wide-angle or a telephoto lens.

The smaller 35-millimeter type also is known as a miniature or a candid camera. The film it uses yields basic prints $1'' \times 1\frac{1}{4}''$, which are about a fourth the size of reflex photographs and require enlargement. However, the camera is excellent for action, color photography, and the preparation of transparencies. An increasing number of models are equipped with a reflex-type viewing unit. In addition, most permit the substitution of one lens for another. These qualities, plus the fact that the 35-millimeter is easy to handle and operate, have made it the most popular camera among amateurs. Eighty per cent of advanced cameras sold are of this type.

There also is another basic difference to take into account. Every camera in a camera shop either is automatic or semi-automatic or is operated manually. An automatic camera has a built-in photoelectric exposure meter which judges the light available, takes into account other information provided and automatically adjusts the lens opening and in many models the shutter speed. Invariably the result is a correct exposure. Some automatic models even flash a light which indicates whether enough illumination is available to take a picture. In some cases, focusing for distance also is handled automatically. The drawback of such cameras is that they leave little to the judgment of the photographer who, for example, may wish to make "mistakes" to achieve various esthetic effects but is not permitted to do so. The fully automatic cameras usually are among the less expensive models.

The more costly cameras are likely to be semi-automatic, offering the photographer the advantages of automation plus the option when he wishes of making his own decisions regarding lens openings and shutter speeds. A non-automatic manually operated camera has no metering system. As a result, the photographer must rely on a separate exposure meter or an exposure table, as discussed later. However, fewer and fewer cameras are available these days in such a primitive state.

Introductory Cameras. Since photography is a costly hobby, it is wise to be certain of your interest before investing large sums in equipment. Many beginners find that $75 or less is a sufficient sum for a first camera. The options include the box-type cameras noted earlier, which include automatic models and a variety of non-automatic Japanese imports that are available in reflex and 35-millimeter models. All such cameras have limited capabilities, but the more you work with them the more you will learn, and the better prepared you will be to make a wise choice of advanced equipment. On the other hand, should you lose interest in photography, you will have a satisfactory camera for snapshots whenever grandma and grandpa arrive in town.

An introductory camera.

59

[LEFT] *A 2¼"×2¼" double reflex model.*
[BELOW] *A 35mm. camera.*

Advanced Cameras. I asked an excellent professional photographer who has illustrated several of my books which camera he would recommend to someone with a serious interest in photography. His choice was a 2¼" × 2¼" reflex model. One reason was its flexibility. Another was the opportunity it provides to make usable prints without the need to purchase an enlarger. As a second camera he recommended a 35-millimeter model which could be used for action and color and any work requiring special lenses. At publication, such cameras ranged in price from about $150 to $600 and more.

Buying a Camera. When you purchase a camera, what you buy essentially is a lens in a box. If you are making a long-term purchase, it is important to buy the best lens you can afford. Unfortunately the typical amateur has no way of gauging the quality of a lens. Instead he must trust both the merchant he deals with and the manufacturer of the camera he ultimately buys. It is wise therefore to consider only well-known brands and to make your purchase from a reputable dealer. If something does go wrong, you are protected. If repairs are necessary, moreover, you are assured of reliable service.

When you enter a camera shop, it is important to have a realistic idea of what your needs are. Extra fast shutter speed, special attachments, and other features add to the cost of a camera. If in the end you don't use them, they are even more expensive. In considering a particular camera, determine how comfortable it is to hold, how efficient the sighting is, how well any push buttons work, and how smoothly the shutter release operates at each setting.

Most dealers also sell secondhand cameras they have taken as trade-ins. Generally they are about half the price of comparable new equipment. In examining such a camera, check the points above and also inspect the lens for scratches, the interior for dirt, which might suggest poor care, and the body for dents and cracks which would indicate that the camera had been dropped and as a result that its lens might be out of alignment.

Whether a camera is new or used, insist on a written money back guarantee under which it can be returned if it does not prove satisfactory within a given period.

Camera Care. To protect a camera from damage, keep it in a camera case. To further protect its lens, cover it with a lens cap. Dust a camera lens at least once a month. Use a camel's hair brush or a soft, clean, well-worn linen cloth, or blow the dust away with a rubber syringe. If a lens is spotted with moisture, remove any dust, then wipe gently with a soft cloth or a lens tissue. If it is soiled, dust the lens, breathe on it gently, and wipe with a tissue or cloth. Also dust the interior of a camera periodically. When a camera is not in use, store it in a cool, dry environment. In addition, record any serial numbers on the camera against the possibility of theft. There may be one on the body and another on the lens.

61

ACCESSORIES

Color Correction Filters. A filter increases the contrast in a photograph, emphasizing certain portions of a scene at the expense of others and thereby adding a degree of drama to the result. A yellow filter, for example, permits clouds to stand out by absorbing blues and violets from the color of the sky. There also are yellow-green, green, orange, red, and ultraviolet filters, each with a different effect. One of the most frequently used filters in color photography is a "skylight" filter, which invests the colors involved with greater warmth.

Exposure Meters. As noted earlier, automatic and semi-automatic cameras have built-in meters. Therefore, a standard separate unit is only used with non-automatic cameras and in those situations where a semi-automatic camera is operated manually. Extremely sensitive special purpose meters are also available.

Flash Guns. These are used principally to provide light for indoor photography. An electronic flash unit provides a permanent rechargeable lighting mechanism. For many photographers it is a wiser investment than a flash gun which relies on bulbs.

Gadget Bag. For carrying cameras, accessories, film, notebooks, and lunch.

Lenses. A telephoto lens provides detail from a distance, a wide-angle lens takes in the width an ordinary lens cannot encompass, and portrait lenses are used, of course, in making portraits. When fitted over a standard lens, a close-up lens permits photographs from a foot or two away or even closer.

Tripod. This equipment is used to support a camera when a time exposure or a slow shutter speed might cause blurring if the camera were held in one's hand while a picture was being made. In such cases the camera is operated by a cable release.

FILM

The kind of film required depends on several factors, the most important of which are the amount of light and the degree of action. Generally two types of film are used in black and white photography. Under normal shooting conditions a panchromatic film is needed. This type has a moderate speed or moderate sensitivity to light.

Eastman Kodak calls its panchromatic film "Plus X"; other firms give it other names. A high speed film ordinarily is used when the lighting is poor, artificial lighting is involved, or the subject is moving at great speed. Since this film has a greater sensitivity to light, it reacts more quickly than the panchromatic type and needs less exposure. The Kodak name for such film is "Tri X." Color films also are available in medium and high speeds.

Each type of film has a speed rating indicated by an ASA number, which is an important factor in determining the correct exposure. For example, many cameras with metering systems have a film speed dial where the number must be indicated. Separate exposure meters also have such arrangements. The number is printed on the package the film comes in or on an instruction sheet inside. Film is available in a wide variety of sizes and packaging arrangements. With a reflex camera, for example, the film needed comes rolled on a spool; with a 35-millimeter camera it is in a cartridge. Since film is expensive, some amateurs purchase it in bulk, then load what they need in the appropriate containers. If one has access to a darkroom, this is not a difficult process.

USING A CAMERA

The Subject. The art of photography is essentially the art of seeing clearly. It relies in large part on the ability to see what is remarkable about ordinary objects and incidents—a flower, for example, or a child at play, or a man at work. Make it a practice to explore the commonplace. You soon will learn to see what you otherwise might have overlooked. If your photographs are successful, moreover, what you once took for granted will take on a kind of wonder.

Selecting subjects is, however, but one of several challenges. Before releasing a shutter, there is a need to visualize just how a subject might appear in a picture. The basic consideration is what to include and, especially important, what to leave out. But there are others as well. Would it be better, for example, to shoot from in close or from a distance, from a low or a high position or from some other angle? Are there predominant lines of movement that can be used to strengthen the picture? Are there textures, tones, or strong contrasts in light or subject matter that would be helpful? How much foreground or background is needed? Would it make sense to "frame" the picture by shooting through a doorway or by including the corner of a building or part of a tree?

As one attempts to answer such questions, he begins to practice the art of composition. There are of course many traditional approaches to organizing a picture. Some are cited below. For others see the manuals listed in the Bibliography.

Subject: Sharply limit the subject matter to those details that directly contribute to your purpose. Also limit the foreground, background, and sky to what is essential.

Position of Subject: Since it is difficult to obtain a good photograph with the subject at the center, be guided by the rule of thirds. Using imaginary lines, divide the picture you are planning into thirds both horizontally and vertically. Position your subject at one of four places where lines cross.

Action: With action photographs increase the size of the foreground at the expense of the background.

Positioning subjects by the rule of thirds.

Use of diagonal lines to enliven a photograph.

Horizon Line: To create a sense of immediacy, keep the horizon line low; to provide an impression of space, position it at a high point in the picture. Never place it at the center; it will appear as if you have two photographs.

Other Lines: Various elements may be used to form lines which will enhance a picture. Horizontal lines, for example, introduce a tranquil effect. Diagonal lines invariably add life to a picture. Vertical lines may lend a sense of dignity, solemnity, uplift, even joy. In all cases, such lines should be arranged so that they seem to move into a picture, not away from it.

Looking at good photographs also is useful in learning about composition. The Bibliography lists several photographic magazines and annual picture collections that are worth studying; the illustrated news magazines also are full of excellent material. In examining photographs, try to understand their strengths and weaknesses; also attempt to visualize how they might be improved.

The most important step in learning to make pictures is, of course, making them. Decide what you want in advance, then try to capture

Use of branches of a tree to frame a subject.

this effect with your camera. Take pictures of a wide range of subjects, but also work exhaustively with a few that interest you most, developing as many versions of a particular subject as you can. Do your shooting at different times of day, include different details, and use different angles. Then decide which of your efforts is the most effective and why.

The Camera. How well you succeed with your pictures also depends on how well you understand your camera's controls and how they can be manipulated.

Focusing: Whether a camera is set for the distance at which it is being used helps determine how sharp a picture will be. As noted earlier, the simplest cameras have a lens with a fixed or non-adjustable focus. This generally means that all pictures taken from about five feet to infinity will be reasonably sharp if you don't jiggle the camera. However, such cameras are not effective at closer range. The more costly models have an adjustable focusing unit, usually a rangefinder, which enables a photographer to work with considerable precision at most distances. At a foot or two, however, the special close-up lens described earlier is needed.

Lens Opening: The speed of a lens is judged by the amount of light it brings to the camera. The larger this opening, the greater the amount of light admitted, and the faster the lens. As might be expected, the more costly cameras have the fastest lenses. They also have a range of smaller lens openings which let in less light. As a result, the photographer (or the camera, if it is automatic) can take lighting conditions into account with considerable precision. With advanced cameras the largest lens opening usually is set at f 1.4 or f 2.8. The lenses in such cameras are described as f 1.4 or f 2.8 lenses. However, these cameras also have settings at 5.6, 8, 11, 16, and 22, and possibly at 32, 45, and 64, each of which provides a progressively smaller opening. An introductory camera is likely to have but one lens opening, which often is fixed at f 8 or f 11. However, some models also have a few smaller openings.

The settings are arranged so that each larger number or smaller opening provides half the light of the preceding opening. As one moves toward the smaller numbers, each setting provides twice the light of the preceding one. On a bright day a photographer generally will move up the scale toward the smaller numbers, since he will need less light for his exposure. When lighting conditions are poor, he moves down the scale. The lens opening also controls the depth of field or zone of focus. This is the portion of the photograph, extending from the closest object, that is in sharp focus. The smaller the lens opening, the greater the depth of field. If a photographer wants less depth of field, perhaps to give greater emphasis to a subject in the foreground, he shifts to a small number and a larger opening.

Shutter Speed: The shutter speed determines the length of the exposure or the amount of time the light admitted by a lens opening is in contact with the film. With advanced cameras, a shutter speed might range from 1/2 second to 1/1000 or 1/1250 of a second. Intermediate settings typically include 1/4, 1/8, 1/15, 1/30, 1/60, 1/125, 1/250, and 1/500 of a second. With introductory cameras, there might be only one shutter speed, which frequently is fixed at 1/50 of a second; or there also might be three or four options, with a maximum speed of 1/200.

Each faster setting provides half the light of the preceding setting; on the other hand, each slower setting doubles the light. The usual recommendation under normal shooting conditions is for a shutter speed of 1/125 and a lens opening of f 8. When the light is poor, the recommendation typically is for 1/30 at ƒ 8. If considerable action is involved, if a faster than ordinary film is used, or if other special conditions intervene, then, of course, other settings would be required, as discussed below.

Exposures: If you own an introductory camera, it will not be possible, of course, to take every kind of picture. The subjects you select and the exposures you make will necessarily be limited by what your equipment can do. If you have an advanced camera, however, you are likely to have all the freedom you require.

To determine the exposure needed in a particular situation, take into account the available light, the degree of action, and any special effects you want. Then select the appropriate film and, with the aid of an exposure meter, the appropriate lens opening and shutter speed. The lens opening and the shutter speed work together to achieve a single effect. A faster shutter speed, for example, typically is combined with a large lens opening and a slow speed with a small opening.

The fact that different combinations of settings yield the same exposure also is of importance. This enables a photographer to take different types of pictures under the same lighting conditions, yet each time obtain a clear, well-lighted photograph. To stop fast action, for example, it might be practical to shoot at 1/500 with a lens opening of ƒ 8. To take other pictures, it might be better to use 1/250 at ƒ 11 or 1/125 at ƒ 16, yet all three settings yield the same exposure. The metering systems on some semi-automatic cameras will provide the guidance for such decisions. Otherwise, you will need a separate exposure meter. You also will need one, of course, with fully manual cameras.

DEVELOPING AND PRINTING PICTURES

Although the work of commercial film processors usually is satisfactory, you will become a better photographer by developing and printing your own pictures. In developing your negatives, for example, you readily will see mistakes you made in planning exposures. You also will learn how to correct for many such errors while printing your pictures and how to make other adjustments that will enhance your work but would be costly to have a commercial firm handle. If you acquire an enlarger, you not only will be able to make bigger pictures, you will be able to strengthen them by "cropping out" distracting or unnecessary detail. This, in turn, will provide a continuing lesson in composition. Of course, producing fine prints comes only with experience. But none of what is involved is very complicated, and much of it is a great deal of fun. Over the long term, moreover, you even might save some money.

A Darkroom. Most beginners use a kitchen, a bathroom, or part of a basement as a temporary darkroom and store their equipment in a box when it is not used. Some rely on other rooms, using a bucket to transport the water they need. Since a darkroom must be dark for part of the process, they cover the windows with black draperies or with opaque black screens fashioned from wood and cloth. To keep light out, they also block spaces around the door with strips of cloth. Since one of the chemicals involved tends to stain, they also must protect work surfaces and furniture. Rather than work in temporary quarters, some try to find a camera club with a darkroom that members may use. But what is most desirable is a permanent darkroom of one's own. The best place to build one is a basement or a utility room, but any area with a water source and an electrical outlet would serve. Plans for simple darkrooms are contained in several of the manuals listed in the Bibliography.

Making Negatives and Prints. The steps are easily summarized. In making negatives, one places the exposed film in a small developing tank. He then bathes the film first in developer, then in water or a commercial "stop bath," and finally in hypo, a fixing solution which makes the film insensitive to light. The film is then washed a second time and hung up to dry.

In making prints, one needs printing paper and a printing device. The beginner ordinarily starts by making contact prints which are the same size as the negative. For this procedure he uses a printing box or a printing frame. At a later date he may acquire an enlarger, which, as noted earlier, will enable him to produce larger pictures and to improve composition by removing irrelevant detail. With an enlarger he also will be able to practice "dodging." This involves making various areas in a picture darker or lighter to achieve an esthetic effect or compensate for poor exposure or a poor negative.

In making contact prints, he places a sheet of light-sensitive paper in contact with the negative, then exposes both to light for a specific period. If he has an enlarger, he projects the image in the negative onto a sheet of printing paper. In either case he then bathes the paper in developer, in water, and in a fixing solution. Finally, he dries the prints and presses them flat.

An excellent introduction to the many techniques involved is provided in *Basic Printing, Developing, and Enlarging*, a booklet published by the Eastman Kodak Company, which is available in many camera stores. Advanced techniques are covered in the manuals listed in the Bibliography.

EQUIPMENT

For Negatives: Developing tanks, chemicals, 16-ounce measuring cup to mix chemicals and large jars to store them, photo thermometer, kitchen timer, film clips for drying.

For Prints: Printing box, or printing frame, three non-metallic trays or baking dishes, safelight, drying blotters or automatic dryer, enlarger (buy one of good quality), printing paper, chemicals, measuring cup, storage jars, thermometer, timer.

Kits: Darkroom kits contain basic equipment and limited supplies for both operations.

Storing Negatives and Prints. Store negatives in glassine envelopes sold in camera stores. Each envelope should carry a serial number which refers to a descriptive entry in a notebook. Photographs should be stored in folders or albums. With albums use rapid mounting cement, library paste, or gummed photo corners. Each photograph should carry its negative number on the reverse side. If a photograph is mounted in an album, the number also should be listed under the picture along with a caption. Of course, photographs also can be framed or mounted separately. In the latter case use dry mounting tissue.

INSTRUCTION

Photography courses frequently are offered in adult education programs conducted at high schools and YMCA's. Some camera clubs also offer their members such courses. There also are a number of formal schools of photography, including some that offer short-term workshops. In addition, some 400 universities, colleges, and community colleges offer instruction in photography and, in some cases, degrees. To answer questions relating to their products, many manufacturers of advanced cameras hold periodic clinics at camera shops and also provide information by mail.

ORGANIZATIONS

There are hundreds of local camera clubs which sponsor competitions for their members and have guest speakers. Some even operate darkrooms and, as noted above, offer photography courses. If you have difficulty in finding a club, ask your local camera dealer.

EARNING MONEY

Some amateurs attempt to sell their work either directly or through a photographic agency with which they share any proceeds. The possibilities for sales include publications, film and camera companies, advertising and public relations firms, and manufacturers of greeting cards and calendars. A number of amateurs become so intrigued with their hobby they make a career of it, taking jobs with newspapers, magazines, or business firms, or operating studios, or freelancing.

BIBLIOGRAPHY

Manuals

The Amateur Photographer's Handbook, Aaron Sussman, Thomas Y. Crowell Co., New York, 1965.

The Complete Book of Nature Photography, Russ Kinne, A. S. Barnes, New York, 1962.

How to Make Good Pictures, Eastman Kodak Company, Rochester, N.Y., 1967.

Hunting with the Camera, Allan D. Cruikshank, Harper & Row, New York, 1957.

Hunting with Camera and Binocular, Francis E. Sell, Chilton Company, Philadelphia, 1961.

Outdoor Photography, Erwin Bauer, Harper & Row, New York, 1965.

Photography from A to Z, Dan Daniels, Amphoto, New York, 1968.

Reinhold's Photo and Movie Book for Amateur Photographers, H. Freytag, Van Nostrand-Reinhold Co., New York, 1964.

There also are a number of manuals devoted to the operation and use of particular cameras.

71

Booklets

The Eastman Kodak Company publishes a continuing series of excellent informational booklets which are sold at camera stores. They include *Basic Developing, Printing, Enlarging; Copying; Enlarging in Black and White and Color;* the *Kodak Master Photoguide;* and *Here's How,* a continuing series on various aspects of photography.

Periodicals

Camera 35. U.S. Camera Publishing Co., 132 W. 31st Street, New York, N.Y. 10001.

Modern Photography. Billboard Publications, 165 W. 46th Street, New York, N.Y. 10036.

Popular Photography. Ziff-Davis Publishing Co., 1 Park Avenue, New York, N.Y. 10017. Monthly.

Travel and Leisure. 132 W. 31st Street, New York, N.Y. 10001. Bimonthly.

Photographic Annuals
International Photography Yearbook.
Photography Annual.
U.S. Camera Annual.

6·PUPPETRY

ALTHOUGH PUPPETS are nothing more than small dolls, they offer a great many pleasures. There is the opportunity to bring them to life and transport an audience to another time and place. There also is the chance to create your own puppets, puppet theaters, and plays. How much time and effort are needed varies. The simplest puppets take but minutes to assemble. The most challenging involve many hours and may require historical research, drawing, sculpture or carving, costume design, and sewing. The same is true of puppet theaters. A few can be assembled on the spur of the moment. But there are others that involve stage design, carpentry, and the preparation of scenery, props, curtains, and stage lighting.

Puppetry is an art so ancient no one is certain where or when it began. There have been puppeteers for thousands of years in Japan, China, and other Oriental countries. Ancient Egyptians and Greeks also used puppets. In Europe puppet theaters have offered performances for hundreds of years. Among the first were those in Italy where the coarse-mouthed hook-nosed Punchinello originated. From Italy he emigrated to Germany as Hans Wurst or John Sausage, to Russia as Petrushka, and to England as Punch, the browbeaten husband of a nag named Judy. In those years Goethe wrote plays for the puppet theater and Mozart and Haydn composed music for it. Puppetry still thrives in parts of Europe and in Latin America and the Orient. Unfortunately, this is not the case in English-speaking countries.

There are four types of puppets considered in this chapter: hand puppets, which are the easiest to make and use; rod puppets, which are operated by wooden or wire rods; shadow puppets; and jointed marionettes, which, of course, are operated by strings.

HAND PUPPETS

A hand puppet is operated directly by hand from a position below the stage. There are many kinds of hand puppets, but most are simple enough to be made by children. The great advantage of these puppets is their flexibility. They are easy to operate, have no trouble holding things in their hands, and bound around with the greatest of ease. They are particularly useful in humorous plays. Their only drawback is that they are not believable. Because they do not closely resemble the people or animals they represent, it is difficult to establish a mood in a performance. However, they are excellent first puppets.

Directions for Making Hand Puppets

Head and Cloth Puppets: Here are three possibilities that take little time to prepare. Form a head from an oil-based clay like Plasticene, place it on your index finger, and wrap a cloth around your hand. Create a head from a potato or an apple with thumb tacks for facial features; then carve a finger-size hole in the bottom. Cut a hole in the bottom of a ball or a matchbox; draw in facial features with a Magic Marker and glue yarn in place as hair.

Paper Bag Puppets: Use a flat-bottomed paper bag with the closed portion serving as the head. Draw a face on one of the broad sides of the bag and glue strips of paper to the top as hair. Place your fist inside and have someone tie the bag at the wrist.

Glove Puppets: These consist of a head attached to a cloaklike glove which has arms and hands. The operator places one of his hands inside the glove, positioning his thumb in one arm, his index finger in the head, and his middle finger in the other arm. The pattern shown is for a basic glove puppet, which should be cut from a sturdy tightly woven fabric. The glove itself should be twelve inches long. If the puppet represents a child, the head should be two to three inches in height; if it represents an adult, it should be three to four inches high.

Cut two pieces from the fabric for the front and the back, then stitch them together and turn the result inside out. Next, cut the puppet's hands from a piece of felt, stitch the pieces together, and attach to the arms. Add the facial features needed with a Magic Marker or paint, or use buttons or scraps of fabric for this purpose and sew them in place. For hair, use yarn, felt, or absorbent cotton. When the head is ready,

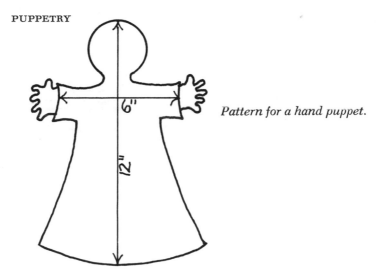

Pattern for a hand puppet.

stuff it with wool or cotton and stitch across the neck, leaving a small opening in the center in which to place your fingers. Insert a tube of paper in the opening to keep the stuffing from falling out.

As another possibility, prepare a glove which you glue to a more solid head. An old doll's head would be excellent. Otherwise, carve a head, neck, and finger opening from a block of close-grained white pine (see Whittling and Woodcarving, Chapter 8) or model a head and neck from papier mâché.

Do your modeling on a paper towel tube which has been inserted in a clay base to hold it erect. Place a quantity of Plasticene on top of the tube and shape the head in rough form. Then dip strips of newspaper in water and use them to cover the head. Next, apply two coats of paper strips, a coat of gauze strips, and two more coats of paper strips, all of which have been dipped in a thin paste. Dry the head in a slow oven, which will take several hours, then scoop out the clay. Finally, add facial features and hair, and glue the glove in place.

A sofa can serve as a simple theater. The performers work from behind the back rest, kneeling on cushions and holding the puppets above them. More complex possibilities are discussed after the section on rod puppets.

ROD PUPPETS

This type of puppet is a slower moving, more dignified species than the hand puppet. It also is more realistic in appearance

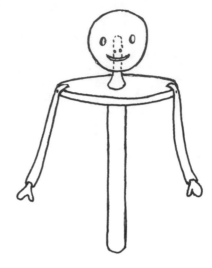

Dowel-type rod puppet.

and action. As a result, it lends itself effectively to drama and to plays that involve pageantry and ceremony. Stiff wires or wooden rods are used to control a rod puppet, which is operated from a position below the stage.

Directions for Making Rod Puppets

Stick Puppets: These are the most rudimentary of the rod puppets, but they are fun to use. One is made from a wooden spoon whose bowl has been turned into a face and whose handle serves as a control. Drape a cloth around the handle and secure it with a rubber band just below the bowl. Another is made from the paper bag puppet described earlier. Stuff the bag with wads of cloth or newspaper, insert a piece of broomstick as a rod, and close the bag over the rod with a rubber band. Another possibility involves cutouts. Sketch heads or complete figures on heavy cardboard or obtain them from magazines and mount them. Then cut them out. Attach small cutouts to Popsicle sticks. Mount large ones—full-size heads, for example—on flat sticks one to two feet long.

Articulated Cardboard Puppets: These puppets have arms and legs that can be moved independently. Experiment first with a puppet that has one leg or one arm that moves. Trace the figure you intend to use on heavy cardboard, substituting a rounded stump for the moving leg or arm. Trace the leg or arm separately, rounding its upper end. Cut out both parts, overlap the rounded sections, and link them with a paper fastener. Then decorate the figure and install two operating rods. Use a stiff wire about a foot long for each. If you have some bicycle spokes, these would work well. Bend each into a loop at the end, then stitch one to the back of the puppet and the other to the back of the foot or hand involved.

Dowel Puppets: This type of puppet might range in height up to 3 feet. However, the one described here is about a foot in height. It has a four-inch head, broad shoulders, and long arms. The main control is a heavy piece of doweling about eight inches long which supports both the head and the shoulders.

Fashion the head and neck from wood or papier mâché. If you use wood, work with a block of white pine. Drill a hole in the bottom of the block for the dowel rod, then carve the features and paint the face. If you use papier mâché, work directly on the dowel stick. Glue strips of cloth to the top to shape the head, then use the method described in the section on glove puppets.

For the puppet's shoulders use thin plywood or extra-heavy cardboard. Shape the material into an oval about six inches across. Also cut a hole in the center for the dowel rod. Then slide the shoulders into position under the neck and glue them in place. For the arms use six-inch lengths of cloth tape. For the hands there are several options. Purchase wooden or plastic hands at a hobby shop, carve your own from wood, make miniature stuffed mittens, or use large wooden beads. Then fasten the hands to the arms and attach the arms to the ends of the shoulders. Either staple them or drill holes and tie them in place. As controls for the arms, use stiff wires about a foot long. Bend the ends into loops and sew or staple them to the hands.

A rod puppet of this type requires a loose flowing gown large enough to hide the dowel rod. All that is needed is a simple garment with slits in the sides for the hands. If costume design intrigues you, however, dressing a rod puppet offers a rich opportunity.

THEATERS FOR HAND AND ROD PUPPETS

The height of a stage opening should be related to the size of the puppets that use it. Usually a puppet stage is about two and one-half times the height of the puppets. In the theaters described below, the stage openings are between two and one-half and three feet, a sufficient size for a puppet about a foot in height. If you plan to use larger puppets, take this into account in constructing your theater.

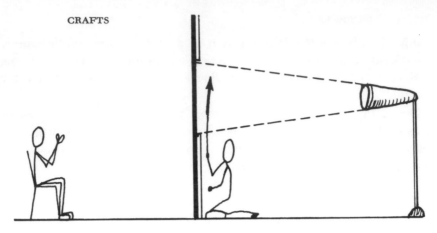

Doorway theater for shadow puppets.

Directions for Making Theaters

Doorway Theater: You will need pieces of opaque fabric, several thumbtacks, and a doorway for this temporary theater. Use fabric a yard wide. Cut one piece four feet long, the other a foot long. Cover the bottom half of the door with the large piece and the topmost portion with the small piece. The uncovered section serves as the stage. The puppeteers sit on stools or kneel on cushions behind the lower curtain.

Box Theater: This theater is derived from a large box of the type refrigerators come in. First remove the back and the top. Then cut an opening about two and a half feet in height in the top half of the front panel. Next add a thin bridge of wood across the top at the back linking the two sides. Install small hooks in the wood at either end to support the scenery discussed later. It would be useful to have a narrow shelf immediately under the opening to serve as a stage. If a refrigerator box isn't available, you can assemble such a theater with three panels of plywood.

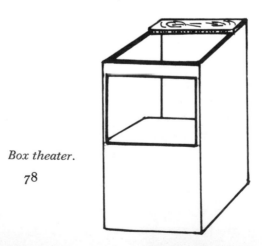

Box theater.

Advanced Theater: Should you develop a serious interest in puppetry, this traditional theater would be an excellent acquisition. To build one you would need the following lumber:

Four pieces 2″ × 2″ × 6 feet long
Four pieces 1″ × 2″ × 3½ feet long
Four pieces 1″ × 2″ × 2½ feet long
One piece 1″ × 3″ × 3½ feet long (for a stage)
One piece 1″ × 6″ × 3½ feet long (for a shelf)

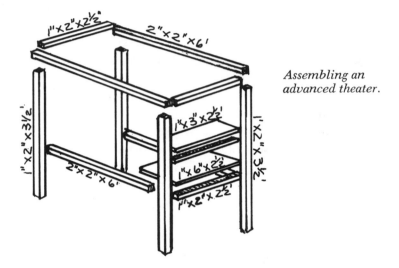

Assembling an advanced theater.

Assemble the theater as shown in the diagram. Install two hooks in the bridge at the back for scenery, as explained below. A proscenium arch of the type illustrated can be cut from a piece of thin plywood 2½′ × 2½′. To simplify the project, have the lumber cut to size. When the theater is assembled, cover the sides and the portion under the stage with fabric.

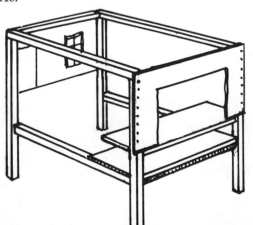

Completed theater, with proscenium in place and flat hung from hooks at rear.

Scenery and Props. Frequently neither scenery nor props are required with such theaters. When they are, a simple set and a few properties are likely to be all that is really needed.

Doorway Theater: Make individual drawings on cardboard of the objects involved or take pictures from magazines and mount them. Then cut the illustrations in outline, fasten sticks to the back, and display from below.

Box Theater, Advanced Theater: In both cases it is possible to make use of traditional scenery. For a backdrop use a sturdy light gray or beige paper slightly larger than the stage opening. Either illustrate the setting with a few bold drawings or paste or pin scenery in place. A window, for example, might consist of several strips of paper pasted in the proper arrangement. Represent a door in the same way. However, place it at one end of the backdrop and only show a portion of it. When a puppet enters from that side, he will look as if he actually is coming through a door. If in the course of the play there are changes in the setting, you will want a separate backdrop for each. Hang the scenery from the hooks at the back of the stage. Scenery can also be used on the stage itself. The possibilities include doll furniture, trees (twigs in clay balls), and one-dimensional cars, houses, and other objects pasted to wooden blocks.

Stage Curtain. A curtain will make things more theatrical. The simplest is an abbreviated window shade installed inside the stage at the top. Emblazon a theatrical-looking design or the name of your troupe on the audience side. For a more traditional curtain, you will need the following: a piece of heavy opaque fabric several inches wider than the stage opening but the same height, a curtain rod or a piece of wire long enough to stretch across the opening, small curtain rings, and

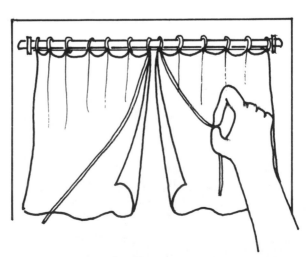

Stage curtain.

two decorative strings each about a foot long. Cut the curtains in half and attach the rings. Then install the rod or the wire inside the stage just above the opening and hang the curtains. They should reach a point just above the floor. Finally, attach the curtain cords as shown in the drawing.

Stage Lighting. Use two floor lamps for general lighting, focusing them on the stage from either side of the puppeteers. For special effects use colored bulbs, or paint standard bulbs with water color. A violet bulb casts a cold, spooky light. A blue bulb yields moonlight, a blue-white bulb cold daylight, a yellow or orange bulb cheerful sunlight. Footlights also are useful. The easiest to install are a string of Christmas tree lights.

Plays, Sound Effects, Music. These subjects are discussed after the section on marionettes.

SHADOW PUPPETS

According to legend, the shadow theater had its origins over 2000 years ago. A Chinese emperor named Wu-Ti, overwhelmed with grief and loneliness at the death of a friend, asked the court magician to summon her spirit. The magician, in turn, produced the shadow of a human figure on a screen, which satisfied the emperor. Puppeteers no longer try to raise the dead, but when they work with shadow puppets, they work with a kind of magic.

Directions for Making Shadow Puppets

Traditional shadow puppets are two-dimensional figures that perform in profile. The only exceptions are dancers, which are presented in a front view. Puppets representing human figures generally are six to eight inches tall. Those representing animals are scaled down accordingly. To create a shadow puppet, either sketch the figure you need or find one in a magazine. Then trace its outline on a piece of heavy cardboard and cut the figure out. Articulated puppets, such as those described earlier, also are used as shadow puppets. However, they must be created in profile.

Although the shadows cast by such puppets are interesting, there are several intriguing possibilities for experimentation. To give the shadows they produce a sense of depth, cut holes for the eyes and the mouth. Also cut slits with a razor blade to suggest the folds in a puppet's clothing. To emphasize its hair or some other part of its body or its clothing, cut out that portion and cover it from the back with a textured fabric or a colored cellophane. The result will be either a textured shadow or a colored shadow. It also is interesting to create three-dimensional shadows. Thus, a head might be fashioned from a wadded ball of paper and glued to a two-dimensional body. Or a pleated skirt of colored cellophane or a cloak of stiff cloth might be added. After any holes are cut, paint the puppet black. Then make any other changes you have in mind.

Once you have created a first draft of a puppet, determine just what kind of a shadow it casts. At times minor alterations will be needed. A shadow puppet is operated from a position below the stage, just as rod and hand puppets are. Its control also is like that of some rod puppets: a stiff wire about a foot long bent into a loop at one end and sewn or stapled to the back.

SHADOW THEATERS

All that is needed for a shadow theater is a semi-opaque screen with a source of light behind the screen. Cotton sheeting, fabric from a white window shade, and heavy white paper all make satisfactory screens. So does a portable movie screen. Ideally a shadow screen should be twice the height of the tallest puppet. It also should be twice as wide as it is high.

Doorway Theaters: Tack a sheet of screening material to the inside of a doorway, making it as taut as you can. Or position a movie screen on a table in a doorway. Or remove the front and back panels from a cardboard carton, cover the opening at the back with a screen, and place the carton on a table in a doorway. In each case cover the open areas around the screen with dark fabric.

Modified Theaters: The box theater and the advanced theater described earlier can both be converted to a shadow theater by installing a screen across the stage opening from the inside.

Scenery. The limited amount of scenery used is pinned to the side of the screen that faces the audience. It usually consists of black cutouts of commonplace objects. Large elements such as trees and houses should be kept to the sides. To turn the lights on in a house, cut open the windows and cover them from behind with red cellophane. To provide a blue sky, cover the top part of the outside of the screen with blue cellophane.

Lighting. A floor lamp with a 150-watt bulb will provide all the light needed. Position it six feet from the screen. If possible direct the shade of the lamp toward the screen. Otherwise remove the shade. If there is a need to create a change in mood on stage, change the color of the light bulb, as discussed earlier, or use a light box with color filters. You can purchase such equipment in a photography store or a hobby shop.

MARIONETTES

Because they are jointed and controlled with strings, marionettes are more difficult to make and use than other puppets, but they also are the most lifelike, and the most satisfying to work with. It is well to start with the simplest of these puppets.

Directions for Making Marionettes

A Two-String Marionette: This marionette has only one moving part, but it offers a good introduction to what is involved. Cut out a cardboard figure nine inches tall. Remove one of its forearms at the elbow and refasten it with a paper fastener. Then attach small weights, such as metal nuts, to each foot with cellophane tape. Make a small hole in the hand of the movable arm and another in the top of the head. Attach a heavy control thread to each. These should be long enough so that they extend about a foot above the puppet when the movable arm is relaxed.

To operate this puppet, attach one string to each index finger. With your hands palms up, hold the puppet erect. Then touch its feet to a tabletop, and move it forward by rocking it gently from side to side. Once you have mastered this technique, learn to operate the puppet with both strings attached to one hand. Then make a second puppet and learn to operate one with each hand.

A Three-String Marionette: Cut apart one of the puppets described above. Remove each arm at the shoulder and also sever it at the elbow. Then remove each leg and cut it again at the knee. Finally, remove the pelvic area at the lower end of the torso. The next step involves refastening these parts so that they move independently. Link them with small loops of thread or wire, using two loops to a joint. When the puppet is reassembled, attach the foot weights and then the control threads. Fasten one thread to the top of the head and one to each hand.

To operate, attach two strings to the fingers of one hand and one string to a finger of the other. It also is practical to attach the strings to small rings and hold these. Practice walking the puppet as described above; then experiment with sitting, standing, falling down, clapping, waving, and any other maneuvers that occur to you. Next learn to do all this with one hand.

If you have a rag doll, you could make a marionette that a young child particularly might enjoy. Cut off the head and the neck, stitch both parts closed, and rejoin with sewing tape. Do the same at the elbows and the knees. Then cut open the feet, add a metal nut or a heavy washer to each, and resew. Then stitch control threads to the back of the head and to the back of each hand and operate as described above. Both the cardboard and the rag doll puppets also can be operated with control bars, a technique described later.

A Six-String Marionette: This type of puppet will enable you to duplicate human or animal movements with greater precision. By adding control threads to the knees and the back, you could turn the rag doll puppet or the cardboard puppet into a six-string marionette. However, a simple wooden marionette would be closer to the real thing. The marionette described below is made from pine and held together at the joints with eye screws and hooks. Heavy pieces of elastic held in place with staples also could be used. You will need the following lumber and materials:

> One piece 1″ × 2″ × 3 inches long (body)
> One piece 1″ × 2″ × 1 inch long (pelvis)
> One piece 1″ × 1″ × 1 inch long (head)
> Four ½″ dowel sticks, 2 inches long (arms)
> Four ¾″ dowel sticks, 2½ inches long (legs)
> Wood scraps (hands and feet)
> Fourteen sets eye screws and hooks

Either round the head slightly or carve rough features. If you feel ambitious, use the wood as a base for a head of papier mâché. The technique is described in the section on glove puppets. Next, roughly shape the hands and feet. Then sand the pieces smooth, wax them, and join as shown in the drawing. To operate this puppet, you will need a control bar described below.

Costumes. The easiest method of dressing marionettes is with loose-fitting scarves, cloaks, and hats which can be readily removed if a puppet has a costume change. It also is practical to create a complete cos-

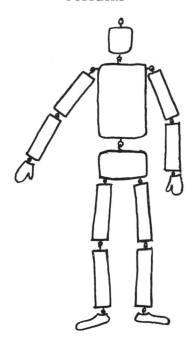

A wooden marionette linked by eye screws.

tume. However, it must be roomy enough so as not to interfere with a puppet's movements. In addition, the controls at the knees and the back probably will have to be attached through the fabric. In such cases, a costume change would not be possible. Instead you would need identical puppets.

Controls. Generally these are threads. Heavyweight nylon or linen thread in white is best for this purpose. If a particularly heavy marionette is involved, use a lightweight flexible wire. Since marionettes are operated from above, the controls should be long enough so that the puppeteer can manipulate them without being seen. What complicates things a little is that the controls are attached to a puppet at different points but must come out even at the top. As a result, they will vary in length. How control threads are attached also depends on the puppet. In some cases they are sewn in place. In others they are held with staples or are attached to tiny eye screws embedded in the puppet's body. In attaching a set of controls, first install those for the head and the back, then move to the hands and knees. To make the task easier, some puppeteers suspend a marionette from a stringing stand. However, it also is practical to string a puppet that has been placed in a prone position on a table. As described earlier, the simplest controls may be held in one's hands. As they grow more complex, however, a control bar is essential.

Control Bars. These are small wooden bars to which the threads or wires are attached. Typically they are about a half-inch wide, a quarter-inch thick, and four to ten inches in length, varying with the size and the weight of the puppet. The threads are fastened to tiny eye screws or are positioned in notches and tied. A hook from which the puppet can be hung when not in use is installed on top of the bar at the center. The controls may be attached to two separate bars or to a single bar. It is best to start with separate bars, particularly with a six-string puppet.

The control bars in the drawing are for three-string puppets. When separate bars are used, one bar controls the arms, the threads required are attached to the back of the hands at one end and to the screw eyes on the bar at the other. The second bar controls the head. With the puppets in the drawing, a thread first was attached to one side of the head, then passed through the screw eye and attached to the other side. To help distinguish between the bars, each should be painted a different color.

Control bars for the six-string marionette look more complicated than they are.

Separate bars: As in the illustration, attach the head and back strings to one bar and the hand and knee strings to the other. Arrange the head string as described above; however, pass it through two eye screws rather than one. With the other bar, position the hand strings at either end and the leg strings side by side between them.

Single bar: This control actually consists of two bars fastened at right angles. It also is called a combination bar. Some combination bars can be dismantled and used separately. However, the one described is permanently fastened. As the illustration shows, it consists of a short bar and a somewhat longer bar which cross slightly off center. String the puppet as follows:

Attach a lightweight wire to the sides of the puppet's head and pass the wire through Position (1) as indicated in the illustration. Then extend a wire from Position (2) to the puppet's back. Next attach a wire to the wrist just above the puppet's left hand, pass it through the eye screw at Position (3), and attach it to the right hand. Attach the wire at Position (4) to the knees in the same way.

86

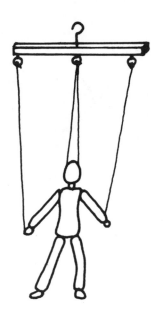

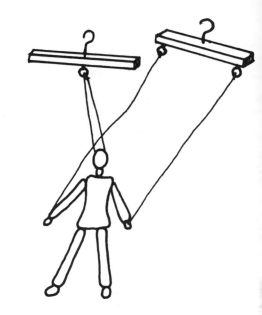

Single control bar for 3-string marionette.

Double control bars for 3-string marionette.

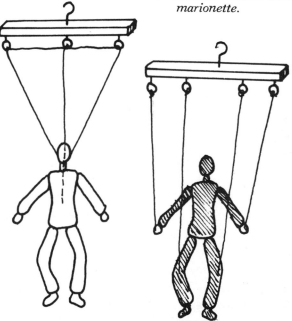

Double control bars, front and rear attachments, for 6-string marionette.

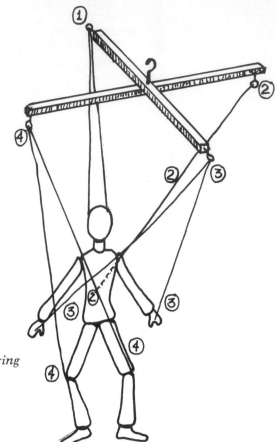

Combination bar for 6-string marionette.

Operating a Control Bar: A wide range of movements may be obtained either by tipping the bar, rocking it, manipulating the strings, or combining all three actions. For example, gently rocking a leg bar from side to side while moving it forward will enable a marionette to walk using one leg at a time. Tilting a bar forward while manipulating a back string will cause a marionette to bow. Pulling up an arm string while tilting the bar back slightly will cause the arm to rise. To use a puppet fully, however, it is necessary to experiment and practice.

Storage. The challenge is avoiding tangled lines. When a marionette is not in use, hang it from the hook on its control bar. You also can roll the strings around a bar, but it is essential to be careful. Prior to a performance place the marionettes you plan to use on a table side by side.

MARIONETTE THEATERS

Since marionettes are operated from above, the kind of theater needed differs somewhat from those used with other puppets. Here are three possibilities.

Directions for Making Theaters

Crate-Table Theater: Place an orange crate on its side in a doorway. Behind it position a card table turned on its side. Behind the table place a bench. Cover the part of the doorway above the table with opaque fabric. The crate serves as a stage and the card table as a backdrop to which a scenery flat could be pinned. The puppeteers stand on the bench, as in the illustration.

Crate-table theater.

Box-Table Theater: Remove the top and one side from a grocery box. Place the box on a table in a doorway with the open end facing the audience. Then cover the doorway above and below the stage. The puppeteers stand behind the table.

Wooden Box Theater: This is an excellent permanent theater. Remove the top and the front from a stout wooden box about the width of a door and two feet in height. Nail two half-inch strips of wood across the top from one side to the other, positioning them between the back and the center of the stage. These are bridges to support wings and scenery. Fasten a neutral-colored strip of paper or fabric four inches wide to both sides of the first bridge. The wings that result make possible graceful entrances and departures. Install hooks in the bridge at the back to sup-

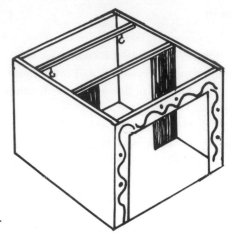

Wooden box theater.

port scenery flats, as with the theaters for hand and rod puppets. Also install curtains as described earlier. Finally, fasten a gaily colored cardboard proscenium to the front of the box. Place the theater on a table in a doorway and operate as described above. Use the lighting arrangements described in the section on hand puppets, except for the footlights, which are not effective with marionettes.

PLAYS
There are many plays designed for puppet theaters to which you might turn. The best place to look is the children's section of the public library. Adapting stories for stage use is another possibility. Material from *Winnie the Pooh, Peter Pan, Just So Stories,* or *Aesop's Fables* would work well. It is important, however, to reduce the number of characters and situations to a bare minimum. You also might put together a variety show in which each of several characters performs briefly. Once you have had some experience, prepare your own plays. In planning plays for shadow puppets, bear in mind that they cannot move with as much spirit or feeling as other types. As a result, a fully narrated play or a performance relying on a combination of narration and dialogue or on mime would be most suitable.

MUSIC AND SOUND EFFECTS
Music. The best use of music is at the start and conclusion of a play and each act. The music should set the mood. If part of a record is being used, mark the sections involved with adhesive tape so that they can be found easily.

Sound Effects. For rain—partially fill a small box with rice, beans, or pebbles, depending on how heavy a downpour is required, and shake. For thunder—strike a cardboard carton with a stick; a rushing river—stir water vigorously in a tub or bucket; shots—use a cap pistol; horses' hoofs—knock together heavy plastic bowls or coconut shells, or alternately strike two wooden blocks on a wooden table. For snow—blow soap flakes across the stage with an electric fan or drop from above; smoke or flashes of fire—use a chemistry set; lightning—rapidly move a small piece of cardboard back and forth in front of a naked light bulb.

ACTING WITH PUPPETS

To maintain the interest of an audience, it is wise to keep your puppets moving and keep their speeches short. Always make clear, moreover, which puppet is speaking. The easiest way is to have the speaking puppet remain still while others on stage move about. Of course, a puppet's movements also can be used to express how it feels. A drooping head, for example, will suggest sadness; a drooping body, despondency; and rapidly waving arms, excitement. One learns to use a puppet effectively only with practice. But the best puppeteers are those who not only have technical competence but are at one with their puppets, investing them with their outlook, ideas, and feelings.

BIBLIOGRAPHY

The Complete Puppet Book, L. V. Wall, Faber and Faber, London, 1956.
Practical Puppetry, John Mulholland, Arco Publishing Co., New York, 1961.
The Puppet Book, L. V. Wall, Plays, Inc., Boston, 1965.
The Puppet Theatre Handbook, Marjorie Batchelder, Harper & Row, New York, 1947.
Puppets and Plays, Marjorie Batchelder, Harper & Row, New York, 1956.
Shadow Puppets, Olive Blackham, Harper & Row, New York, 1960.

Books for Children
Penny Puppets, Penny Theatre, and *Penny Plays*, Moritz Jagendorf, Plays, Inc., Boston, 1966. Includes "The Winning of Wildcat Sue," "Beauty and the Beast," and seven other thrillers.
Puppets for Beginners, Moritz Jagendorf, Plays, Inc., Boston, 1966.

7·WEAVING

THE TECHNIQUES of the hand weaver may seem at first more mysterious than they actually are. What the weaver does essentially is interlace lengths of yarn. First he installs in his loom a taut bed of warp threads. Frequently there are hundreds of these arranged parallel to one another. Then at right angles he inserts a series of weft threads, weaving them over and under the warp threads. Thousands of weft threads may be involved. Although the weaver's work varies in terms of the patterns, colors, and yarns he uses, in every case he interlaces weft threads with warp threads, a method that also was used by craftsmen in the Middle East 7000 years ago.

Of course, the role of the weaver has changed. Two centuries ago hand weavers were responsible for producing all the fabric needed in the world. Since that time machines have taken over this work. Each year they manufacture over 90 billion square yards of fabric, but none of what they produce possesses the beauty and individuality of hand-woven textiles. As a result, there still are craftsmen who weave by hand. In fact, a number spin and dye their own yarn, then use the fabric they weave to create original garments and household accessories. Some weavers are professional craftsmen, but the largest proportion are amateurs who weave for the pleasure of it.

GETTING STARTED

If you are diligent, it is quite possible that you can learn to weave using a handbook as a guide. There are many books which describe the basic techniques on an illustrated step-by-step basis. Some of the best are listed in the Bibliography. Many beginners also learn the essentials at classes conducted in museums, YMCA's, and art studios. At the outset you will need equipment, yarn, an understanding of how a loom works, and a sense of the opportunities and the pitfalls. These matters are discussed below.

LOOMS

You can obtain a taste of weaving with a simple, inexpensive frame loom. This consists of a wooden frame studded with raised nails which hold the yarn in place. First the warp threads are strung between opposite ends of the loom. Then the weft is passed over and under the warp with a shuttle or a long needle. In this way one easily can produce a sizable square of fabric of his own design, but it is tedious work.

Several weavers I consulted recommend that a beginner with a serious interest in weaving acquire a 15-inch four-harness table loom. Such a loom would be capable of weaving a piece of fabric 15 inches wide. What its harnesses are and do is discussed later. However, a loom with four harnesses makes it possible to produce a great many designs, whereas looms with a smaller number are limited in this regard.

A 4-harness table loom.

A floor loom.

Ultimately many amateurs acquire a floor loom, which is more costly but weaves still wider pieces of fabric. Though the warping process is arduous, a floor loom is easier to use than a table loom, since the treadles that control the harnesses are operated by foot rather than by hand, thus leaving the weaver free to work the shuttle with both hands. Floor looms are available in stationary and folding models. They range upward in price from $200 for new equipment. Suppliers are listed at the end of the chapter.

OTHER EQUIPMENT

Shuttles. A shuttle is used to insert the weft between the warp threads. New looms usually come with a shuttle. But it is best to have several. If threads of different colors are used, for example, a separate shuttle is needed for each. The same is true if different yarns are used in combination. A common shuttle is the stick type around which the yarn is wrapped. Experienced weavers also use boat shuttles, which include a bobbin that carries the yarn. They also rely on a bobbin winder, which is available in both manual and electric models.

Warping Board. This device enables the weaver to arrange his yarn into warp threads of the appropriate length. The simplest type consists of a flat board with a number of pegs inserted at right angles. When a weaver purchases a floor loom, he may replace his warping board with a warping reel, which has still greater capacity.

Threading Hook. This is used in threading a loom, a procedure described below. Ordinarily a threading hook comes with a loom.

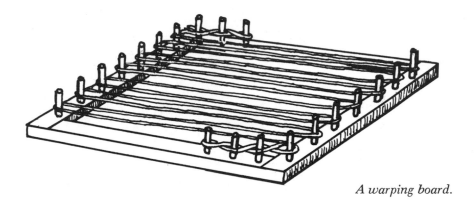

A warping board.

PATTERNS FOR FABRICS

There are a great many patterns available. In fact, there are books which concern themselves only with patterns. One of the best is listed in the Bibliography. Of course, some of the deepest satisfactions in hand weaving come from creating one's own patterns. Two basic patterns a beginner might experiment with are a plain weave and a twill weave.

In its variations the plain weave is called tabby, calico, homespun, basket weave, and taffeta. Basically it is a simple "over and under" weave. However, the weaver might go over and under one, two, or more warp threads. He also might combine yarns of various weights and textures. The same is true for colors. In fact, through the appropriate arrangement of colors, he can create stripes, checks, and plaids.

A twill weave is characterized by the use of diagonal lines which might yield a zigzag effect or a herringbone, a diamond, or a diagonal

95

pattern. In a twill design, the weft crosses over and under a fixed number of warp threads. However, each time a new weft thread is installed, it intersects with a warp thread to the left or right of the previous intersection.

Drafts. Frequently there are three sets of instructions, or drafts, for re-creating a pattern. All are depicted on graph paper. A profile draft describes the position of the warp and weft threads. If a warp thread is on top at a particular intersection, the square is black; if the weft is on top, the square is white. A threading draft indicates the way in which the loom is threaded. A treadling draft specifies the sequence in which to operate the treadles that control the harnesses.

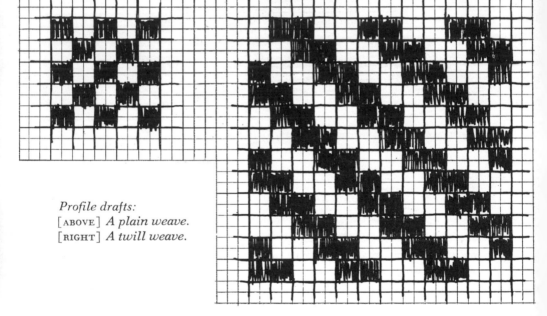

Profile drafts:
[ABOVE] *A plain weave.*
[RIGHT] *A twill weave.*

PROJECTS

The most useful first project would be a sampler of swatches depicting different patterns and color combinations. In developing such a sampler, the beginner not only learns the basic techniques of weaving but begins to get a sense of the potentialities. This also is an opportunity for experimentation. In fact, experienced weavers also experiment with swatches made on table looms, storing the more promising patterns and color combinations in a notebook for future reference.

Having mastered the basic techniques, a beginning weaver might attempt a place mat, a table runner, or a scarf. Other possibilities include pillow covers, hangings, ties, baby blankets, and draperies. However, with the blankets and the draperies, it would be necessary to sew lengths of fabric together to achieve the width needed. With a floor loom, tablecloths, rugs, and fabric from which garments can be made also become possibilities.

YARN

The options include cottons, linens, wools, synthetic fibers such as dacron and acetate, and blends. There are at least 2000 kinds of yarn available to the hand weaver. He may use them separately or in various combinations, depending on his objectives in regard to texture, weight, finish, durability, draping, and other requirements.

At the outset, however, it is wise to work with a crocheting cotton. This probably is the easiest yarn with which to learn the techniques of weaving. On the other hand, wool and linen are difficult "first" yarns. The former is too stretchy for this purpose and the latter too rigid. Since only a limited number of yarns can be obtained in most communities, the weaver soon finds that much of what he needs must be purchased by mail from mills and specialized suppliers. A list of such outlets is at the end of this chapter. Most distribute literature, yarn samples, and/or color cards.

Yarn typically is sold in two-ounce and four-ounce packages and by the pound, which usually is a better buy. However, initially yarn should be purchased in small quantities. It also is available "ready-warped" on spools or in braids, which eliminates the need for the warping process described below. At this writing, a major drawback of "ready warp" is cost. The yarn on spools, for example, is at least twice as expensive as ordinary yarn.

DYEING YARNS

A growing number of weavers use dyes extracted from common plants to dye their yarns in colors not ordinarily available from commercial sources. Creating such dyes is a fascinating pursuit. If you live in the country, the sources are virtually limitless. If you are a city dweller or a suburbanite, finding useful plants may be more of a challenge, but generally at least some are available. In addition, courses in natural dyeing are offered in many urban areas. For information check your local craft council, botanical garden, or Audubon Society. The American Craftsmen's Council (see Organizations) also may be a source of help. In addition, consult the handbooks listed in the Bibliography.

USING A LOOM

With their harnesses, heddles, reeds, pulleys, and bars, even the simplest looms are fearsome-looking devices. But they look, and in books like this may seem, far more confusing than they actually are.

Installing the warp threads, or threading the loom, may take but an hour or two or an entire day, depending on the size and complexity of the fabric and the weaver's experience. After he has decided on a pattern, he estimates the amount of yarn needed for the warp. This is based on the number of warp threads or warp ends called for and on their length. Then he estimates the amount of yarn needed for the weft. To determine this, he multiplies the number of threads per inch by the projected length and width of the fabric. Since yarn is sold by weight, he also must determine how many yards a package will yield. If a package doesn't provide this information, a supplier should be able to do so.

The yarn needed for the warp is then organized on the warping board into threads of the required length. Finally the warp is braided into a chain, cut into pieces, and fastened to the "warp beam"* of the loom. As noted earlier, there may be several hundred threads involved.

In threading the loom, the weaver first passes the warp threads through a series of perpendicular steel wires called "heddles," each of which has an eyelet at the center. The heddles are arranged side by side in wooden frames called "harnesses." The table loom recommended earlier has four harnesses arranged one behind the other, each with a row of several hundred heddles. In line with the threading pattern selected, each warp end is passed through a particular heddle in but one harness. The warp ends then are threaded through a "beater-reed," which keeps them properly spaced. The reed consists of a series of perpendicular wires in a frame, arranged like the teeth in a comb. The

---

* It can also be fastened to the "breast beam." In that case, the steps described below would be reversed.

spaces between the wires, through which the warp ends are threaded, are called "dents." Once the threads have been passed through the dents, they are attached to a "cloth beam," on which the fabric is stored as it is woven.

After the warp has been installed, the weaver loads his shuttle with yarn for the weft. As noted earlier, he will need separate shuttles for each type of yarn and for each color he uses. With the frame loom already described, a flat shuttle or needle is used to pass over and under the warp, pulling the weft into place. The procedure with a more advanced loom is far easier. Using a treadling draft as a guide, the weaver depresses a treadle which raises a particular harness. The harness then raises those warp ends that pass through its heddles, creating a "shed" that makes way for the weft. The weaver then moves his shuttle through the shed, laying the weft thread, or "pick," on top of the warp ends which were not raised. Next the beater-reed is used to beat the new pick against the fabric that already has been woven. Then the weaver raises a second harness which lifts other warp threads, and another pick is laid and beaten into place. With a more complex pattern, still other harnesses would be used to create additional sheds. In every case, however, the procedure is the same: shedding, picking, beating.

ORGANIZATIONS

It would be helpful to join a guild of amateur weavers. Such organizations provide an opportunity to meet experienced weavers, and they often sponsor lectures, demonstrations, and shows of their members' work. If you have difficulty locating a group, write for information to the American Craftsmen's Council, 29 W. 53rd Street, New York, N.Y. 10019.

SOURCES OF SUPPLY

Each of the firms listed below provides literature, yarn samples, and/or color cards. In some cases there may be a nominal charge.

Looms and Other Equipment

Bailey Manufacturing Co., 118 Lee Street, Lodi, Ohio 44254.
Gilmore Looms, 1032 N. Broadway Avenue, Stockton, California 95205.

Floor looms.

Grant, 6404 Golden Chain Drive, Salt Lake City, Utah 84107.

I. W. Macomber, 166 Essex Street, Saugus, Massachusetts 01906.

Norwood Loom Company, Box 272, Baldwin, Michigan 49304. Folding floor looms.

School Products Company, 312 E. 23rd Street, New York, N.Y. 10010.

Yarn

William Condon & Son, Ltd., 65 Queen Street, P.O. Box 129, Charlotte-town, Prince Edward Island, Canada.

Conlin Yarns, P.O. Box 11812, Philadelphia, Pennsylvania 19128.

Contessa Yarns, P.O. Box 37, Lebanon, Connecticut 06249.

Craft Yarns of Rhode Island, P.O. Box 385, Pawtucket, R.I. 02862.

Frederick J. Fawcett, Inc., 129 South Street, Boston, Massachusetts 02111.

Home Yarns Co., 1849 Coney Island Avenue, Brooklyn, N.Y. 11230.

Lily Mills Co., Shelby, N.C., 28150.

Tinkler & Co., 237 Chestnut Street, Philadelphia, Pennsylvania 19106.

Troy Yarn and Textile Company, 603 Mineral Spring Avenue, Paw-tucket, R.I. 02880.

Yarn Depot, Inc., 545 Sutter Street, San Francisco, California 94102.

BIBLIOGRAPHY

Handbooks

Handweaving, Iona Plath, Charles Scribner's Sons, New York, 1964.

Handweaving for Pleasure and Profit, Harriette J. Brown, Harper & Row, New York, 1952.

Key to Weaving, Mary E. Black, Bruce Publishing Co., Milwaukee, 1957.

On Weaving, Anni Albers, Wesleyan University Press, Middletown, Connecticut, 1965.

The Shuttlecraft Book of American Handweaving, Mary M. Atwater, The Macmillan Co., New York, 1951.

The Weaver's Book, Harriet C. Tidball, The Macmillan Co., New York, 1961.

Weaving as a Hobby, Marguerite Ickis, Sterling Publishing Co., New York, 1968.

Handbooks on Dyeing Yarns

Dye Plants and Dyeing, Handbook #46, Brooklyn Botanical Garden, 1000 Washington Avenue, Brooklyn, N.Y. 11225. Write for current price.

Natural Dyes and Home Dyeing, Rita J. Adrosko, Dover Publications, Inc., New York, 1971.

Pattern Book

Designing and Drafting for Handweavers, Berta Frey, The Macmillan Co., New York, 1958.

Periodicals

Craft Horizons, 44 W. 53rd Street, New York, N.Y. 10019. Monthly.

Handweaver & Craftsman, 220 Fifth Avenue, New York, N.Y. 10001. Quarterly.

8·WHITTLING AND WOODCARVING

THE BEST WAY to learn how to carve in wood is to acquire a piece of white pine and a sharp pocketknife, find a comfortable place to sit, perhaps under a tree, and whittle away. The result may be an impressive pile of chips or, if you have better fortune, a flower, a cow, or some other simple figure. In any case you will have made a start and also spent a relaxing hour or two. Some people like whittling so well they continue to rely on their pocketknife and become quite skillful. Others eventually turn to instruments such as gouges, chisels, and skews. They work with larger, more complicated projects, pay close attention to the kinds of woods available and the pattern of the grain, finishes, and related matters, and at times produce remarkable work.

Man has been carving in wood for thousands of years. He has created statuary, masks, altarpieces, choir stalls, figureheads for ships, architectural embellishments, and decorative and utilitarian objects of every description. One need only visit a museum of art or natural history to gain a sense of the possibilities. As might be expected, some of what has been preserved was created by great artists whose primary medium was wood, men such as Michael Pacher, Veit Stoss, and Grinling Gibbons and more recently William Zorach and Robert Laurent. What is intriguing, however, is that much of what has endured is the work of anonymous craftsmen and amateurs.

A year before this book was written, for example, the work of John Scholl came to light. When Mr. Scholl was eighty, he gave up working his Pennsylvania farm and spent the remaining ten years of his life whittling, using his jackknife, as one critic put it, the way a painter uses pigment. In his ten years as a whittler he created religious objects, giant snowflakes, toys, a Ferris wheel, birds, flowers, and other commonplace objects he endowed with beauty, humor, and understanding. Nothing he created was for sale. He whittled for the fun of it.*

The whittler who does best at his craft is one with a keen eye and a sense of the intricacy of life. He also needs patience, for results can be a long time in coming. If one does not have these characteristics, he can acquire them. The best way is by whittling.

TOOLS

As already noted, all one needs to start is a jackknife. To make the most intricate cuts, a penknife, which has far smaller blades, would also be useful. A number of whittlers prefer knives with fixed blades, such as sloyd knives. In addition, a knife that is bent or hooked at the end is a good supplementary tool. Other whittlers I've talked to like the knife handles that come with interchangeable blades.

The chisels, gouges, and other tools referred to earlier make cuts of different sizes, shapes, and depths and make it possible to do more intricate work with great efficiency. There is a vast and confusing range of these available. They are described in manuals in the Bibliography and in the catalogs under Sources of Supply. The neophyte would be wise to purchase one of the beginner's sets many manufacturers offer. Ordinarily these include four or five cutting instruments and a small mallet for driving chisels when working in hardwood. A vise and wood clamps also would be useful.

When it is necessary to remove large quantities of unwanted wood, a rasp, a coping saw, and a spokeshave play useful roles. Some woodworkers with power tools also turn to a hand saw or a jig saw for this purpose.

Sharpening Tools. Carving tools must be razor sharp or they cannot do the job for which they were designed. In addition, new tools need sharpening before they can be used.

Sharpening Equipment and Supplies: One or more oilstones are essential. Many woodcarvers rely on a manufactured stone, either a Carborundum or an India type. These come in coarse, medium, and fine grades. A combination stone with coarse and fine faces is a good invest-

---

* Some 50 years after his death, however, his work was sold at prices ranging up to $2500 for a single object.

ment. To produce an exceedingly fine edge, also acquire an Arkansas or Washita stone. These are fine-grained natural stones. For sharpening gouges and other tools with contours, you also will need a number of slipstones. These are small oilstones in various shapes.

To keep a stone from moving while in use, it should be mounted. Some suppliers sell mounts. You also can make your own by using four strips of wood to enclose the space a stone is to occupy on a wooden block. In using an oilstone, you also will need a quantity of light machine oil. Ordinarily the final step in sharpening is stropping. For this procedure, acquire a piece of leather 4″ × 12″, mount it on a wooden block, and impregnate it with emery paste.

Techniques: Depending on the condition of the tool, use either a coarse or a medium grade Carborundum or India stone. Position the tool on the stone so that it rests flat on its bevel and maintain this angle in sharpening. To start, place a few drops of oil on the stone.

If you are sharpening a knife, place it at the far end of the stone with the back of its blade toward you and pull it in your direction. Then turn the blade over and pull it in the opposite direction, repeating until sharp. If you are sharpening a chisel, push the tool forward a number of times with its beveled side down, exerting pressure on the blade as you do so. This step produces a burr or a wire edge. To remove, place the chisel face down on the stone and move it forward. In sharpening a gouge, move the tool forward as with the chisel; as you do so, however, slowly rotate the gouge along the width of its blade. Remove the wire edge that forms on the inside of the blade with a slipstone. To sharpen tools further, use a finer stone.

In stropping a straight-edged tool, pull the blade across the leather several times. With a curved tool, rotate the blade as you pull. When you have finished, wipe the tool with an oily rag.

Storage. If a tool is to remain sharp, it must not come in contact with other metal surfaces. Therefore, carving tools usually are stored in racks or in divided drawers. If you don't have a great many tools, however, you can keep them in a tool roll. You can buy one or you can make one. To do so, you will need a piece of baize, Pacific cloth, or tightly woven lightweight canvas about two feet long and a foot wide. Form a two-inch cuff at the bottom of the fabric and another at the top and stitch in place at the ends. Then stitch individual pockets into the cuffs at two-inch intervals and fasten a length of tape at each of the outside vertical edges. When the tools are in place, roll them up and secure with the tape.

WOOD

A clear, close-grained white pine is one of the most satisfactory woods with which you can work. Birch, spruce, basswood, yellow poplar, and red cedar are others. However, balsa is too soft and is not durable. Hardwoods such as mahogany, pear, apple, and cherry are excellent, but generally require the use of gouges, chisels, and a mallet. On the other hand, walnut and oak are so dense they are difficult to carve.

Some projects require flat broad pieces, which can be obtained from planks an inch thick. Others need the bulk provided by a two-by-two, a two-by-four, or a four-by-four. In any case, purchase a substantial length, cut off what you need, and save the rest for another day.

Sources of Supply. Lumber yards are, of course, a primary source of wood. Hardware stores and hobby shops are likely to have the carving and sharpening equipment you need. If you become deeply involved, you may find it useful to turn to suppliers such as those listed below who specialize in carving equipment and exotic woods. Each will send a catalog on request.

Albert Constantine & Son, Inc., 2050 Eastchester Road, Bronx, N.Y. 10461.

Craftsman Wood Service Company, 2727 S. Mary Street, Chicago, Illinois 60608.

Woodcraft Supply Corp., 313 Montvale Avenue, Woburn, Massachusetts 01801.

PROJECTS AND TECHNIQUES

One of the possibilities is carving in relief. Sketch a design on tracing paper, transfer it to the wood,* then cut away the unneeded material at a depth of an eighth or a quarter of an inch, with the result that the design stands out. When carved in a thin, flat piece of wood, the work may be used as a plaque. However, furniture, bookends, trays, and other objects also may be decorated in this way.

Three-dimensional figures are, of course, another possibility. If the figures are carved from a relatively flat piece of wood, they may be fastened to a plaque. Carved birds frequently are displayed in this fashion. Otherwise, a figure may be mounted on a base or, if it is thick

* See Chapter 2, Making Prints, for the technique involved.

enough, may be free-standing. In addition to birds, one might try mammals, fish, or flowers. Human figures are more difficult. Some carvers also enjoy making useful objects such as trays, plates, bowls, and salad spoons and forks. The books listed in the Bibliography are filled with detailed plans for such projects.

Getting Started. The most sensible first step is to learn what your tools can do. Acquire a piece of white pine and experiment until all that remains is a pile of chips. Then create something. One of the pleasantest of projects, and one of the easiest, is carving an egg, either life-size or larger. Use a two-by-two four inches long or a four-by-four six inches long. Carefully rule a series of lines which bisect the wood horizontally and vertically on all sides, as the drawing indicates. This will help to keep your egg from becoming lopsided. Then sketch views of the egg as it would be seen from all sides. Remove most of the unneeded wood with a rasp, a coping saw, or a knife with a large blade. After you have carved a rough shape, work with smaller blades. When you are satisfied with your effort, sand the egg and apply a finish, as described below.

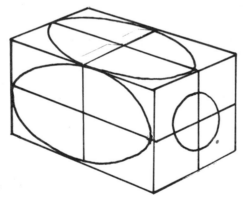

Carving an egg.

Next experiment with a figure such as the cat shown in the drawings. Work with a two-by-four about six inches long. Draw the horizontal and vertical lines described above. Then sketch the cat in all its dimensions on all four sides and the top. Remove most of the unneeded wood at the top, front, and back, but maintain the width of the block. Then rough in the sides. In the final step add the detail.

In developing their ideas, some carvers create a clay model before sketching a design on wood. Some also devote a good deal of time to

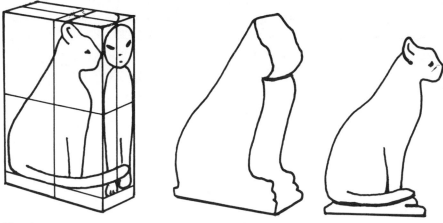

Carving a cat.

selecting the most appropriate wood for the project in terms of color and texture. Incorporating the grain in their design also is of importance to them.

When you are ready to begin cutting, work with the grain, using your thumb and perhaps other fingers to guide and steady the tool. Make certain, of course, that your hand is behind the cutting edge at all times; otherwise you risk a serious injury. When working with gouges, chisels, and similar instruments, use a vise or clamps to hold the wood firmly in place.

Finishing. Some objects benefit from a light sanding which eliminates scratches but retains the faceting left by the tools. Others look better if some or all of the facets are removed. This is a decision only the craftsman can make. Whatever sanding is required should be done under light pressure with the utmost care. With curved areas, use pieces of sandpaper rolled into cylinders.

A paste wax designed for use on raw wood is an effective finish for most projects. One such product is Minwax. Generally three light coats are used, with a half-hour for drying and a period for polishing between each application. Penetrating sealers also are practical; however, varnishes are not satisfactory. Some carvers stain their work before waxing, but it is well first to test the stain on a sample of the wood to determine if it yields.the color you are seeking and provides uniform coverage. Carved objects also may be painted. In such cases the wood first should be sealed. If water color is used, two coats may be necessary; then apply wax. If an enamel or lacquer is used, one coat is likely to be sufficient, and an additional finish is not necessary. Certain woods require the application of a wood filler before finishing. Your lumber, hardware, or paint dealer can advise you.

INSTRUCTION

At times a museum or an adult education program will offer instruction in woodcarving, but generally the neophyte is on his own except for help provided by other, more experienced carvers and by the authors of books such as those in the Bibliography.

BIBLIOGRAPHY

The Art of Wood Carving, John Upton, Van Nostrand-Reinhold Co., New York, 1958.

Bird Carving, Wendell Gilley, Van Nostrand-Reinhold Co., New York, 1961.

Contemporary Carving and Whittling, W. Ben Hunt, Bruce Publishing Co., Milwaukee, 1967. A good book for beginners.

Creative Wood Craft, Ernst Rottger, Van Nostrand-Reinhold Co., New York, 1963.

Whittling and Woodcarving, E. J. Tangerman, Dover Publications, New York, 1936.

Wood Carving, Freda Skinner, Sterling Publishing Co., New York, 1963.

Woodcarving for Beginners, Charles Graveney, Watson-Guptill Publications, New York, 1967. An excellent literate introduction.

9·WOODWORKING

ALL KINDS OF PEOPLE work with wood, but they have many things in common. They like using their hands, they like making things, and they love wood—its coloring and grain, the way it smells, and, above all, the kinds of things it enables them to do. Woodworkers I know create doll houses, toys, shelving of all types, furniture, cabinets, virtually anything you might name. In fact, a librarian in the next town, a middle-aged lady of great skill and determination, even built her own house.

A PLACE TO WORK

Initially a basement, a spare room, or an attic might make an admirable place to work. With some projects, a kitchen also could be used. If you decide to invest in a permanent shop, try to acquire a work area that is at least 8′ × 10′ in size with a sturdy floor, good lighting, and lots of electric outlets. If possible, it should be isolated, or at least insulated in some way, from the rest of your home.

A WORKBENCH

An old table will serve if you screw or clamp a ¾-inch sheet of plywood to the top. But eventually a real bench would be needed. You can buy one for relatively little or can build one without too much difficulty. Several of the publications in the Bibliography contain plans for workbenches. A bench should be equipped with a woodworking vise, support pegs, a bench stop, and a bench hook. A vise holds a piece of lumber in place while it is being worked with a plane, a chisel, or

Bench hook.

some other cutting instrument. Purchase one that is bolted rather than clamped to a bench and that has at least a four-inch opening. Support pegs and a bench stop are holding devices used primarily with longer pieces of wood, usually in conjunction with a vise. A bench hook helps hold shorter pieces in place for sawing and other operations. As the drawing suggests, it is a simple matter to make one.

HAND TOOLS

One catalog lists over 1500 different hand tools for woodworking. However, initially a dozen would be sufficient, and these should be purchased only as the need arises. If you buy the highest quality tools you can afford, they will provide years of efficient operation. A hardware store usually is a good place to buy tools, but if there is a shop nearby that specializes in tools, it might prove more satisfactory, since the salesmen are likely to be more knowledgeable. Sooner or later you will need the following basic tools.

Measuring. Straight-edge ruler, eight-foot retractable steel tape, try square for insuring right angles, pencil, scratch awl.

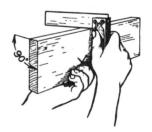

Testing squareness with try square.

Later: a sliding T-bevel for determining various angles, dividers for marking circles and arcs, calipers for various small measurements, and a marking gauge for marking wood for sawing and other operations.

Holding. Workbench accessories noted above, clamps for gluing and other purposes.

Cutting. Twenty-four-inch crosscut saw with a 10-point blade (10 teeth to the inch). This tool is used primarily to cut against the grain but will also cut with the grain of soft woods. Eight-inch coping saw for making curved and other irregular cuts. Mitre box, to assure accurate 45- and 90-degree cuts.

Later: a 24-inch 5-point ripsaw for cutting with the grain, a 12-inch 14-point backsaw for fine work, a keyhole saw for cutting holes.

Removing Wood. A Stanley "Surform" tool, which functions both as a small plane and a rasp.

Later: a 12-inch jack plane for producing a smooth surface with the grain, a six-inch block plane for planing across the grain, a set of woodworking chisels from one-quarter to one inch in size for cuts of various types, a wooden mallet for driving the chisels.

Boring Holes. Brad awl or gimlet for making small holes to start nails or screws, hand drill with one-quarter-inch chuck for drilling small holes, 8-inch ratchet brace with bits up to one inch, plus an expansion bit for larger holes, nail set for sinking nail heads below a surface.

Fastening. A claw hammer for pounding and removing nails, with a wooden handle to absorb the shock of impact. A 12-ounce hammer ordinarily is used for general work and a 16-ounce model for heavy work, but the weight you select should also depend on the ease with which you can use the tools. A set of screwdrivers, including standard and Phillips models, for driving screws of different sizes and types.

LUMBER

Lumber is sold in boards of various widths and thicknesses, as moldings and other forms of trim, and as panels. It is available either as a hardwood taken from a deciduous tree or as a softwood from a faster-growing conifer, or evergreen. Generally softwoods are less expensive, easier to work with, and useful in all sorts of simple, casual projects. They are by far the best types of wood for the beginner. The hardwoods generally are sturdier, more difficult to manipulate, more costly. They are best suited for projects such as building furniture, where durability as well as appearance is of importance. Boards, trim, and plywoods come in both softwoods and hardwoods. Bear in mind, however, that not all lumber classified as "hardwood" (i.e., from a deciduous tree) is hard. Basswood is a good example of a soft hardwood. The opposite also is true. Softwoods such as fir are harder than some hardwoods.

Quality. A wise approach is to buy the least expensive grade of wood that will satisfy your needs. But be certain that what you buy is dry and well seasoned. Otherwise your project may shrink, warp, or crack. All lumber is graded in terms of the relative number of knots, holes, twisted fibers, and other defects. There are times when the only wood suitable for a project must be free of defects. In most cases, however, less expensive wood will meet your needs. The standard grades of lumber and the uses for which they are suited are as follows:

1 and 2 Clear: Both sides have no defects. Suitable for the highest quality cabinet work.

C quality: Very small knots, other minor defects; one side may have no defects. For quality cabinet work.

D quality: A somewhat larger number of imperfections, but highly useful for general projects that may be finished or painted.

No. 1: Larger, more numerous knots, but the knots are sound and smooth. Useful for general projects that require painting.

Nos. 2, 3: A still larger number of knots, including at times knotholes. Useful for rough work such as shelving in work areas.

Nos. 4, 5: Lowest quality. Generally not suitable for home workshop projects.

The type of plywood made from softwoods ranges in quality from grade A-A, in which both sides are perfect, to grade D-D, in which both sides suffer from serious defects. An A-D grade would be perfect on one side but imperfect on the other. Plywood made from hardwoods ranges in grade from "custom" to "reject."

Recommended Woods. In your first projects use woods such as pine, black willow, spruce, and redwood, all of which are relatively soft and, as a result, are easy to cut, fasten, sand, and finish. Plywood also should be useful, since it will neither warp nor split and is exceedingly strong. Initially it might serve as the back of a bookcase or the top of a workbench. Eventually you might want to use plywood in cabinetry and paneling. As you grow more skillful and more concerned with craftsmanship, consider such woods as walnut, maple, birch, ash, mahogany, and cherry.

Lumber Sizes. One buys boards by the board foot, a unit a foot long, a foot wide, and about an inch thick. A board six inches wide, six feet long, and an inch thick, for example, would consist of three board feet. But dimensions can be misleading, since a board is usually slightly narrower and thinner than the standard sizes indicate. This is a result of drying and milling. Boards up to six inches in width actually are three-eighths of an inch narrower than the specified size. Those more than six inches wide are a half-inch narrower. Boards designated as one inch thick actually are 25/32 of an inch thick. Two-inch boards or more are three-eighths of an inch thinner than the stated measurement. Trim is sold by the running foot and panels by the square foot.

Saving Money. The cheapest lumber frequently will yield excellent wood for small jobs once the knots and other defects are cut away. For rough work consider wood from old crates and boxes and also the secondhand lumber sold by salvage companies.

OTHER MATERIALS

Abrasives. In the early nineteenth century carpenters used sharkskin to smooth wood. Today we rely on garnet paper for general sanding and aluminum oxide for sanding that requires extensive removal of wood. Purchase several sheets of each in medium and fine grits. However, traditional sandpaper is not a good buy, for it is not durable.

Fasteners. There are thousands upon thousands of different types, models, and sizes. They include nails, screws and bolts, and devices used in forming or strengthening joints.

Nails: Brads are the smallest nails, starting at a quarter-inch in length. Common wire nails range in size from one inch to six inches. Usually they are used for the rougher kinds of work. However, they include box nails, which are somewhat thinner and not as likely to split a piece of wood. There also are finishing and casing nails, which have smaller heads than other types and may be set below the surface.

Casing nails are most useful in fastening interior trim. Heavier, longer nails are designated as spikes. They range in size from three to twelve inches.

A nail generally should be two to three times as long as the thickness of the wood being fastened. For most jobs common wire nails have sufficient holding power. If more is needed, use cement-coated nails or threaded nails. If outside work is involved, be certain that the nails are made of copper, aluminum, or some other rustproof material.

Nails from one to six inches in length are categorized by a penny size represented by the letter "d." The scale is as follows:

2d, 1″; 3d, 1¼″; 4d, 1½″; 5d, 1¾″; 6d, 2″; 7d, 2¼″; 8d, 2½″; 9d, 2¾″; 10d, 3″; 12d, 3¼″; 16d, 3½″; 20d, 4″; 30d, 4½″; 40d, 5″; 50d, 5½″; 60d, 6″.

Screws: Wood screws should be used instead of nails when the object being assembled is large or may be subject to heavy use or repeated vibrations. They also should be used with pieces that must be dismantled and with hardware such as hinges and drawer pulls.

There are three basic types of screws. The flat-head screw is used when a flush surface is desired or when the screw head is to be countersunk below the surface. Screws with round and oval heads are used primarily for decorative purposes. All three varieties are available with single slots or with crossed Phillips slots which permit greater pressure to be exerted in tightening.

Screws are designated by length and by gauge numbers ranging from zero to 30, which indicate the diameter of the unthreaded shank. A zero-gauge screw, for example, has a diameter of .0578 inch. A 30-gauge screw is .4520 in diameter. Methods of installing screws are described in the section Using Hand Tools. Since screws are relatively expensive, purchase only those you need for a particular project.

Bolts, Other Fasteners: When a project requires exceedingly rugged fasteners, carriage bolts, lag screws, and similar devices often are useful.

Glues. In certain situations glue is more practical than a mechanical fastener. These include forming joints, creating larger pieces of wood from narrower or thinner pieces, and attaching small pieces to reinforce the framework of larger objects.

STORAGE OF TOOLS AND FASTENERS

A panel of pegboard or plywood provides one practical method. Install the panel on the wall immediately above your workbench. Then suspend the tools with hooks and clamps. Cluster related tools. To be certain tools are returned to their proper place, draw their outlines on the panel. There also are tool cabinets available which may be installed on a wall. Fasteners often are stored by type and size in covered glass jars arranged on shelves. Metal cabinets with "see-through" plastic drawers also are available for this purpose.

MAINTENANCE OF HAND TOOLS

All hand tools need lubrication. Metal parts should be wiped several times a year with an oily rag. If rust has developed, remove it beforehand with a commercial solvent. At least once a year oil all moving parts, such as those in braces and drills. In addition, regularly sharpen drills, planes, chisels, auger bits, saws, and other cutting devices. A professional should sharpen your saws. However, you can sharpen other tools in your workshop. The manuals listed in the Bibliography contain detailed instructions. When wooden handles and other wooden surfaces become rough, they should be sanded smooth, then refinished with a penetrating sealer. If a hammer handle becomes loose, the addition of a thin wedge at the top may solve the problem. If not, swell the wood by applying a mixture of water and glycerin.

PROJECTS AND PLANS

Concentrate first on small, simple projects. In this way you can learn the techniques and develop the skills you need without too great an investment in materials. A first project might be a workbench, a bookshelf, a bird house, a toy, or a shoe rack. Your library is likely to have many books of plans for projects at all levels of complexity. In addition, lumber yards sell plans at nominal costs. So do a number of companies and associations such as the following, which offer free lists of what they have available.

Douglas Fir Plywood Association, 9225 Westmont Place, S.W., Tacoma, Washington 98498

Masonite Corporation, Home Planning Service, 29 N. Walker Drive, Chicago, Illinois 60606

Stanley Tools, Advertising Services Dept., 195 Lake Street, New Britain, Connecticut 06052

Western Pine Association, Yeon Building, Portland, Oregon 97204

USING HAND TOOLS

Initially learn how to use a saw, a plane, a brace and bit, a hammer, and a screwdriver. Also learn how to make measurements. Before undertaking your first project, practice with your tools on scrap wood. Basic techniques are described below. Advanced approaches, such as joinery, are covered in the manuals listed in the Bibliography.

Measuring and Marking. You will make many of your measurements with a rule of one type or another. When sawing is required, the best tool for marking a line parallel to the grain is a marking gauge. For small measurements, calipers are useful. To test the squareness of edges, ends, and work faces, use a try square. To inscribe circles and arcs, use a divider. For many projects, a well-sharpened lead pencil may be used for marking; if the highest degree of precision is needed, use a scratch awl.

Using a Saw. The first step is to draw a guideline. The second is to position the lumber for cutting. Rest the wood on a workbench or a pair of sawhorses, then steady it with one knee and one hand. Bear in mind that the cut, or kerf, of the saw removes one-eighth of an inch of wood. Therefore make your cut in the waste wood at the edge of the guideline, or the wood will not be cut precisely to size. With both a crosscut and a ripsaw, cut down from above. Start the cut near the handle, raising and lowering the saw with long rhythmic strokes in which the greatest pressure is exerted on the downstroke. Periodically check the position of the blade with a try square to assure that the

Using a ripsaw.

cut is true. As noted earlier, a crosscut saw is designed primarily to cut against the grain, while a ripsaw is used for cutting with the grain. The crosscut saw should be held at a 45-degree angle; the most efficient angle for a ripsaw is 60 degrees. If the wood on either side of a cut tends to bind a saw, use a case knife to keep the opening clear.

Using a crosscut saw.

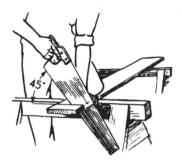

Using a Plane. Either a plane or a "Surform" tool will serve. Make certain the tool is sharp. With a plane be sure the blade extends only far enough to produce a thin ribbon of shavings. Use long continuous strokes. Check your work periodically with a try square to avoid creating hills and valleys.

Using Abrasives. A sandpaper holder will help you achieve a perfectly flat surface. This device takes about a quarter of the standard 9" × 11" sheet in which abrasives are sold. Fold the sheet carefully, then tear off what you need with a straight edge. Power sanders are described in the section Power Tools.

Drilling Holes. To start a hole for a nail or a screw, use a brad awl. To drill a small hole, use a hand drill. To drill a larger hole, use a brace and bit. When the tip of the bit cuts through the wood, remove it and complete the hole from the other side. This reduces the possibility of rough edges and splintering.

Operating a brace and bit.

117

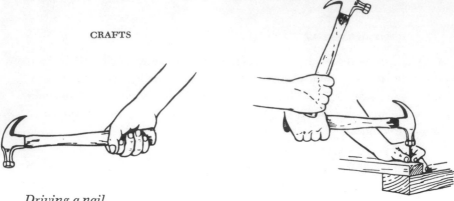

Driving a nail.

Using a Hammer. As noted earlier, a nail should be two to three times as long as the thickness of the wood being fastened. While a nail usually is started with an awl, it may be necessary to drill a pilot hole if a hardwood is involved. It also will be easier to sink a nail if you first rub it with paraffin or graphite. In driving a nail, grasp the hammer near the end of the handle. Then strike the nail head with relatively light rhythmic taps, not deadly blows. Your hand should be at the level of the nail head when the hammer makes contact. If it is higher, the nail will be driven forward; if it is lower, it will be bent back.

Should a nail bend, remove it and start a new nail in another location. To remove a bent nail, position the claw of the hammer under the nail head. Then slowly pull back the hammer until its handle is at right angles to the wood. If the nail does not readily come free, place a small block of wood next to it. Using it as a lever, pull the hammer back until the nail is released. To avoid splitting a piece of wood, stagger a series of nails rather than inserting them in a line. Blunting the point of a nail by striking it with a hammer also will reduce the danger of splitting. To countersink a nail, use a nail set. Then fill the resulting hole with a putty stick the color of the wood.

Drawing a nail.

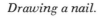

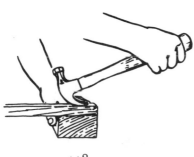

118

Using a Screwdriver. The procedure depends on the project. If you are fastening two thin pieces of wood or are fastening hardware to a piece of wood, punch the necessary pilot holes with a brad awl and place the screws in the holes. Then tap the screws gently with a hammer and drive them into position with a screwdriver of the appropriate size. If you are fastening two thick pieces of wood which require long screws, a somewhat different procedure is needed. There are three steps.

(1) Drill a pilot hole that is slightly smaller than the circumference of the threaded portion of the screw. The hole should be about three-quarters of the overall length of the screw and penetrate both pieces of wood.

(2) Using a larger bit, broaden the top portion of the hole so that it is slightly larger than the circumference of the unthreaded shank. In this instance drill only through the top piece of wood.

(3) To countersink the screw, widen the topmost portion of the hole so that it equals the diameter of the screw head. Fill the resulting hole with putty or with a piece of dowel that matches the wood and the grain. The manuals in the Bibliography contain tables which list the bits needed with each screw size.

Safety. The National Safety Council suggests the following:

Use tools only for the purpose for which they are designed.

Be certain cutting tools are sharp. Otherwise they require additional force, which can lead to accidents. Also check handles to make certain they are tight and sound.

Carry tools with cutting edges or sharp points face down. Never place such tools in your pockets. Carry only that number of tools at one time that you can manage safely.

In using chisels, knives, or other cutting tools, keep both hands behind the cutting edge.

Store tools so that they cannot fall.

POWER TOOLS

When you undertake projects that require more sawing, drilling, and sanding than is practical to do by hand, it is time to purchase one or more power tools. There are two categories of power equipment: relatively inexpensive hand-held portable tools and larger more costly stationary tools mounted on pedestals. Both types are operated by electric motors. Both also are available with a variety of attachments that enable them to perform not only their basic functions but many others as well.

Portable Tools. Usually it is these to which the amateur turns first. They include saws, drills, sanders, and routers. Each type is available separately or in a kit with a number of attachments.

Saws: A power saw is used to do basic cutting or to reduce a piece of wood to a size where hand cutting is practical. Through the use of interchangeable blades, a portable saw may be used for crosscutting, ripping, creating grooves (dadoes), rabbet cuts, and joints of various types, and handling other specialized work. The most versatile of the portable saws is a saber-type saw. The most desirable of these is equipped with a control that regulates the speed of the cutting edge.

Drills: Aside from drilling holes, a power drill may function as a sander for curved and flat surfaces, a grinder, a polishing and buffing unit, a screwdriver, even a paint mixer. It also may be mounted on a stand and used as a drill press. The most practical sizes for drills are three-eighths-inch and half-inch.

Sanders: Although a power drill may be used as a general sander, a reciprocating sander is more satisfactory in preparing a surface for a finish. A belt sander with a vacuum attachment is the best tool for sanding a large surface.

Routers: These devices are mechanized chisels which make decorative cuts in pieces of wood, create moldings, grooves and other decorative edges, fashion joints, and do mortising and countless other jobs.

Stationary Tools. Equipment of this type usually serves the advanced amateur and the professional. It includes lathes, shapers, jointers, and saws and drills of various types. Individual units may cost as much as several hundred dollars. At this writing a complete "home factory" might cost $2000 or more.

Safety. The National Safety Council suggests the following:

In purchasing power tools, be certain that all moving parts are properly enclosed.

Prior to operating such a tool, remove jewelry, your watch, and tie, replace loose clothing, roll sleeves above the elbow, and cover loose hair.

Carefully follow the manufacturer's directions.

Wear an eye shield where appropriate. However, do not wear gloves.

Make any adjustments with the power fully disconnected. Do not trust snap switches.

Do not leave a tool until it has completely stopped. If young children have access to the area, remove any cutting attachments and "lock out" the power supply.

Clean all equipment with a bench duster rather than your hands.

The Safety Council's booklets *Home Workshops* and *Safety in the Woodshop* cover in detail precautions necessary for operation of each of the standard power tools. For information on these and related publications write The National Safety Council, 425 N. Michigan Avenue, Chicago, Illinois 60611.

INSTRUCTION, ORGANIZATIONS

Many adult education programs offer courses in woodworking and furniture refinishing. If a course is not available, school officials may organize one if there is enough interest. In some communities there are woodworking clubs that provide instruction. At times they provide tools and other materials at a discount. Individual hobbyists also may be excellent sources of advice.

BIBLIOGRAPHY

Books, Pamphlets

Awful Handyman's Book, George Daniels, Harper & Row, New York, 1966.

Better Homes and Gardens Handyman's Book, Meredith Publishing Co., New York, 1951.

Carpenters and Builders Guide No. 1, Frank D. Graham, Harry F. Ulrey, Theodore Audel & Co., Indianapolis, 1966.

Complete Book of Home Remodeling, Improvement, and Repair, Arthur M. Watkins, Doubleday & Co., 1963.

How to Work with Wood and Tools, Educational Department, Stanley Tools, Pocket Books, New York, 1968. Includes plans for 39 projects. Available through Advertising Services Dept., Stanley Tools, New Britain, Connecticut 06050. 75 cents.

Stanley Tool Guide, Educational Department, Stanley Tools, New Britain, Connecticut. Available through Advertising Services Dept. 50 cents.

Unhandyman's Guide to Home Repairs, R. O'Neill, The Macmillan Co., New York, 1965.

Periodicals
Family Handyman, 235 E. 45th Street, New York, N.Y. 10017.
The Home Craftsman, 315 S. Washington, Alexandria, Virginia 22314.
Workbench, 4251 Pennsylvania, Kansas City, Missouri 64111.

PART II

COLLECTIONS

AUTOGRAPHS
COINS
POSTAGE STAMPS
PRINTS AND REPRODUCTIONS
OTHER COLLECTIONS

10·AUTOGRAPHS

ON APRIL 10, 1867, in Honolulu, a mariner named Montross and a sea captain named Soule signed an agreement in which Montross accepted the post of first mate aboard the whaling ship *St. George* bound for Alaskan waters. In return for his services he would receive one-eighteenth of "all oil and bone caught during the time he . . . [was] on board."

On April 7, 1895, the humorist Eugene D. Field wrote to a friend about P. T. Barnum's circus, "I felt under lasting obligation to Barnum, for he had discovered me when I lived in a tree in Missouri."

On December 2, 1932, the black poet Countee Cullen wrote to a friend about the roots of racial prejudice, "Negroes and whites cannot get to know each other by remaining apart; what we do not know we either fear or suspect."

Letters and documents dealing with people, events, ideas, occupations, and daily life are attracting a growing number of collectors. The fascination, as one collector put it, is "owning a piece of history." However, the average collector usually does not start with correspondence. Instead, he focuses first on signatures and on public documents signed by well-known persons. It is only after he has acquired some experience and has determined precisely what his interests are that he considers letters, manuscripts, and similar materials, some of which are quite expensive.

The items described above could have been purchased at from $40 to $100 each when this book was written. However, there are also countless signatures and documents available for far less. The signatures of contemporary baseball players, politicians, musicians, authors, and astronauts are in this category. Although such material is not of historical significance, much of it is intriguing to own. In building such a collection, moreover, the beginner learns the essentials of what can be an exciting avocation.

125

TERMINOLOGY

The first thing to understand about autograph collecting is that an autograph is not a signature. A "signature" is what results when a person writes his name. An "autograph" is the body of a hand-written letter. Back in the 1850's, when autograph collecting first developed in the United States, it was the practice of collectors to clip signatures from letters and throw away the autograph portion. Today no one in his right mind would do this. An autograph in combination with a signature is called an "Autograph Letter Signed" or an ALS. A typewritten letter with a signature is a "Letter Signed" or an LS.

The term "document" has a far broader definition. Some of the most common documents are land grants, civil appointments to Federal positions, and military commissions and discharges. In the early days of this country such documents had to be signed by a President. However, official documents also include accounts and records, contracts, reports, receipts, customs house papers, ships' papers, even government lottery tickets if they are sufficiently old. A document written and signed by the same individual is called an "Autograph Document Signed" (ADS). If it is typed or printed and signed, it is a "Document Signed" (DS).

The term "manuscript" includes books, musical scores, speeches, diaries, logbooks of ships' voyages, and poetry. When a manuscript is written and signed by the author, it is called an "Autograph Manuscript Signed" (AMsS). When it is typed and signed, it is a "Manuscript Signed" (MsS). Material of this sort is the most costly in this field, but occasionally one encounters a poem or a speech that is moderately priced. An example is James Whitcomb Riley's manuscript of his famous children's poem "Little Orphant Annie." When this book was published, the item cost $90. By the time you read this, its value may have risen considerably. Written in ink, decorated with a drawing, and signed by the author, it consists of fourteen lines, concluding:

> And he'p the pore and needy ones, 'at clusters all about—
> Er the Gobble-uns'll get you
> Ef you
> Don't
> Watch
> Out!

Autograph material also is categorized by size. The standard sizes are octavo (abbreviated 8vo), which is about 6″ × 8″, quarto (abbreviated 4to), which is about 8″ × 12″, and folio (fol), which is 9″ × 13″ or larger.

SPECIALIZATION

The possibilities for specialization are virtually infinite. In many cases a single specialty is broad enough to occupy one for a lifetime. Some collectors focus on individuals such as Lincoln, the Roosevelts, or Grover Cleveland, assembling documents, letters, and manuscripts by them and about them. If signed photographs are available, these also may become part of a collection. Others concentrate on wars, particularly the Civil War, collecting documents, letters, and the diaries of soldiers and the women they left behind. Still others are concerned with a particular period in history such as the Great Depression of the 1930's, or with the experience of a particular people such as the Jews, or with a group such as Presidents or signers of the Declaration of Independence, or with an occupation such as medicine, baseball, or whaling.

GETTING STARTED

There are several useful steps. One is writing to the dealers listed later in this chapter for their catalogs. These are fascinating documents which offer a sense of the many possibilities. Another is doing some additional reading. Relatively few books have been written on this hobby, but for the beginner one of the best is *Collecting Autographs and Manuscripts* by Charles Hamilton. It also would be useful to visit a history museum and inspect the autographs, manuscripts, and documents on display, viewing them as a prospective collector. The largest such collection is in the Library of Congress in Washington, D.C.

If your interest matures, join a collectors' organization. The best one for beginners is the Universal Autograph Collector's Club, 9 Normandy Lane, New Rochelle, N.Y. 10804. It publishes an informative newsletter and provides opportunities for purchasing material at auction and through trading with other members. A membership also will place your name on the mailing lists of several autograph dealers. As you grow more experienced, you also might want to join the Manuscript Society, a group of advanced collectors. Write to the Executive Secretary, Manuscript Society, Southern Illinois University, Carbondale, Illinois 62901.

SOURCES OF MATERIALS

Attics. If you have good fortune, you might find interesting material stored in trunks and boxes in attics or in dresser drawers or even in old books, including bibles. The chances of this are somewhat better if your family has lived in one location for a long period, or if it has been in this country for many generations, or if a family member at one point was active in public life. If your attic is bare, consider your mother's, or your grandmother's, or your great-aunt Addie's.

Celebrities. Some collectors write to well-known persons with a request for a signature or even a brief signed letter. It is surprising how many such requests are granted. In some cases, however, the signatures are those of a secretary or an automatic signing device called an "Autopen." If you use this method, ask for only one signature or letter and enclose a stamped, addressed return envelope.

Other Collectors. Persons with relatively inexpensive collections often do a good deal of trading with one another. Usually this is done on a personal basis or through advertisements in which a collector lists what he has available and what he is seeking.

Dealers. There are relatively few dealers in autograph material in this country. However, virtually all buy, sell, and trade. Some accept "want lists" from collectors which they fill as required material becomes available. All provide identification and evaluation services for a fee.* Some also make repairs in material that is torn or otherwise damaged. Most are reputable, but as in all occupations there are individuals who do not hesitate to take advantage of a neophyte. A dealer's reputation among experienced collectors is an important indication of his status. Most dealers sell material in all price ranges. However, some may concentrate on items in a particular range. This becomes clear as one studies their catalogs. A number of better-known dealers are noted below. Most provide catalogs or lists of their offerings.

* Curators at history museums ordinarily undertake identifications without charge, but they do not estimate value.

Conway Barker, P.O. Box 35, La Marque, Texas 77568.

Walter R. Benjamin Autographs, 790 Madison Avenue, New York, N.Y. 10021.

Bruce Gimelson, Fort Washington Industrial Park, Fort Washington, Pennsylvania 19304.

Charles T. Hamilton Galleries, Inc., 25 E. 53rd Street, New York, N.Y. 10022

Doris T. Harris, 1300 S. Beacon Street, San Pedro, California 90731.

King Hostick, 901 College, Springfield, Illinois 62704.

Milton Kronovet, 75 Ocean Avenue, Brooklyn, N.Y. 11225. An excellent source of low priced materials.

Paul C. Richards, 101 Monmouth, Brookline, Massachusetts 02146.

Auctions. Auctions are conducted by dealers, specialists in the disposal of artistic and literary materials, and autograph collectors' clubs. All involve bidding from the floor, although in some cases it is possible to arrange for a dealer to bid in your behalf if you cannot be present. The standard commission for this service is 10 per cent. Some firms sell exclusively at auction and may execute bids by mail. Although a great deal of material is purchased at auctions, they are not likely to be a good source for the beginner. The techniques of bidding are complicated, the other bidders generally are dealers or advanced amateurs, and a well-developed sense of values is essential if one is to get his money's worth. The one auction where a beginner might try his hand is sponsored annually by the Universal Autograph Collector's Club.

VALUES

The value of an item is determined by what someone is willing to pay for it. This might be based on any or all of the following factors.

Type of Material. A clipped signature of U. S. Grant, for example, might be worth about $15. A document signed by him while he was President might have a value of $45 or $50. A letter written during his term of office might be worth $125. As a rule, signatures are worth less than signed documents. In turn, documents usually have less value than signed letters. An Autograph Letter Signed (ALS) or-

Common signatures: William Cullen Bryant, Daniel Webster, Henry Clay, James Russell Lowell, Samuel F. B. Morse, Henry Wadsworth Longfellow.

dinarily is more valuable than a typed letter which has been signed. A signed photograph might be worth even more.

Individual or Event. Items involving individuals who have established themselves as historic figures are likely to command large sums. Such persons might include Presidents, kings, prime ministers, dictators, literary figures, artists, musicians, and scientists. When a person in modern times has clearly established himself—an Einstein, a Franklin Roosevelt, or a John Kennedy, for example—his material also acquires great value.

Items involving persons whose fame is fleeting or not well established have less appeal. The signatures of most modern politicians, artistic figures, and athletes are in this category. When Hubert Humphrey was defeated in a Presidential election, for example, the value of his signature and his papers dropped precipitously, even though he was a former Vice President and United States Senator. On the other hand, once Richard Nixon defeated Humphrey, the value of his material rose sharply. In fact, Humphrey's signature was worth only a dollar or two when this was written, while Nixon's had a value of at least $30.

If an event is historic, then items associated with it also acquire value. An eyewitness account of the first explosion of the atom bomb or of the assassination of a President is likely to be worth a great deal, no matter who the author is.

130

Content. Subject matter, detail, and length all are of importance. Letters, diaries, and documents that shed new light on historic events are in great demand. So is material that offers information about the private life of an important person. A letter written by George Washington, for example, brought a record price because he discussed problems he was having with his false teeth. Diaries and letters that offer a picture of domestic life in the past or of life in battle also may have considerable value, even when written by ordinary persons.

Rarity. Because they are relatively scarce, the signatures and letters of Daniel Boone, Nathan Hale, John Paul Jones, Edgar Allan Poe, and Thomas Lynch, Jr., a signer of the Declaration of Independence, are worth a good deal. On the other hand, the signatures and letters of Daniel Webster, Henry Clay, William Cullen Bryant, and Henry Wadsworth Longfellow are so plentiful they have relatively low values.

The value of Presidential materials also is affected in this way. Since the early Presidents signed thousands of routine documents, their signatures on such items have little value. However, the same signature on a letter probably would be worth a great deal. Handwritten letters of modern Presidents are particularly rare and valuable. The reason

Preferred signatures: Daniel Boone, Edgar Allan Poe, Nathan Hale, John Paul Jones, Thomas Lynch, Jr., Joseph Smith.

for their rarity is an automatic device that signs routine correspondence for them. The machine-made signature is identical to the human signature. The only difference is that it is worthless.

Current Interest. Value also is affected by current interest in an individual or event. In 1900, for example, a signed letter by the English novelist William Makepeace Thackeray brought $300. At this writing such a letter is worth about $40.

Condition, Appearance, Age. If an item is damaged or has been repaired, it is likely to be worth less than if it were perfect. The same is true if the ink has faded or the paper is stained or the writing is not completely legible. An older item may or may not be worth more than contemporary material, as was noted earlier. But the value of such material generally has greater stability.

PITFALLS

One of the most important involves authenticity. It is necessary, for example, to beware of forgeries. One of the most celebrated forgers of autograph material was a Philadelphian named Joseph Cosey who specialized in duplicating letters of such figures as Benjamin Franklin and Abraham Lincoln. His work was so good it has value in its own right. Another hazard involves purchasing letters or documents that were written by ordinary people with the same name as a celebrated figure. John Adams, the second President of the United States, had many namesakes whose correspondence occasionally appears on the market as his work. To protect yourself, deal only with merchants and collectors who will guarantee in writing that the material they sell or trade is authentic. The other major pitfall is paying more for an item than it is worth. Here all one can do is expand his knowledge of values and deal with someone he trusts.

DISPLAY, STORAGE, RECORDS

Some collectors have their prize material matted and framed. The mats should be made from the highest quality acid-free plyboard. Others display their best items on sheets of black velvet in glass-enclosed cases. It also is practical to display autograph material in albums with transparent holders or to store it flat in file folders. However, do not tape or glue your material to anything. In addition, do not mark, fold, or cut an item or make repairs on your own. When these are needed, consult a dealer or the curator of prints at an art museum. A few advanced collectors ultimately acquire the knowledge to do their own repairs, but the techniques are extremely complicated.

For each acquisition prepare a 5" × 7" file card. Enter an identifying number, a description of the item and its source, price, date of acquisition, and condition. Also cite whatever you know of its background and significance.

BIBLIOGRAPHY

Autographs: A Key to Collecting, Mary A. Benjamin, R. R. Bowker Co., New York, 1946.

Collecting Autographs and Manuscripts, Charles Hamilton, University of Oklahoma Press, Norman, 1961.

11·COINS

THE EARLIEST KNOWN COINS are staters, which were struck by hand over 2500 years ago in the Kingdom of Lydia in what is now western Turkey. They were made from a natural alloy of gold and silver called "electrum" and carried an impression of the Lydian state seal. Over the centuries, staters, nomismas, ducats, doubloons, Indian-head cents, Liberty-head nickels, and thousands of other coins have exerted a fascination far greater than their intrinsic value might suggest. Their remarkable diversity, their age and historical associations, the fact that some offer tangible links to a dimly perceived past and that a great many are lovely works of art, all have played a role in creating the coin collector. Even the ancient Romans collected the coins of the ancient Greeks. And little has changed since, except that there are more coins and more coin collectors.

STARTING A COLLECTION

If collecting coins seems like something you would enjoy, initially don't collect anything. The options are so vast you are likely to become confused and turn to other things in disgust. As a first step, spend some time reading. To start, read one of the histories of coinage listed in the Bibliography, such as J. Earl Massey's book *America's Money*. Then explore in a few of the basic catalogs. Among these, the ones compiled by Richard Yeoman are among the best. One of the first things you will learn is that coin collectors collect not only coins but also paper money, tokens, and medals.

If you still are intrigued, it would be useful to find a collector, talk to him about collecting, and attend a meeting of a local coin club. A coin dealer or your newspaper can tell you whom to contact. If you decide to start a collection, it would be wise to join such a club. From contact with members and from formal programs, you will learn a good deal that otherwise only experience could teach you.

Some coin collectors start by concentrating on a coin of a particular denomination and design—oftentimes it is the Indian-head cent. They attempt to collect each of the dates it carries and also each of the mint marks, which identify the mints where it was produced. Others try to assemble one representative coin from each country. Both approaches are points of departure that lead in many directions. Here are but some of the possibilities for other collections.

Issues of one country throughout its history or a particular period, including ancient and medieval coins of various countries.

Commemorative coins issued to honor individuals or mark historic events.

Commemorative medals struck by various governments.

Coins which depict a particular subject, such as ships, birds, hats, buildings, famous men, and coats of arms, or the mottoes they carry.

Unused coins, including "proof" or "specimen" sets, which are struck especially for collectors, or rolls of uncirculated coins.

Paper money, in terms of many of the above possibilities.

Tokens—either a general collection or one organized by the use for which particular tokens were issued.

Unusual money, including currency with errors and objects such as dog teeth, fish hooks, and shells that were used as money before the development of modern coinage.

EQUIPMENT

One of the pleasant aspects of coin collecting is that it requires little equipment. All one needs is a good quality magnifying glass, an inexpensive catalog to help in identifying specimens and determining their value, and coin holders, envelopes, and other devices in which to store your possessions. For storage equipment see the section Care and Storage.

SOURCES OF COINS AND OTHER CURRENCY

Dealers. Coin dealers are a primary source of material. Some deal in currency of all types. Others specialize in United States and Canadian coins or in foreign coins. A few also maintain extensive markets in medieval and ancient coins. Many operate out of small shops or stalls in department stores. To find dealers in your area, look in the classified section of the local telephone directory under "Coin Dealers" or "Stamp Dealers." There also are dealers who specialize in mail order sales and advertise their wares in coin magazines and newspapers. In addition to selling coins, most dealers buy coins and many are also willing to trade.

Although the vast majority of coin dealers are reputable businessmen, there are exceptions. Beware of overstatements regarding value, condition, and rarity. Also beware of "bargains." These are few and far between. To determine which dealers are satisfactory, consult experienced collectors.

Some dealers list their coins in catalogs they distribute to a regular mailing list. Frequently a request to be listed is all that is necessary to receive such materials. Many dealers also are willing to work with "want lists" of coins a collector is seeking. If you submit want lists, also provide a stamped addressed envelope in which the dealer can reply. Ordinarily he will indicate which coins he has available and their prices and set them aside. If he does not hear from you within a reasonable period, he will return the material to stock. On the other hand, if you make a purchase, you have the privilege of returning it if it does not meet your expectations. In making purchases by mail, bear in mind that insurance and postage substantially increase the cost. In such cases it is wise to buy several coins at a time rather than only one.

Other Collectors. A great deal of buying, selling, and trading is done at meetings of local coin clubs. In fact, many clubs conduct periodic auctions to assist members in acquiring and disposing of material.

Mints and Banks. The United States Mint in Philadelphia and the United States Assay Office in San Francisco sell special sets of unused coins in current circulation. The mint in Philadelphia sells "proof sets" prepared especially for collectors on dies which operate at slower than normal speeds. The coins that result have highly polished surfaces and are extremely attractive. The assay office in San Francisco sells uncirculated sets of coins struck under standard procedures. Both types of sets are sold by mail. The Philadelphia mint also sells medals which commemorate the careers of Presidents and other public figures as well as events with which they were associated. Some 400 are available. A list is sent on request. The address of the Philadelphia mint is Independence Mall, Philadelphia. The address of the assay office is 350 Duboce Avenue, San Francisco, California 94117. Mints do not sell rolls of uncirculated coins.

Canadian proof sets are available from the Bank of Canada in Ottawa. Proof sets of foreign coins, or "specimen sets" as they are known, are difficult to obtain directly from the issuing mints. It is best to purchase those from a domestic firm with an agent abroad or from a foreign dealer.

Auctions. Many of the most desirable coins are sold through auctions at which bids by mail frequently are permitted. In such cases a dealer sends his auction catalog to those persons who wish to participate. They in turn submit their bids by mail. It is far better, of course, to be present so that you can inspect the coins and enjoy the competition. In either case, before submitting a bid, carefully read the conditions of the sale to avoid misunderstandings. If you aren't sure what to bid, check the standard coin catalogs for a valuation of the items that interest you and also ask a dealer for his opinion. Then submit a bid that reflects your estimate of the value and your *need* for the item. Resist the impulse to make overly large or unlimited bids. On the other hand, do not submit a bid that clearly is too low. In fact, absurdly low mail bids might cause your name to be removed from auction lists, since dealers will not regard you as a serious collector. Before bidding by mail, establish credit at the auction house involved with a letter of identification from your bank.

Spare Change. The coins and bills in your possession could include rare or unusual items. Regularly check your wallet or change purse.

CONDITION AND RARITY

These two factors determine the value of a coin, its cost to the collector, and the ease with which it can be sold should he wish later to dispose of it. In building a collection, therefore, it is essential to acquire the best material you can afford. If only a poor specimen is available or is within your means, replace it with something better when the opportunity arises. The American Numismatic Association has adopted the following scale in grading the condition of coins. It is also used in standard coin catalogs.

Uncirculated or Mint Condition. No sign of wear or damage.

Extremely Fine. A somewhat less desirable surface, but no definite signs of wear.

Very Fine. Insignificant signs of wear, but almost as desirable as an "extremely fine" specimen.

Fine. Clearly distinguished signs of wear, but desirable.

Very Good. Somewhat more wear, but not unattractive.

Good. Worn, although letter, date, design are legible.

Fair. Badly worn; ordinarily not desirable.

Poor. Poorest condition.

Serious collectors of American material strive for items which are, at a minimum, "fine" or "very fine." Since much European material often is far older, an item in fine condition may be regarded as quite satisfactory. The primary emphasis with medieval and ancient coins is, of course, on rarity.

In collecting paper money, try for crisp, unfolded, uncreased notes.

UNITED STATES CURRENCY

Colonial, State Issues. Many of the coins in this group were in use prior to 1792, the year the Federal government opened in Philadelphia its first mint. They are among the most fascinating of American coins because of their age, historical significance, and great diversity. In fact, the origin of some of these coins still is not known.

The earliest settlers brought European money with them, with the result that, when trade developed, coins such as pieces of eight and doubloons became part of the currency here. The first colonial coins the British government issued appeared in 1616 for use in Bermuda, but they migrated to the mainland. In the years that followed, a Lord Baltimore series was issued in Maryland, "elephant tokens" appeared in North Carolina and New England, and Irish coins were imported to combat a shortage of change. The first coins minted in the American colonies were issued by the Massachusetts Bay Colony starting in 1652. They were the famous Willow, Oak, and Pine Tree series. In this period, Virginia and New Hampshire also issued coins.

After the Revolutionary War, New Jersey, Connecticut, and Vermont produced their own coins. So did a number of private citizens, including Ephraim Brasher, whose gold doubloon minted in 1787 is highly valued. At one point there were 33 different coinages in circulation plus many kinds of coins from abroad. The confusion was so great that exchange tables were commonly used to determine equivalent values. It was not, in fact, until 1857 that the last of these issues finally was removed from circulation.

Regular Issues. Since Federal coins were first minted in Philadelphia, over a hundred major denominations and designs have been issued. These range from the "dismes" and "half-dismes" made from Washington's silver plate to the magnificent $20 double-eagle gold piece, which was discontinued in 1933. Denomination, design, designer (whose initials appear on some issues), and date of issue all are of consequence to the collector. So is the mint mark indicating the mint that produced a coin. Recent coins carry an "S" for the former San Francisco mint and a "D" for the Denver mint. Those coins without mint marks come from Philadelphia. Earlier coins may carry designations for mints which no longer function, such as "CC" for Carson City, Nevada; "C" for Charlotte, N.C.; "D" for Dahlonega, Georgia; and "O" for New Orleans.

A representative collection of American issues might include the following coins:

Half-cents (1793–1857).

Large cents and small cents (1793–1864).

Indian-head cent (1859–1909).

Lincoln cent. Issued since 1909, with the designer's initials VDB for Victor D. Brenner.

Two-cent, three-cent pieces (1864–1889).

Five-cent pieces, including the silver half-dime (1794–1873), the Liberty-head nickel (1883–1913), the Buffalo-head nickel (1913–1938), and the Jefferson nickel (since 1938).

Dimes, including the Liberty-head dime (1892–1909) designed by Charles E. Barber, the Mercury dime (1916–1945) designed by A. A. Weinman, and the Roosevelt dime (since 1946) designed by John R. Sinnock.

Quarters, including the Liberty head (1892–1916), the Liberty standing (1916–1930), and the Washington head (since 1932).

Half-dollars, including the Liberty head (1892–1915), the Liberty standing, which is the only American coin with an American flag (1916–1947), the Franklin (1948–1963), and the Kennedy (since 1964).

New Jersey cent, 1786.

Indian small head penny, 1884.

Liberty head dime, 1916.

Columbian Exposition half dollar, 1893.

Silver dollars, including the Liberty head (1878–1921) and the Peace
Dollar (1921–1935), the last silver dollar to be minted.
Golden Eagle gold pieces, including various quarter-eagles ($2.50,
1796–1929), half-eagles ($5, 1795–1929), eagles ($10, 1795–
1933), and double-eagles ($20, 1849–1933).

Proof Sets. See the earlier paragraph on mints and banks.
Commemoratives. A commemorative coin commemorates a
significant event or the career of an important individual. Almost 50
were issued from 1892 through 1951, when the practice was discontin-

ued. Typically they were silver half-dollars, although a few were struck in gold. The first American commemorative was issued to mark the opening of the Columbian Exposition in Chicago. Some others commemorate the birthdays of Daniel Boone and Booker T. Washington, the discovery of the Old Spanish Trail, the completion of the Bay Bridge between San Francisco and Oakland, and the establishment of various cities and states.

Patterns. These are coins issued to test new designs and denominations and changes in weight and in raw materials. The most interesting are, of course, the ones with changes that were not adopted.

Tokens. Although tokens are not coins, they circulate and have intrinsic value. They include tokens used in the past by steamboat and horsecar passengers, sales-tax tokens issued by states, the strikingly beautiful gambling tokens of Siam, tokens issued by merchants to meet shortages of small change, and, of course, the wooden nickels issued as promotional devices by many American communities.

Medals. Commemorative medals serve the same purpose as commemorative coins, except that they do not circulate. A collector's emphasis might be historical or biographical, or it might be artistic, since many medals are the work of famous artists. See the earlier paragraph on mints and banks.

Paper Money

Colonial and Revolutionary War Notes: In 1690 Massachusetts became the first American colony to issue paper money when it produced notes to cover military expenses. Later other colonies followed suit. From 1775 through 1779 the Continental Congress printed over $200 million in notes to pay the cost of the Revolutionary War. Their denominations ranged from one-sixth of a dollar to eighty dollars. But by 1781 their value had dropped precipitously. As much as $500 in paper was needed to obtain a single dollar in specie. From this decline came the expression "not worth a Continental." In collecting the paper money of these periods, beware of modern-day replicas, which also are "not worth a Continental."

Broken Bank Bills: These were issued by banks which no longer function, including many which operated prior to the Civil War.

Fractional Currency: These bills were used as substitutes for coins in a period during and after the Civil War when metal was in short supply. The Federal Treasury Department continues to redeem them at face value.

Regular Notes and Certificates: There are two kinds—the large notes issued prior to 1929 and the small notes which have been issued since. The large notes include the following: Federal Reserve Bank Notes with brown seals, National Bank Notes with brown seals, Gold Certificates with yellow seals, and United States Bank Notes with red seals.

Most of these notes and certificates come in a range of denominations and in various series. They also carry the signatures of numerous Secretaries of the Treasury and Treasurers of the United States. As with coins, some collectors focus on a single denomination in all its permutations. Others try to develop a complete series of one of the categories above or assemble a more broadly focused collection. Collecting notes and certificates is a costly pursuit. If necessary, however, one can always spend his collection.

Military Currency: Notes of this type are used by members of the armed forces engaged in military operations abroad. Some of the most interesting items were issued during World War Two.

Oddities and Rarities: Most collectors of paper money also have a deep interest in oddities. One type is the creased note which inadvertently was folded in printing with the result that a blank space was produced where the plate and the ink did not make contact. Another is the inverted reverse in which the back of a note is printed upside down. Low serial numbers also are sought after, particularly those on a note

$500 Confederate note, 1864.

with a new motto or a new signature. So are notes with unusual serial numbers, such as those consisting of the same or consecutive digits.

Confederate Money. Perhaps the rarest of the Confederate coins is the half-dollar cast at the Federal mint during the Civil War in New Orleans after it was captured. One side of the coin acquired a new Confederate design, but the other side was left just as it was. In addition to a full range of coins, there were seven series of Confederate notes with denominations from 50 cents to $1000. Most types of Confederate notes still are available to collectors, but the many modern replicas on the market make it something of a challenge to acquire a completely authentic collection.

CANADIAN CURRENCY

One of the intriguing things about Canada's money is that a good deal remains to be learned about its development, far more than is the case with United States currency. The possibilities for collections include material from the period of French colonization as well as currency dating from 1870, when decimal coinage began. In addition, there are attractive contemporary coins bearing maple leaves, beavers, fishing schooners, caribou heads, even an oil refinery. Some collectors also find interesting the coins Canadian provinces issued prior to the establishment of a national monetary system. Early Canadian paper currency includes cardboard money which was inscribed, signed, and circulated when currency from France was late in arriving. It also takes in government issues and issues by various banks, merchants, lumber firms, and trading companies. A standard series of notes has been issued since 1870.

CURRENCY OF OTHER COUNTRIES

It is possible to collect material from virtually every country, although doing so is more difficult and costly in some cases than in others. As a first step, select several countries that interest you and explore the possibilities with coin dealers and other collectors. Also write the embassies of these countries for advice on how to proceed efficiently. If the results of your investigation are encouraging, decide on one nation and learn what you can about its history and monetary system. Dealers with agents abroad might be an excellent source of coins and notes. So might travelers and firms that do business in that country. If you can get the names of coin collectors there, they also might be a resource.

MEDIEVAL COINS

The coins in use from the waning days of the Roman Empire in the fifth century to the advent of the Renaissance in the fifteenth are classified as medieval. They reflect a dramatic evolution from the crude bronze coins of the barbarians who succeeded the Romans to the complex monetary systems of the nations that emerged a thousand years later. The earlier coins gave way first to a standard silver coin which was used in many areas. Invariably it carried a cross or a portrait of a local monarch. In what was to become Germany, the pfennig was such a coin; in Spain, the dinero was. Toward the end of this period, nationalistic designs began to appear, such as the fleur de lis on French currency.

ANCIENT COINS

Although there were earlier coins, the first of consequence were products of the Greek cities. Some were so beautifully crafted and designed they are minor works of art. These include the silver "turtle" stater of Aegina, where the first European mint operated; the silver "foals" of Corinth, which depicted the flying horse Pegasus; the tetradrachms of Athens, graced on one side with the head of Athena, the

The two sides of a Roman didrachm, circa 222–187 B.C.

goddess of wisdom, and on the other with a sprightly owl, and the "victory" decadrachm of Syracuse with its charioteer drawn by four spirited horses. Roman coins, on the other hand, are far less intriguing in design and content. They usually celebrate political figures, ruling families, and important events.

Assembling a collection of ancient coins and also the instruments of barter that preceded them is one of the more fascinating pursuits open to the collector. It is pleasant to discover, moreover, that many ancient coins are reasonably priced. However, there are two pitfalls. One is the large number of counterfeits extant. The other is the uninformed dealer. A knowledgeable dealer or collector can be of great help. So can study and research.

CARE AND STORAGE

Handling. Always grasp coins on the rim between the thumb and the forefinger. Never hold them flush against the fingers or in the palm, since oil and perspiration tend to color and corrode them.

Cleaning. It is best not to clean coins, since this may result in damage or additional wear and a reduction in value. If a coin is so dirty and tarnished that cleaning is essential, consult an expert. If this is not practical, wash the coin very gently in tepid water with a mild soap, not a detergent. Then dry it gently with a soft cloth. But *never* use a polishing or burnishing preparation. If you wish to bring up the outline of a badly worn coin, wipe it with a soft cloth that has been dipped in vegetable oil. To protect their coins against tarnish, some collectors apply a coat of lacquer, but this is a task for an experienced person.

Storage. There are many possibilities. A series of coins might be stored in coin cards or in special loose-leaf binders. Some collectors use glassine envelopes, with one coin to an envelope. Then they file the envelopes systematically by series, type, or nation in airtight storage boxes or cabinets. Collectors also use opaque envelopes of different colors to specify particular characteristics. Plastic tubes are used to store rolls of uncirculated coins. In addition, lucite holders are useful to display highly priced coins.

In any case, do not store coins loose in a container, since they are likely to become scratched. Also do not hold them together with rubber bands, or they will tarnish.

Each container should carry a catalog number which refers to a file card that identifies the material and its age, condition, source, and cost.

145

ORGANIZATIONS

It will be extremely useful to join a local club, as noted earlier. As your interest in coin collecting develops, also consider joining the American Numismatic Association, the national amateur group. The address is 818 N. Cascade Avenue, P.O. Box 2366, Colorado Springs, Colorado 80901. A membership includes a subscription to the monthly magazine *The Numismatist.* Many advanced amateurs and professional numismatists also hold membership in the scholarly American Numismatic Society. Its address is Broadway at 155th Street, New York, N.Y. 10032.

MUSEUMS

Many historical and art museums have collections of coins and other currency. The major collections are at the following institutions: New York—American Numismatic Society, Metropolitan Museum of Art, Money Museum of the Chase Manhattan Bank, Brooklyn Museum; District of Columbia—Museum of History and Technology of the Smithsonian Institution; Buffalo—Buffalo Museum of Science; Newark—Newark Museum; Detroit—Money Museum of the National Bank of Detroit.

BIBLIOGRAPHY
Introduction to Coin Collecting

America's Money, J. Earl Massey, Thomas Y. Crowell Co., New York, 1968. A history.

Coin Collecting, Robert I. Masters, Fred Reinfeld, Sterling Publishing Co., New York, 1960.

The Coin Makers, Thomas W. Becker, Doubleday & Co., New York, 1969. A history.

The Complete Book of Coin Collecting, Joseph Coffin, Coward-McCann, New York, 1959.

How to Build a Coin Collection, Fred Reinfeld, Sterling Publishing Co., New York, 1958.

Introduction to Numismatics, American Numismatic Association, Colorado Springs, 1967.

Select Numismatic Bibliography, Elvira Clain-Stefanelli, Stack's, New York, 1965. A 400-page bibliography of specialized works.

Catalogs

A Catalog of Modern World Coins, Richard S. Yeoman.

Coins of the World, Wayte Raymond.

Domestic and Foreign Coins Manufactured by the Mints of the United States, Superintendent of Documents, Washington, D.C. 20402.

A Guide Book of United States Coins, Richard S. Yeoman.

The Official Guide of United States Paper Money, Theodore Kemm.

Standard Catalog of Canadian Coins, Tokens, and Paper Money, J. E. Charlton.

The Standard Catalog of U.S. Coins From 1652 to the Present, Wayte Raymond.

Revisions of these catalogs are issued periodically. In some cases there are annual editions. A large number of specialized catalogs are also available.

Periodicals

Coin World, Sidney News Building, 19 E. Court, Sidney, Ohio 45365. Weekly.

Numismatic News, 160 N. Washington, Iola, Wisconsin 54945. Weekly.

The Numismatic Scrapbook, Hewitt Brothers, 7320 Milwaukee Avenue, Niles, Illinois 60648. Monthly.

The Numismatist, American Numismatic Association, P.O. Box 2366, Colorado Springs, Colorado 80901. Monthly.

12·POSTAGE STAMPS

To MOST PEOPLE a postage stamp is a piece of paper they buy so that they can mail a letter. The collector, of course, sees things differently. The great variety of stamps fascinates him. So do the beauty and the age of many and the stories some possess. And so does the process of searching them out. In fact, there are so many stamps extant that the opportunities for collections are almost without limit. What also is intriguing about this hobby is the ever-present possibility, however slight, of finding a rare stamp that commands a large sum because of its age, an error in production, or simple scarcity. In recent years such stamps have sold for prices as high as $380,000.

It is through such appeals that the art of philately has grown into one of the world's most popular hobbies. The term "philately" was coined in the 1860's by an avid French collector, Georges Herpin, who tradition has it became tired of being referred to as a "timbromaniac" or stamp maniac. In coining "philately," he combined *philos*, which is Greek for "loving," and *ateleia*, which is Greek for "tax exempt." Since there wasn't a Greek word for stamp, but stamps were tax exempt, that was the best he could do. In the United States and Canada alone it is estimated that there are over 25 million adults and children who share his love of stamps.

STARTING A STAMP COLLECTION

To assemble a complete collection of all the stamps ever issued would be impossible. As a result serious collectors specialize, concentrating on one or more of the many aspects of collecting discussed below. For the beginner, however, it is wise to start with a small general

148

collection, focusing on a representative group of stamps from all countries or from a region such as North America. Assembling such a collection provides a useful apprenticeship. You will learn what the sources of stamps are, what stamps cost, how to select them, how to interpret them, and how to care for them. You also learn at first hand what the possibilities for a specialized collection are.

OTHER FIRST STEPS

When you first start collecting, you will need a 5x to 10x magnifying glass, a pair of tongs with rounded ends to handle stamps, and one of the guidebooks and catalogs noted in the Bibliography. Your library is likely to have several. Joining a local stamp club also would be useful. If the club is reasonably vigorous, it will provide a chance to learn more of philately through lectures, films, workshops, and study groups. It also provides an opportunity to buy, sell, and trade stamps. To determine if there is a club in your area, check with the local postmaster, a stamp dealer, or the club editor of the newspaper. Or write for information to the National Federation of Stamp Clubs, 153 Waverly Place, New York, N.Y. 10014.

TYPES OF COLLECTIONS

There are a half-dozen major specializations, each of which offers a great many possibilities.

National or Regional Collections. The emphasis is on stamps of a particular country and/or its possessions; or on stamps of a region, such as Central America, the Caribbean, or the islands of the South Pacific; or on stamps from nations of a particular type, such as very small countries.

Historical. Such collections are composed of stamps from a particular period in history. They might further be restricted to a particular nation, such as nineteenth-century German stamps, or a particular event, such as stamps issued by the Confederacy and the Union during the Civil War.

Topical or Pictorial Stamps. Such collections are organized by the subject matter of the stamp. A collector might focus on stamps used for propaganda; on stamps which commemorate important events (commemorative stamps); on those carrying portraits or reproductions

A Liberian postage stamp.

U.S. stamp, Civil War era.

U.S. topical issue, 1961.

of great art; or on stamps depicting animals, automobiles, flowers, or sports events.

  Mechanical Characteristics. Some collectors assemble stamps of a particular denomination, such as two-cent stamps of the world, or a particular type such as air mail, special delivery, or postage-due stamps. Others collect envelopes with stamps and a postmark, which are known as "covers." Some concentrate on "first day covers," which are postmarked on the date a stamp is officially released. There also are collec-

Postmark Uniontown, Pa., 1965.

tions of stamps with unusual shapes, such as triangular and diamond-shaped stamps, and of plate blocks or stamps attached in blocks of 4 or 16, with their serial numbers. In addition, there are collections of stamps with printing errors or errors in their perforations.

Postal Stationery and Postmarks. Some collections are concerned with postal stationery, such as stamped envelopes, postal cards, picture post cards, and wrappers in which publications are mailed. Others are composed of postal markings, such as cancellation marks, postmarks, or postal slogans. Just like collectors of stamps, these collectors emphasize historical materials, collections representative of various areas, mechanical characteristics, and subject matter.

A first day cover.

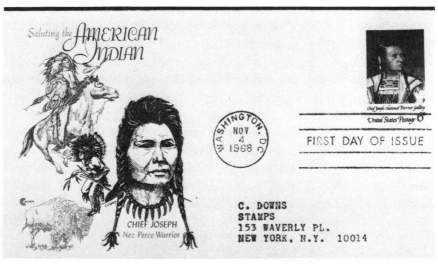

"*Non-Stamps.*" These include so-called "local stamps" issued in the past by private firms that delivered mail within a municipality or along a particular route. When a steamship company was the carrier, they are known as "steamship stamps." Another type is the government revenue stamp. Some are used on alcoholic beverages, playing cards, and tobacco products. Others are used in connection with stock transfers, customs inspections, and the issuance of hunting and boating permits. Still other types collected are Christmas seals, advertising stickers, and counterfeit or "bogus" stamps.

SOURCES OF STAMPS

A dollar is all that is needed to get a beginner started in stamp collecting. This sum will purchase a packet of several hundred assorted stamps from countries throughout the world or from a particular country. Beware, however, of purchasing an unsorted mixture. Such stamps are scooped at random from large piles and are sold by weight. They invariably include many duplicates and many items in poor condition and are not a good value. Many amateurs also find it easy to assemble a sizable number of stamps free of charge. A search of drawers and attics frequently turns up letters with stamps that were in use some years ago. In addition, a canvass of friends, neighbors, business firms, and libraries, particularly those that receive mail from abroad, often is useful. It is surprising in fact how many will set aside stamps for you.* Some collectors also have "pen pals" abroad with whom they exchange stamps. For assistance in developing such a relationship, write People-to-People Program, P.O. Box 1210, Kansas City, Missouri 64141.

As a collector develops a clear sense of his needs, he also begins purchasing stamps in sets and on an individual basis. There will be many sources to which he regularly turns.

Dealers. A great many responsible and expert stamp dealers do business throughout the United States and Canada. When a collector develops a working relationship with such a man or woman, he acquires an invaluable asset. Such dealers are not only sources of stamps but sources of help in solving philatelic problems that sometimes arise.

* To remove a stamp from an envelope, soak it in tepid water until the stamp floats free. Then dry the stamp on paper towels and press between the pages of a heavy book.

In addition to selling stamps over the counter, many dealers serve their customers by mail. This usually is done in two ways. A collector prepares a "want list" he sends to his dealer. The dealer then indicates which of the stamps he has and their prices, and the collector makes his decision. A dealer also may keep want lists on file, notifying customers as stamps become available. He also may send booklets of stamps on approval to steady customers. Each stamp in a booklet is marked with a price. The customer removes those he wants and sends the rest back with a check for his purchases. Unfortunately not every dealer is scrupulous in his relationships with collectors. It is best to deal only with well-established firms or with those recommended by other collectors whose judgment you trust.

Some firms specialize in auctions at which collectors bid for stamps. These are the best places to find stamps that are hard to obtain. The auctioneers publish detailed catalogs of the items available and distribute these to extensive mailing lists so that collectors may bid by mail if they wish. Ordinarily a minimum bid ranges between $5 and $10.

Collectors of postal stationery, postmarks, and other postal markings also find secondhand bookstores and junk shops a useful source of material. From these they sometimes obtain bundles of old letters and postal cards available for small sums.

Government Agencies. For a commission some dealers will routinely provide all the new issues released by a particular country. However, many collectors prefer, where practical, to obtain such stamps directly from the government involved. It is less costly, and frequently they are able to obtain selected stamps which are perfectly centered. At times stamps issued several years earlier still may be available. Write to the following agencies for information on the services available.

United States Stamps: Philatelic Sales Unit, City Post Office, Washington, D.C. 20013.

Canadian Stamps: Post Office Department, Ottawa, Canada.

Latin-American Stamps: Philatelic Section, Organization of American States, 17th Street and Constitution Avenue, N.W., Washington, D.C. 20036.

United Nations Stamps: United Nations Postal Administration, United Nations Building, New York, N.Y. 10017.

Stamps of Other Nations: Director of Posts, capital city.

A number of post offices in the United States maintain special philatelic windows to serve collectors. All United States post offices also provide a first day cover service. Collectors of such items keep close track of when and where new stamps are to be released. The stamp publications listed in the Bibliography are the best sources of such information. To obtain a first day cover, send the postmaster involved a self-addressed envelope with the number of new stamps you wish marked in the upper right hand corner. Place the envelope in a larger one along with payment for the stamps and a request for "first day service." On the release date the stamps are affixed and the envelope is stamped "first day of issue" and returned to you. Collectors who specialize in contemporary postmarks use a similar procedure. To obtain a mark they do not possess, they send the postmaster of the community involved a self-addressed stamped envelope with a request that it be stamped with a clear postmark and returned.

Clubs and Collectors. One of a stamp club's many services is to provide a marketplace where members can informally trade or sell stamps to other members. In addition, some clubs circulate among their members circuit books or exchange books of stamps that other members want to sell. A number of clubs conduct periodic auctions of such material. In addition, some collectors with stamps to trade or sell place classified ads in stamp publications.

VALUE, CONDITION, AND OTHER CONSIDERATIONS

The key factors in purchasing any philatelic item are relevance and value. Relevance is easily determined. Can you make use of a stamp? Does it fit into your collection? Value reflects the soundness of your investment. If you decide to spend several dollars for a stamp, you first want to be sure it is worth the money and will maintain its value over the years. Standard catalogs provide estimates of current value, as is discussed later. However, determining future value is not always easy. One factor at work is the law of supply and demand. A scarce stamp clearly will have a higher value than one that is plentiful. Since commemorative issues, for example, are not reprinted, they are exceedingly popular at the time they are released.

The physical condition of a stamp also is of great importance in determining its value. Condition usually is described in two ways. One is in terms of use. A stamp either is in mint condition, fresh from the press; in unused condition, although it may be part of a collection; or in used condition, as a result of having been sent through the mail. The other is in terms of its physical characteristics. These include the quality of the printing, the extent to which the stamp is centered on the paper, the condition of the teeth or perforations, the presence or lack of creases, tears, or thinning, the quality of a cancellation mark, the condition and the amount of the gum on the back, and other factors. Using these criteria, stamps are classified as follows:

Superb. Excellent, fresh-looking color; free from dirt, creases, tears, and thin spots; perfectly formed, perfectly spaced teeth; if not perforated, wide even margins; all of the original adhesive gum; a light but clear cancellation mark.

Very fine. A few minor defects.

Fine. A somewhat larger number of minor defects.

Good. A serious defect, such as a heavy, illegible cancellation mark.

Average, Poor, Bad. With each category a larger number of serious defects.

The standards for modern stamps are, of course, higher than for older stamps, which will have experienced greater wear. Thus, a 100-year-old stamp regarded as superb would not have the equivalent condition of a superb 25-year-old stamp. In every case the wisest procedure is to purchase the best you can afford, then when possible replace what you have with a finer stamp.

CATALOGS

1961, Dec 4   Perf 11½   Unwmkd.

97	A48	3c	brown, gold, orange & yellow	6	4
98	A48	4c	brown, gold, blue, & emerald	40	5
99	A48	13c	dp. green, gold, purple, & pink	40	20

United Nations stamp marking 15th anniversary of UNICEF, 1961.

This listing describes the three denominations of a United Nations stamp which commemorates the fifteenth anniversary of the establishment of the United Nations International Children's Fund. It is taken from *Scott's Standard Postage Stamp Catalogue*, a leading annual reference work which describes the stamps of all nations. There also are many specialized catalogs which describe the postal material of individual countries in great detail. A stamp catalog performs two important functions. It is the principal tool the collector uses in identifying his material and, as noted earlier, it serves as a rough guide to current values.

The stamp listed above was issued December 4, 1961. The term "Perf 11½" next to the date indicates that there are 11½ perforations or teeth in every two-centimeter space, a key characteristic which a collector checks with a perforation gauge, described below. When a stamp does not have perforations, it is listed as "imperf," or imperforate. The notation "Unwmkd." means that the paper the stamp is printed on does not have a watermark. When there is one, a model number and often an illustration are provided. To examine a stamp for this characteristic, you would need a watermark detector.

The numbers 97, 98, and 99, on the lines below, are the catalog numbers for the denominations in which the stamp is available. In ordering the stamp from a dealer, it is only necessary to request United Nations 97, 98, or 99, depending on your preference. These designations also appear in stamp albums which include the stamp. The number-letter combination to the right (A48) refers to the type of design. The remaining information is concerned with the denomination (3c), the colors, and the estimated current retail price for a stamp in fine condition. The first estimate (6) represents the value of an uncanceled stamp; the second is for a canceled stamp. Actually you may find dealers selling at less than catalog prices.

To find a stamp in a catalog, first determine which country issued it. If you cannot translate the inscription, check the identification list in your album. Then look in your album for the stamp and its catalog number. If the album does not have the stamp, turn to the catalog and inspect all the stamps illustrated for the country involved. Usually you will find the stamp or a related version with your stamp listed underneath. If there isn't an illustration, it will be necessary to match the characteristics of your stamp against those listed.

STORAGE

Albums. One of the early stamp collectors thought stamps so attractive she used them as wallpaper. Today, of course, most collectors use an album. There are many types available. The least satisfactory is the small bound album, which offers limited space and cannot be expanded. The best album for a beginner is a loose-leaf or spring binder with separate preprinted pages which can be supplemented as necessary. A useful homemade album can be assembled with a sturdy binder and prepunched graph paper, whose lines will serve as a guide in mounting stamps or other material. In addition to general albums, there are available single country albums, albums of blank paper for topical stamps or postmarks and cancellation marks, and special albums for covers. Scrapbooks are practical for storing postal stationery. Picture postal cards may be stored by categories in shoe boxes.

Many collectors also make use of a stock book for storing material that has not yet been mounted. It consists of pages with strips of transparent plastic that hold items in place. Duplicate stamps ordinarily are mounted on stock cards or stored in glassine envelopes.

Mounting Techniques. The most commonly used mounting device is a peelable hinge, a small rectangle of glassine coated on one side with an adhesive. To attach a hinge to a stamp, place the stamp face down on a clean surface. Fold back the top third of the gummed side of the hinge so that a gummed flap results. Moisten the flap and carefully fasten it to the back of the stamp just under the perforations at the top. Moisten the remainder of the gummed portion, turn the stamp face up with your tongs, move it to the appropriate space in the album, cover with a clean tissue, and press down. When properly affixed, the hinge and stamp lift easily, which makes it possible to examine the back of the stamp without removing it from the album.

To mount a block of four stamps, affix hinges to the back at the top corners. In mounting larger blocks, attach hinges at all four corners even though this prohibits lifting the stamps. Triangular stamps are mounted in terms of the page they occupy. If they are on a right-hand page, the hinge is attached to the left side of the stamp. If they are on a left-hand page, it is affixed to the right side. With diamond-shaped and circular stamps, attach the hinge as close to the top as possible. Some col-

 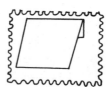

Mounting a stamp with a peelable hinge.

lectors use transparent acetate mounts instead of hinges. These are small envelopes with adhesive on the back. The stamp is placed inside and the unit is attached to the album. Covers, postmarks, cancellation marks, and postal stationery all may be mounted with hinges. With postal stationery, photo mounts also are practical. Do not use glue, rubber cement, or cellophane tape for mounting stamps or other postal material.

Background Data. It is sound to maintain a record of each item in your collection, noting its characteristics, history, source, and cost. Some collectors enter this information in the album itself either under or alongside the material involved, or on a blank facing page. Others assign each item a number and a file card.

STAMP CARE

Removing Grease, Dirt. If grease is the problem, place a stamp briefly in boiling water, then dry on paper towels and press flat in a heavy book. If dirt must be removed, soak in warm water or, if badly soiled, in benzene. Then dry and press. However, not all stamps can be cleaned with these techniques. A small number have been canceled or printed with ink that runs if the stamp is placed in a liquid. A violet-colored cancellation mark on some Latin-American stamps behaves this way. If a stamp is valuable and you have doubts as to how it might react to cleaning, check with an expert before proceeding.

Removing Old Hinges, Paper from a Stamp. Soak in tepid water until the paper floats free, then dry and press as described above. Beware of stamps whose colors might run.

Restoring Color to Faded Stamps. The primary colors used in some older stamps have a tendency to fade and turn brown or black. To restore the original color, paint the surface with a light coating of hydrogen peroxide, using a camel's hair brush. After waiting a minute or two, brush on a light coating of water. Then dry and press flat.

Removing Creases. Dampen the back of the stamp with water, then cover with a celluloid playing card and press with a warm iron.

ORGANIZATIONS

Local stamp clubs have already been discussed. There also are two major national organizations: The American Philatelic Society, P.O. Box 800, State College, Pennsylvania 16801, and the Society for

Philatelic Americans, P.O. Box 266, Cincinnati, Ohio 45201. For a membership fee, each organization offers a variety of services: identification and evaluation of stamps, translation of foreign inscriptions and postal markings, inexpensive stamp insurance, the use of circuit books for selling and buying stamps, national and regional conventions, and a monthly magazine and various handbooks. There also are many specialized organizations concerned exclusively with air mail stamps, first day covers, and other categories to which these national groups and the National Federation of Stamp Clubs noted earlier can direct you.

BIBLIOGRAPHY
Guidebooks
The Complete Guide to Stamp Collecting, Prescott H. Thorp, Grosset & Dunlap, New York, 1953.
Postmark Collecting, R. K. Forster, Stanley Paul & Co., Ltd., London, 1960.
Scott's Guidebook to Stamp Collecting, L. N. and M. Williams, Simon and Schuster, New York, 1963.
Stamp Collecting and Postal Specialties, Merit Badge Booklet, Boy Scouts of America, North Brunswick, N.J., 1966.
Standard Handbook of Stamp Collecting, R. N. Cabeen, Thomas Y. Crowell Co., New York, 1965.

Catalogs and Listings
Postage Stamps of the United States, Superintendent of Documents, Washington, D.C. 20402.
Minkus Regional Catalogs, Minkus Publications, New York. Various volumes. Annual.
Minkus World Wide Catalog, Minkus Publications, New York. Annual.
Scott's Standard Postage Stamp Catalogue, Volumes I, II, Scott Publications, New York. Annual.
Scott's United States Specialized Catalogue of Stamps, Scott Publications, New York. Annual.

Periodicals
The American Philatelist, The American Philatelic Society, Box 800, State College, Pennsylvania 16801. Monthly.
Linn's Weekly Stamp News, 220 S. Ohio Avenue, Sidney, Ohio 45365.

Mekeel's Weekly Stamp News, 13 Milk Street, P.O. Box 1660, Portland, Maine 04111.

Minkus Stamp Journal, Minkus Publications, 116 W. 32nd Street, New York, N.Y. 10001.

SPA Journal, Society for Philatelic Americans, P.O. Box 266, Cincinnati, Ohio 45201.

Stamps, 153 Waverly Place, New York, N.Y. 10014.

Western Stamp Collector, P.O. Box 10, Albany, Oregon 97321.

13·PRINTS AND REPRODUCTIONS

FEW PERSONS TODAY can afford an original painting by a well-known artist, yet many can afford the work of a fine printmaker. Good quality original prints, signed by the artist, are available for as little as $20 or $25. One of the pleasures in collecting prints is, of course, finding something you regard as beautiful or fascinating and buying it and displaying it. Another is the exploration involved. There are art museums, art galleries, print shops, and secondhand bookstores to visit. There is reading to be done about artists whose work interests you and the techniques they use. There also is the process of learning to see and understand quality in art.

An original print is the result of a design an artist has created in a metal plate or a wooden block or on a stone or a silk screen. The design is inked and the copies are printed individually by hand.* Contemporary printmakers customarily do their own printing or supervise the process, then number and sign each print that meets their specifications. Typically they print an edition of from ten to two hundred copies, then destroy or change the design so that additional prints cannot be made from it. In the nineteenth century and earlier, prints often were produced in far larger quantities, were not numbered, and frequently were not signed.

Many collectors are concerned primarily with contemporary prints, including lithographs, woodcuts, etchings, engravings, and serigraphs by artists throughout the world. Others have an interest in old prints. A number who are prepared to spend relatively large sums stress the

* See Making Prints, Chapter 3.

work of well-known artists of the past. Others focus on material of more modest origin which often is of historic interest in that it depicts how people lived. Such material offers countless opportunities for a collector to specialize. There are, for example, prints that depict city life, ships and harbors, railroads, aspects of the cotton trade, hunting and fishing, costumes, architecture, military affairs, and sports events.

REPRODUCTIONS

A reproduction is an illustration of an original art work published in thousands of individual copies by photomechanical methods. Reproductions also are available in bound books, which usually are organized by period, nation, subject, or artist. A good quality reproduction that is faithful to the color and line of the original can be a satisfying possession. Since the range of material reproduced takes in all types of prints and paintings, including old masters, there also are interesting opportunities for specialization. In addition, as old prints grow scarce, reproductions may be used to fill gaps in collections.

The low prices also are appealing. Some months before this was written, I purchased for $3 at the Chicago Institute of Art a handsome reproduction of an Indian painting by Frederic Remington. Earlier I had acquired for 50 cents a reproduction of a stunning poster announcing an exhibition by Edgar Degas. There also are reproductions in miniature available for 10 or 15 cents which some young people collect in scrapbooks or simply tack to a wall. If you keep your eyes open and have a bit of luck, you also may encounter reproductions that cost nothing. I find them occasionally in the advertisements and feature stories of expensive magazines like *Fortune, American Heritage,* and *Realités* and in various graphic arts publications. If you gain access to *Lithopinion,* a handsome publication issued by Local One, Amalgamated Lithographers of America, in New York, you also will find many treasures.

MAKING CHOICES

Some collectors restrict themselves to well-known works by established artists. But this approach is self-defeating, for the adventure of collecting lies in developing one's taste and knowledge, in making choices in terms of personal appeal, and, if necessary, in making mistakes and learning from them. Before making a purchase, the wise beginner will do a good deal of browsing to learn what he likes. In fact, after several years of collecting he may see his first acquisitions in quite a different light than when he bought them. At times his enthusiasm will have diminished, but not always. One dealer told me of a customer who had bought his first prints three years earlier. A few days before our conversation the customer had returned to look at several others. "The prints you sold me get better and better," he observed. "No," he was told, "it is only that you are learning to see better and better."

SOURCES OF PRINTS

Art Galleries. These are major sources of original prints. Not all galleries sell prints, but a growing number do. One of the outstanding print galleries is Associated American Artists, 663 Fifth Avenue, New York, N.Y. 10022, which, for a small fee, distributes catalogs of current offerings. Two leading sources of old prints are the Old Print Shop, 150 Lexington Avenue, New York, N.Y. 10016, which issues monthly catalogs to customers, and the Old Print Center, 981 Second Avenue, New York, N.Y. 10022. Of course, art dealers, like other merchants, vary in responsibility and expertise. So it is important to exercise caution in making purchases from dealers you know nothing about. The membership list of the Art Dealers Association of America is a useful guide to reliable dealers. For a free copy write the association at 575 Madison Avenue, New York, N.Y. 10022. However, it is by no means the only criterion of reliability.

IGAS. The letters stand for International Graphic Arts Society, a non-profit organization that sells quality prints to its members. Each year it offers some 40 different prints by artists throughout the world at modest prices. Typically a print is available in a numbered edition of 210 copies. To join IGAS, one pays a membership fee and agrees to purchase at least three prints every two years. Five bulletins a year describe the current offerings. In addition, the prints are displayed in museums and libraries in major cities. The address is IGAS, 410 E. 62nd Street, New York, N.Y. 10021.

Print Clubs. There are a number of such groups which provide the opportunity to purchase prints at reasonable prices. See the section Organizations.

Other Sources. Shops in some art museums and libraries sell contemporary prints. Sources of old prints of historic interest include print shops, bookstores, secondhand stores, attics, and grandmother's parlor. It also is possible to purchase prints at auctions.

Renting Prints. A number of art museums rent framed prints for small sums which may be applied to their purchase price. Some universities and colleges also rent prints to their students for nominal sums. In addition, a slowly growing number of public libraries lend framed prints as they do books and records.

SOURCES OF REPRODUCTIONS

Shops in art museums are the best and least expensive source. These include the outstanding shop at the National Gallery of Art in Washington, D.C., which also houses the world's greatest collection of original prints. Commercial sources include print shops, dealers in art supplies, and reproduction specialists. The largest of the latter is Oestreicher's, a dusty cavern on a New York side street which offers over 300,000 different reproductions, and a handsome catalog. For information write: Oestreicher's, 43 W. 46th Street, New York, N.Y. 10036.

PRICES

Prints. Most original prints are priced between $25 and $300, with a large number available at under $50. However, prints by celebrated artists like Picasso, Braque, and Chagall are likely to cost far more. The best and rarest of the Currier & Ives prints are in this category. Prints by old masters like Rembrandt ordinarily are available only to the very wealthy or to museums.

With the exception of rare items, it always is possible that another copy of a print may be available at a lower price. However, you also may find another copy available at a higher price. Shopping can be useful, but bear in mind that there are few bargains in this field and even fewer "exciting finds" at low prices. Should you encounter a dealer generous enough to offer you such an opportunity, thank him and go on your way.

Reproductions. The prices of full-size reproductions start at but a few dollars, but range upward at times to surprisingly large amounts. Miniature reproductions cost very little, as noted earlier.

MISREPRESENTATIONS

When you decide to purchase an original print from a dealer, have him state on the invoice that he is selling you an original work by the artist indicated. If he refuses, take your business elsewhere. If you are planning to spend a large sum on a print, obtain one or two independent evaluations before proceeding. If a print is being resold, determine if a history of its previous ownership is available.

The possibility always exists that what is offered as "original" is not original. Instead it may be a photochemical reproduction that has been numbered and signed. At times the signature may be a forgery; in other cases the artist himself will participate in the fraud by signing the item. There are also situations in which the work of an artist is reproduced by a copyist who then makes prints of his copy. In addition, "restrikes" pulled from old worn plates long since discarded may be offered as originals. The best protection against such misrepresentation is caution, a knowledge of prints, and a relationship with established dealers.

DISPLAY, STORAGE, CARE

Original Prints. Those prints you wish to display should be matted and enclosed under glass in a narrow, unobtrusive frame. A mat consists of two portions hinged together: a backboard to which the print is attached and a front piece or "window" through which the print shows. At the outset have your prints framed commercially, but be certain the framer takes certain precautions. The print must not be trimmed. The mat should be 100 per cent rag to protect the print from staining and deterioration. The print should be hinged to the backboard, not mounted. In addition, the hinges must not stain the print or cause deterioration. Thus, masking tape, other gummed paper tape, and plastic and cellophane tapes should not be used. Ultimately, you may wish to do your own matting. The procedures are discussed in *A Guide to the Collecting and Care of Original Prints*, which is listed in the Bibliography.

Several precautions also are necessary in displaying and storing prints. They require a moderate stable temperature and humidity. They should be displayed only in a subdued light, since constant exposure to direct light will fade them. If prints are to be stored, ideally they should be matted, then kept flat in a solander box which comes lined with rag paper. You also can store them unmatted either in solander boxes or oversize folders. In such cases, they should be separated by sheets of glassine paper. If a print is torn or needs other repairs, consult the curator of prints at the nearest large art museum.

Reproductions. These also may be framed, but you may find the cost of the frame far exceeds the cost of the reproduction. It also is practical to display reproductions in mats in which a sheet of clear plastic has been placed between the picture and the window opening. Inexpensive precut mats are sold for this purpose, or you can cut your own. Should you wish to change your display periodically, it is simple to do so. Those reproductions not in use should be separated by tissue paper and stored flat in folders. As noted earlier, miniature reproductions lend themselves to scrapbook displays. Use photograph mounts to hold them in place.

EXHIBITS, LECTURES, CLINICS

One of the best ways to learn about prints is to look at them. Art museums, art galleries, and the print clubs discussed below often have several exhibits a year that are worth studying. Museums and clubs also may have lectures, demonstrations, and other educational programs relating to prints. Some museums also schedule clinics at which curators evaluate art works and provide advice on repairs and other matters.

ORGANIZATIONS

Several cities have print clubs whose purpose is to foster printmaking and print collecting. They sponsor shows and lectures and offer their members opportunities to buy original prints, frequently at lower than normal prices.

BIBLIOGRAPHY

The Bite of the Print, Frank and Dorothy Getlein, Clarkson N. Potter, Inc., 1963.

The Book of Fine Prints, Carl Zigrosser, Crown Publishers, New York, 1956.

Catalogue of Color Reproductions of Paintings, UNESCO, Paris, 1965. Two volumes.

A Guide to the Collecting and Care of Original Prints, Carl Zigrosser, Christa M. Gaehde, Crown Publishers, New York, 1965.

Modern Prints and Drawings, Paul J. Sachs, Alfred Knopf, New York, 1954.

What Is an Original Print? J. B. Cahn, Print Council of America, New York, 1967. Available for a small fee from the council, 527 Madison Avenue, New York, N.Y. 10022.

14·OTHER COLLECTIONS

The list below suggests but some of the other possibilities. Part III, which deals with nature study, suggests still more.

Barbed wire
Books
Bottles
Buckles
Buttons
Cartoons: humorous, political
Chessmen
China: eggs, figurines
Clocks, watches
Comic books
Earrings
Folk art
Furniture: antique, miniature
Glassware
Greeting cards
Guns
Keys, locks
Kitchen utensils
Medical nostrums

Models: airplanes, cars, ships
Motion pictures
Nuts, bolts, nails
Phonograph records
Photographs
Political campaign materials
Posters
Puzzles
Recipes
Riddles
Shaving mugs
Sheet music
Snuff boxes
Swords
Theater programs
Toys: antiques, dolls, soldiers
Type faces
Weather vanes

BIBLIOGRAPHY

Specialized Publications

Many of the subjects listed are fully covered by specialized books and periodicals. With others, however, you will find little or nothing to help you find your way. In such cases, other collectors, dealers, and manufacturers will be your primary source of information.

General Publications

Auction, Parke-Bernet Galleries, 980 Madison Avenue, New York, N.Y. 10021.

Hobbies, the Magazine for Collectors, 1006 S. Michigan Avenue, Chicago, Illinois 60605.

PART III

NATURE STUDY

BIRDS
FISHES
FOSSILS
INSECTS
PLANTS
ROCKS, MINERALS, AND GEM STONES
SEA SHELLS

15·BIRDS

By DEFINITION, a bird is a warm-blooded egg-laying vertebrate which is believed to have evolved from the reptiles. It is covered with feathers, which in the distant past may have been scales, and endowed with wings, a relatively large brain, keen sight, and acute hearing. In most cases it is beautifully adapted for flight. Air sacs in the hollows of its bones help keep it aloft, and its few heavy parts are strategically positioned to improve balance. There are roughly 8600 kinds of birds, of which about 700 species are found in the United States and Canada.

This past winter some neighbors of mine, Tom and Margot Southerland, journeyed 1500 miles to Florida in search of two specific birds. One was the Cape Sable sparrow, which is found only in the region between Miami and Tampa. The other was the dusky seaside sparrow, whose habitat is the Cape Kennedy area. They managed to see the Cape Sable sparrow, but alas not the other. The Southerlands spend much of their free time looking for and at birds. They have climbed mountains, explored islands, and searched in marshland and desert and along rocky coastlines to find birds they had not yet seen. At the time this book was written, they had identified 515 of the 700 North American species. When they reach 600, they will join a select group of fewer than two dozen persons who have identified that many. Among the tens of thousands of bird watchers, reaching 600 is a remarkable achievement. It is something like hitting sixty home runs in a single season or scaling an exceedingly difficult mountain.

What initially attracts bird watchers is a game in which one hunts for a beautiful but progressively more elusive quarry that won't stay put the way a wild flower does or a rock. As a birder becomes more experienced, looking for birds often leads to other things as well. Some birders become experts on a single species such as the osprey or an entire family such as the warblers, preparing papers for learned journals, serving as resources for ornithologists. Others make a hobby of photographing or sketching birds or recording their call notes and songs.* Others become interested in bird banding or serve as cooperators in university research projects. Some acquire an additional interest in mammals, plants, minerals, and other aspects of nature. A growing number also become ardent conservationists who work with vigor and determination to preserve the natural environment for birds and for other creatures, including humans.

GETTING STARTED

The best first step would be to sit quietly in your back yard or walk in a park or the countryside and see how many birds you already can recognize. You probably can identify quite a few: a house sparrow, a robin, a crow, a starling, a pigeon, a duck, a gull, a woodpecker, a cardinal, a blue jay, a red-winged blackbird, an owl, and perhaps others. If looking for birds intrigues you, the next step is to acquire a field guide which describes the birds in your area and suggests where to find them. At the outset a local or state guide would be the most useful. These frequently are prepared by state governments (usually conservation departments), natural history museums, and bird clubs. If a local or state guide isn't available, acquire a regional or national guide, which you would need eventually anyway. Among the best are three by Roger Tory Peterson which describe separately the birds east of the Rocky Mountains, those farther west, and those in Texas and adjoining states. One of the best one-volume guides is *Birds of North America* by Chandler Robbins, Bertel Bruun, and Herbert Zim. At first borrow a guide from your library; if you find your interest continues, then buy one. In this exploratory stage it also would be useful to participate in a bird walk. Local bird clubs frequently sponsor such events. It is a good way to learn some of the techniques of bird watching, meet other birders, and expand your knowledge of local birds.

Should you decide to become a bird watcher, it will be necessary to make a few purchases. A field guide already has been mentioned. Be

* Frequently call notes and songs are the same. When they differ, call notes may relate to alarm, territorial defense, aggression, feeding, and nesting, while a song is used in mating.

certain to buy one with a separate listing of the species described so that you may check off those you sight. However, you also should have a notebook or a diary for observations and comments regarding each new species you see. Field glasses also are needed to check the field markings and color of a bird, two key criteria in making identifications. Purchase a pair with a magnification of seven power and a wide field. You also will need a small knapsack for carrying books, equipment, and food for yourself and, as we shall discuss, for the birds.

In addition, the serious birder eventually may acquire bird whistles or tape recordings of bird calls with which to attract birds and a tape recorder for playing and recording calls. He also may want a telescope and a tripod for observing birds offshore, and a camera.

WHERE AND WHEN TO FIND BIRDS

Birds may be found virtually anywhere, but you will find the largest number where and when they feed. The most likely places are where one type of terrain or growth ends and another begins. Thickets and hedgerows on the edge of a field or a lawn are good places to look. The edge of a wood, the bank of a stream or a river, the margin of a beach or a marsh are others. The best times to go birding generally are in the early morning and an hour or two before sunset, although this varies to a degree with particular species. If you live along one of the four flyways that migratory birds use, you are likely to see a greater number of species than otherwise. These flyways encompass the Pacific Coast, the Rocky Mountains and Western Great Plains, the Mississippi Valley, and the Atlantic Coast. The migrations southward start in the fall and extend through Christmas. The northward migration may begin as early as January or February and conclude in May or June. Experienced birders can give you the optimum periods for your area.

As suggested earlier, you might start birding in your back yard or a nearby park. Dozens of species are likely to be found in both places. Next begin exploring in the countryside or in nearby bird sanctuaries. Initially the emphasis should be on seeing as many birds as possible. As you grow more experienced, however, you will seek out particular species rather than birds in quantity. In such cases it is necessary to take into account a bird's habitat and range.

Habitat refers to the type of surroundings a bird prefers. Meadowlarks, swallows, and bobolinks, for example, often are found in fields.

Sage thrashers, road-runners, and red-tailed hawks frequent the desert regions of the Southwest. Blackbirds, yellowbirds, and coots like ponds and marshes. Chickadees, flickers, and owls are found in wooded areas. Terns, willets, knots, and sandpipers, along with gulls, inhabit coastal sections.

A bird's range is the geographical area within which it ordinarily is found. This may be highly limited, such as the range of the dusky seaside sparrow the Southerlands sought, or it may cover hundreds, even thousands, of miles. A good field guide will provide detailed information on both habitat and range.

Attracting Birds. There are steps one can take to increase the likelihood that he will see the birds he is seeking. Sunflower seed distributed on the ground or on a board near a tree or a dense shrub, or placed on a feeder in a back yard, may attract chickadees, house finches, and other species. Buy the seed in 50- to 100-pound sacks, but don't buy mixtures. A quantity of suet placed in a wire container or a plastic milk carton and hung from a tree also will attract birds, including woodpeckers and tufted titmice. If you use this method in a park or a wild area, plan to sit quietly nearby to await the results. The installation of a bird bath or bird house in a back yard also may result in some interesting visitors. For a detailed discussion of these approaches, see the booklet *Attracting Birds,* which is listed in the Bibliography.

Imitating a bird in distress or a mouse underfoot is a traditional method of encouraging birds to come out of a thicket. This involves kissing the back of your hand. If the kiss is applied with tight lips, a mouselike squeak will result. If the kiss is drawn out, it will resemble the distress signal a bird uses. As already noted, birders also use whistles or tape recordings to attract birds. These either duplicate the call of the bird they are seeking or that of some other creature likely to attract it. A whistle that gives the death squeal of a rabbit or a mouse, for example, is often used to attract birds of prey.

IDENTIFYING BIRDS

A successful bird walk requires preparation. Determine the types of birds you are likely to see in the section you are exploring. Then study their pictures and descriptions in your field guide. Some advanced birders also listen beforehand to recordings of birds they may encounter, but this is not necessary at the outset. One is likely to see birds at any time of day but the ideal periods, as noted earlier, are at daybreak and in the late afternoon. After dark the principal attraction is, of course, the owl.

During the day it is best to walk with the sun at your back so that the colors and markings of the birds you see are more readily visible. If you walk facing the sun, you may have to identify the birds by their silhouettes. The principal field guides show these, but they are a relatively difficult means of identification.

In looking for birds, it is important to check everything that moves. The National Audubon Society recommends the following procedure in examining a tree. Starting at the top, move your eyes slowly from left to right; then drop your eyes slightly and look from right to left. Continue in this zigzag fashion until the entire tree and its trunk have been inspected. To double check, start at the bottom and zigzag your way to the top. The same system is effective in examining a section of a thicket or a hedgerow.

It is easier to see birds in wooded areas, where they move from tree to tree, than it is in brushy areas, where they tend to remain inside a thicket or quickly dive into one if startled. It is under such conditions that the use of "squeaking," whistles, and recorded bird calls is most effective.

In every case, however, it usually is difficult to observe a bird from closer than 20 or 30 feet, which is why field glasses must be used to make accurate identifications. At times you might get closer in a car or on horseback; if so, take care not to roll down a window, open a door, or dismount, or the bird will fly away.

When you first see a bird, ask yourself what family or group it might belong to, based on your previous reading or experience. Might it be a warbler, for example, or a sparrow or a wading bird or a swimming bird? Also estimate its relative size, contrasting it with the size of a bird you already know, such as a robin, a crow, or a sparrow. Then consider its shape (the length and size of its bill, tail, and legs, for example) and its color and its field marks (such as the markings above or below its eyes or on its tail or breast). Also be alert for its behavior in flight (whether it flaps its wings continuously or glides, for example) and its behavior on the ground (whether it hops or walks).

After but a few months of bird watching, you will come to know many new birds by sight. You may see a long-tailed brownish bird that seems to explode upward and know immediately that it is a mourning dove. Or you may spot a large bird overhead holding its wings in the shape of a V, and know at once it is a turkey vulture.

After a few months you also may begin to pay closer attention to bird calls and songs. In a few cases a call or a song is the only distinguishing feature among otherwise identical birds, such as various flycatchers. With many other birds, however, it makes identification easier and more interesting. Some experts base most of their identifications on the call or song of a bird, but this requires considerable experience. The best approach is to learn a few calls at a time and use them as a basis for comparison in learning others. The best teacher is a good recording, a number of which are listed in the Bibliography.

As you make observations, list them in a notebook, then check them as soon as possible against the descriptions in your field guide. In looking for particular birds, you will, of course, already have their characteristics in mind. In all cases it is important to be absolutely certain of your identification before claiming a bird for your list.

The Southerlands work together in checking identifications. Only after one has called out all key characteristics and the other has double checked them, do they feel free to list a bird as one they have seen. In fact, on occasion when doubt has nagged at them, they have gone back to check again. There are other birders, however, who are less stringent in their requirements.

In his first year an energetic bird watcher may log 200 species or more. From that point, however, enlarging his list becomes an increasingly difficult task. Eventually, he may see but a few new birds each year and do so only by traveling great distances to out-of-the-way places. Thus, one ordinarily must journey to Big Bend National Park in Texas if he is to see the Colima warbler, to the lower Florida Keys for the white-crowned pigeon, and to the Carlsbad Caverns in New Mexico for the cave swallow. As a result, there are several lists bird watchers may attempt to develop. Most maintain a "life list" of all the birds they have identified. A refinement is a "joint life list" of birds a husband and wife or a parent and child have jointly identified. Birders also maintain lists of birds they have seen in their back yards or in their town or state.

One of the great satisfactions in bird watching lies in accounting for the relatively rare species. In North America these include about 100 subspecies. Such birds actually are members of other species, but are geographically isolated from them and, as a result, have developed subtle differences in their appearance or in the sounds they make. Rare birds also include "accidentals" that enter an area where they are seldom if ever seen. When an accidental is sighted, it is of importance to

178

check its characteristics with great care before claiming it. A responsible birder first may obtain the corroboration of another birder, if possible, or take photographs, or examine the skins of the species at a natural history museum. If an unusual bird is sighted, it is customary in many communities to let other birders know. Usually this is done by telephone. In the Boston area one calls the local Audubon Society, which then reports the event as part of a recorded telephone announcement. To learn what is going on, dial 617-536-4050. In the New York area, where there is a similar arrangement, dial 516-485-2170 for unusual sightings.

COUNTING BIRDS AND OTHER ACTIVITIES

Counting Birds. Each Christmas season birders throughout the United States and Canada, usually members of clubs, devote a day or more to counting the birds in their areas. The results give the National Audubon Society a continuing picture of changes in the bird population in the two countries. In a recent year over 10,000 men, women, and children in 839 different communities participated in the Christmas Count. In my town about 35 observers were at their stations on the chosen day before 7 A.M. in 16-degree temperatures. Working within a 15-mile radius, they counted 21,537 individual birds and 77 different species, including the great blue heron, the green-winged teal, the pileated woodpecker, and a pair of yellow-bellied sapsuckers. In many communities local clubs sponsor another count day in May. Often referred to as the Big Day, it is a local affair which enables members to compete against one another or against their previous records.

Banding Birds. As part of a continuing study of bird migration, over 3000 volunteers serve as bird banders in the United States and Canada. Their job is to trap birds with mist nets and other harmless devices, place an identifying band around one of their legs, and release them. Persons who later encounter these birds are asked to report their findings to the Bird Banding Office, Patuxent Wildlife Research Center, U.S. Fish and Wildlife Service, Laurel, Maryland 20810. Each year 40,000 persons do so, some from as far away as South America and Europe.* The banding office, in turn, notifies the bander as to where the

* If you find a dead banded bird, remove the band and submit it with information on where and when the bird was found and under what circumstances. If you find a live banded bird, the band should not be removed; instead the number it carries should be submitted and the bird released.

179

bird was found and the finder as to where it came from. Prospective banders must be at least 18, possess a thorough knowledge of birds in their area, and have the recommendation of three naturalists, ornithologists, or banders who can testify as to their fitness. Applications are available in the United States from the Bird Banding Office at the above address and in Canada from the Canadian Wildlife Service, Ottawa.

Nest Research. Bird watchers also cooperate in research into the breeding habits of birds by providing ornithologists with regular reports on nesting birds in their areas. For information write Laboratory of Ornithology, Cornell University, 159 Sapsucker Woods Road, Ithaca, N.Y. 14850.

ORGANIZATIONS

There are scores of local bird clubs and naturalist clubs. Some are particularly helpful to beginners in that they conduct bird walks and are sources of information and advice. Others are essentially study groups for advanced amateurs or action groups working in behalf of the conservation of natural resources. The major national organization concerned with bird life is the National Audubon Society, 1130 Fifth Avenue, New York, N.Y. 10028. In addition to its leadership in the conservation movement, it conducts an extensive educational program in the natural sciences. It operates nature centers, conducts nature camps for adults, and publishes pamphlets, books, and a magazine. The publications of its Junior Audubon Program are particularly helpful to bird watchers with children. There also are state Audubon societies with which a number of local clubs are affiliated. Many birders also maintain membership in two other conservation organizations, the National Wildlife Federation, 1412 16th Street, N.W., Washington, D.C. 20036, and the Sierra Club, 220 Bush Street, San Francisco, California 94104.

BIBLIOGRAPHY
Field Guides
Birds of North America, Chandler S. Robbins, Bertel Bruun, Herbert S. Zim, Golden Press, 1966.
A Field Guide to the Birds, Roger T. Peterson, Houghton Mifflin Co., 1947. Birds east of 100th meridian.

A Field Guide to the Birds of Britain and Europe, Roger T. Peterson, Guy Mountfort, P. A. D. Hollom, Houghton Mifflin Co., 1966.

A Field Guide to the Birds of Texas and Adjacent States, Roger T. Peterson, Houghton Mifflin Co., 1963.

A Field Guide to Western Birds, Roger T. Peterson, Houghton Mifflin Co., 1961. Birds west of the 100th meridian.

Guides and Picture Books

Birds of the Eastern Forest, J. F. Lansdowne, J. A. Livingston, Houghton Mifflin Co., 1968.

Birds of the Northern Forest, Lansdowne, Livingston, Houghton Mifflin Co., 1966.

Birds of Prey of the World, M. L. Grossman, John Hamlet, Clarkson N. Potter, 1964.

The Bird Watcher's Anthology, Roger T. Peterson, Houghton Mifflin Co., 1957.

How to Watch Birds, Roger Barton, McGraw-Hill Book Co., 1955.

The Shorebirds of North America, Gardner D. Stout, Viking Press, 1967.

Song and Garden Birds of North America, National Geographic Society, 1964.

Song Birds in Your Garden, John K. Terres, Thomas Y. Crowell Co., 1968.

Water, Prey, and Game Birds of North America, Alexander Wetmore et al., National Geographic Society, Washington, D.C., 1965.

Books for Young People

Audubon Land Bird Guide, Richard H. Pough, Doubleday & Co., New York, 1951.

Audubon Water Bird Guide, Richard H. Pough, Doubleday & Co., New York, 1951.

Booklets, Pamphlets

Attracting Birds, U.S. Fish and Wildlife Service, Superintendent of Documents, Washington, D.C. 20402. A complete list of Fish and Wildlife Service pamphlets is available from the Superintendent of Documents.

The Story of Birds for Audubon Juniors, Shirley Miller, National Audubon Society, 1130 Fifth Avenue, New York, N.Y. 10028. With membership in Junior Audubon Program for young people. A list of other Audubon materials is available on request.

Periodicals

Audubon Magazine, National Audubon Society, 1130 Fifth Avenue, New York, N.Y. 10028.

The Auk, American Ornithological Union, San Jose State College, San Jose, California 95114. Advanced.

The Condor, Museum of Vertebrate Zoology, Berkeley, California 94720. Advanced.

Natural History, American Museum of Natural History, Central Park West and 79th Street, New York, N.Y. 10024.

Recordings of Bird Songs

A Field Guide to Bird Songs. Two 12-inch LP records, Cornell University Laboratory of Ornithology, Ithaca, N.Y. 14850. Related to Peterson's *A Field Guide to the Birds.*

A Field Guide to Western Bird Songs. Three 12-inch LP records, Cornell University Laboratory of Ornithology. Related to Peterson's *A Field Guide to Western Birds.*

Recordings of tropical, Mexican, African, and other bird songs are also available from the above source.

16·FISHES

My DAUGHTER BETSY shares her room with three small goldfish and two small snails. The tank they occupy is equipped with a bed of gravel, a filter to keep the water clean, an aerator to maintain the necessary oxygen level, and a small jungle of floating plants.

An engineering student at the university in my town shares his apartment with hundreds of brightly colored, curiously constructed tropical fish. Many are kept in his living room in four large tanks whose aerators bubble in concert like a gentle brook. In addition, a bedroom serves as a kind of nursery where guppies, white clouds, and bettas he has bred, some no larger than grains of sand, make their way to maturity.

One of his most amusing possessions is an angel fish that looks out of his tank with seeming arrogance at whoever presumes to look in. One of his most interesting is a fish that breeds by blowing a nest of bubbles which cling together on the surface. After the female lays her eggs, the male fertilizes them and blows them into the nest, where he guards them.

Other aquarists raise fish taken from brooks and ponds and from tide pools and coral reefs. Many trap the fish they need and create displays of uncanny beauty. Whether one is starting out, however, or is an established aquarist, the result of his efforts is an intimate view of a way of life as remote from ours as anyone could imagine.

GETTING STARTED

In considering this hobby, visit a pet shop or a museum aquarium to determine if fish really intrigue you. Then talk to an aquarist (a pet shop dealer will know of several) and do some specialized reading. The best primers are William T. Innes' classic *Exotic Aquarium Fishes* and Clifford B. Moore's *The Book of Wild Pets.* A young person with an interest in raising fish should read the *Aquarium Book for Boys and Girls* by Alfred Morgan. The next step is buying a small tank, some of the other equipment described below, and a few fishes. Still later, consider joining an aquarium society. A membership in a well-run organization teaches one a good deal. It also provides a place to trade fish and offers opportunities to buy fish and equipment at discount.

EQUIPMENT

The challenge is to create an environment inside four glass walls that duplicates as precisely as possible the natural world of a fish. You can establish a modest but satisfactory aquarium for under $25. Some pet shops have package deals for beginners which reduce the cost somewhat. In addition, the Aquarium Club of America sells supplies at discount. See the section Organizations.

Tanks and Bowls. To start, purchase a five- or ten-gallon tank. The larger size is a better investment. The best type of fresh water aquarium has a stainless steel frame and a slate bottom. For marine specimens use a metal-free fiberglass model or some other type that is impervious to salt. Of course, the size of a tank determines the number of fish you can keep. The general rule is one gallon for each inch of fish, excluding the tails. Tropical fish actually need somewhat less room. In a ten-gallon tank you could keep ten small goldfish or 15 small tropicals. However, as the fish grow it would be necessary to re-move some to another tank, or overcrowding and a shortage of oxygen would result.

If you plan to breed fish, you also would need a second tank or one or two squat fish bowls. However, a bowl should never be used as a general tank. Its surface is too limited to provide sufficient oxygen, and the water it contains cannot be kept at a stable temperature. Moreover, the rounded walls distort the image of the fish.

Tables and Stands. A tank should be kept on a rubber pad on a sturdy table. The pad serves to cushion the tank in the event it is jarred and reduces the possibility of cracking the cement that holds it together, which could result in leaks. Ultimately you might want an aquarium stand, some of which are designed to hold several tanks.

Aerator-Filter. This unit adds oxygen to the water, filters out pollutants, helps maintain healthy fish, and sharply reduces the need for cleaning a tank. There are inexpensive models suitable for a five- or ten-gallon aquarium. Larger tanks require proportionately larger and more costly units.

Gravel. A two-inch bed of aquarium gravel or coarse sand generally is needed to hold plants in place. With marine plants, use fine sand.

Heater. This unit is necessary only with tropical fish. Purchase a heater with a thermostatic control. To determine the size of the heater needed, multiply the number of gallons to be heated by five watts. Thus, a ten-gallon tank would require a fifty-watt heater.

Thermometer. A thermometer is used to make certain the temperature of the water is correct. It is essential equipment with tropical fish, marine varieties, and certain native fish. There are thermometers that float and others that stay put. The latter type is more desirable.

Lamp, Cover. The light from an aquarium lamp helps plants grow, helps maintain the water at an even temperature, is beneficial to the fish, and enhances the appearance of the tank. A cover for the top of the tank prevents evaporation of water, keeps the dust out, and restrains fish with a tendency to jump. A piece of heavy glass cut to size will serve as a reasonably effective cover, and a gooseneck lamp positioned above the glass will provide the needed light. A better arrangement is a hood with a built-in light.

Feeding Equipment. Many aquarists feed their fish by dropping the food on the surface of the water. A floating food feeder concentrates food in one area and facilitates cleaning. Specialized feeders for specialized foods also are available.

Cleaning Equipment. A dip tube is used to remove uneaten food and other debris which otherwise would foul the water. A battery-powered vacuum cleaner does a still more thorough job. If algae has begun to obscure the walls of a tank, remove it with a single-edged razor blade. If a tank has become polluted or its use has been changed or it must be moved, use a siphon to remove the water. A four-foot length of $3/8''$ hose seems to work best. The filter discussed above and the plants and scavengers discussed later also help keep a tank clean.

Fish Net. This is used in moving fish from one tank to another and in removing dead fish. A nylon net is the most durable type.

185

Ornaments. Sea shells, coral, and similar objects frequently are used in tanks for decorative purposes. They are suitable in marine tanks but not in fresh water aquaria, since they may increase the amount of lime in the water, which can have a negative effect on the fish. They also create a housekeeping problem in that they tend to catch debris.

WATER

A tankful of tap water may have an adverse effect unless it is treated. There are three potential hazards.

Chlorine. Either use a commercial preparation to neutralize the chlorine or let the water stand for a week before introducing fish.

Hard Water. A simple kit sold in pet shops will determine the hardness of water. If it is above 8 on the hardness scale, add a quantity of water softener to the filter. If you can obtain soft water from a stream or a well, so much the better. However, do not transport it in a metal container.

Acidity and Alkalinity. An excess in either case also may create problems. Measuring the degree of acidity or alkalinity involves the use of a kit and a pH (potential hydrogen) scale. The scale ranges from zero to 14. Water that is neutral has a pH of 7. A higher reading indicates acidity, a lower reading, alkalinity. Acceptable tap water has a pH of 4 to 9. Pet shops sell both the pH kit and chemicals to make adjustments. If you are breeding fish, it is particularly desirable first to determine their pH needs. The handbooks listed in the Bibliography contain such information.

The water needed for marine species and for native specimens from ponds and brooks is discussed later.

PLANTS

Aquarium plants meet a variety of needs. They contribute to a more natural environment for fish and help provide them with oxygen. They also play an important role in breeding. Many fish lay eggs on their leaves, and baby fish use plants as hiding places when pursued by adults that wish to eat them. The fish, in turn, contribute the carbon dioxide plants need and also nourishment in the form of droppings and uneaten food which they absorb through their roots. This process also helps clean the tank.

There are over three dozen varieties of fresh water plants, many of which are quite beautiful. Some grow under water and must be rooted in the gravel or sand at the bottom of a tank. Others float unrooted on the surface. One of the most popular rooted plants is sagittaria. It is available in dwarf, regular, and large varieties, which makes it useful in tanks of all sizes. Vallisneria is a rooted plant appropriate for larger tanks. Cabomba, anacharis, and myriophyllum may be grown under water or floated. Lesser bladderwort and crystalwort are common floating varieties. However, do not overlook such lovely possibilities as hair grass, spatterdock, the swordplants, and the Madagascar lace plant.

Plants used with native and marine specimens are discussed separately.

SETTING UP A TANK

First select an appropriate location. You will want a spot that is not too close to a heating vent or a radiator, that will not be in a draft, and that receives only indirect sunlight. Wash the tank thoroughly. Then add the gravel, banking it so that it slopes from back to front, an arrangement which will make cleaning easier. In filling the tank, position a saucer on the gravel and pour the water on the saucer. Initially add enough to fill two-thirds of the tank. Then install the plants. If they are the rooted variety, you probably will need a dozen for the back and a half-dozen for either side. Wash them carefully in cold water and place them in the tank one at a time. Make certain the roots are fully spread, then pack gravel around each plant up to where the leaves begin to branch, but no higher. When all the plants are in place, fill the tank within an inch or two of the top and remove the saucer. Finally, add the anti-chlorine preparation, set the aerator and filter in operation, and position the cover and the light. Wait several days before introducing the fish. This period will enable the plants to establish themselves and permit any cloudiness in the water to dissipate. Meanwhile acquire your fish.

BUYING FISH

Initially purchase just a few fish. Add others as you acquire more knowledge and a sense of your interests. Various fishes you might start with are suggested below. In all cases be certain that those you select are about the same size and will live peacefully together.

Sources. The place to acquire your first fish is a pet shop unless you are concentrating on native fish. The techniques of acquiring these are discussed separately. As you grow more experienced, you may reach a point at which a pet shop no longer can supply your needs. Then it will be necessary to turn to suppliers in larger cities, like the famous Aquarium Stock Company in New York. A pet shop dealer will be able to advise you. Many such firms have catalogs, ship by mail, and guarantee live delivery. A number of professional breeders and collectors also sell by mail. They advertise in the magazines listed in the Bibliography. Another source is the Aquarium Club of America, which is discussed under Organizations. There also may be amateur breeders in your area or other aquarists who wish to dispose of surplus fish. You are likely to learn of such persons through aquarium societies and pet shops.

Health. The primary consideration in purchasing a fish is its good health. The likelihood is that a fish is healthy if it swims vigorously, holds its fins in a normal position, and has a good appetite. In addition, its body will be free of white spots that indicate the presence of the disease "ich," discussed later. It also is important to check the appearance of other fishes in the same tank. If even one seems ill, don't buy any from that tank. Once you have established your aquarium at home, it would be sound to place new acquisitions in a quarantine tank for a week, no matter how healthy they seem, to make sure they do not have an illness which might affect your other specimens. Add a sterilizing preparation to the tank to destroy potentially harmful organisms they might carry. A pet shop will have several such preparations.

Cost. The cost of fishes varies widely. The least expensive are common goldfish and guppies, which cost about 20 cents each. The most expensive are exotic species, which range upward in price from $5.

Introducing Fish to a Tank. A fish usually is placed in a plastic bag of water for the trip home. So that the shock of moving from one environment to another is minimized, float the bag in your tank until the temperature in each is the same. This takes about an hour. Then cut the bag open and release the fish.

Scavengers. Snails and catfish traditionally have served as the garbage men of the aquarium. What the filter, dip tube, and plants don't remove, they do. Three or four snails are all you will need for a 10-gallon tank. Since they propagate rapidly, you may, in fact, soon find yourself with a far greater number. Catfish should be selected in terms of whether a tank requires relatively low or relatively high temperatures. One catfish will suffice.

FEEDING

Food appropriate for various fishes is discussed below. As a general rule, feed a fish once daily what it can consume in five minutes. Actually a fish will suffer no great harm if it goes without food for a week or more. It will suffer, however, if it is given more to eat than it can manage and the water is polluted by decaying food. What is not eaten should be removed immediately, unless it is live food which will survive in the tank.

TREATING ILLNESS

Fish may become ill for any number of reasons. These may include temperatures that are too low or too high, sudden chilling, a lack of oxygen, overfeeding, or being fed the wrong food.

Among fresh water fish, the best known disease, and one of the most common, is "ich," which is short for ichthyophthirius. This disease is caused by a parasite which entrenches itself just under the skin of a fish, causing white spots to appear. It is highly contagious and may be fatal, but it responds to treatment. One treatment calls for the addition of a teaspoon of sea salt per gallon of water. Another involves adding five drops of 2 per cent Mercurochrome per gallon. Some aquarists add streptomycin to the water. Others, with tropical fish, raise the temperature of the water to 85 degrees for a week or more. The heat kills the parasite but not the fish.

Fungus growths also are relatively common, highly contagious, and potentially fatal. Such growths generally are white and scummy-looking. They affect the eyes, mouth, fins, and other parts of the body. In such cases a fish should be removed to a separate hospital tank. If it has just become ill, a sea-salt bath as described above may be sufficient treatment.

For more serious cases various fungicides are available. In the case of an eye fungus, one cure involves swabbing the eyes of the fish with silver nitrate. Many commercial preparations also are available to deal with these problems. In fact, one firm sells a complete first aid kit for about $4. Treating diseases of salt water fish is discussed separately.

GOLDFISH

Since goldfish are naturally hardy creatures, they are an excellent species for a first aquarium. If they are treated well, they may live for several years: It is not unusual, in fact, for goldfish to survive a decade or longer. The common goldfish is a native of China. The fancy varieties were bred there and in Korea and Japan. Their descendants in the United States and Canada are produced at extensive fish farms in the Midwest and the East.

Types of Goldfish. The common goldfish also is called a "wakin." The fancy varieties, which are somewhat more expensive, include the comet, a large-finned fish which tends to jump and must be kept in a hooded tank; the fringetail, which is characterized by a long tail; the fantail, which possesses a double tail; and the colorful shubunkin or calico fish which is colored with dark reds, blacks, browns, and blues. There also are two rather ugly varieties: the telescope, which has "pop" eyes, and the lionhead or buffalo head. These generally range in length from one to three inches. If they are free in ponds or brooks, they grow far larger.

Temperatures. Sixty-eight degrees is the best temperature at which to keep goldfish, although 55 to 75 is an acceptable range.

Food. There are many dried preparations available. It is wise to mix two or three different kinds and serve the result. Supplement this occasionally with finely chopped lettuce and bits of clam, earthworm, and ground beef.

Breeding. When goldfish breed, ordinarily this first occurs in the spring of their second year. The signs that mating is imminent are quite clear. The female swells with eggs and the male pursues her around the tank. At this point it is desirable to move the pair to a separate breeding tank which has been planted with myriophyllum. After the female deposits her eggs on the leaves of the plant, and the male fertilizes them, the two fish should be returned to their original tank or they will eat the eggs. If the fish mate before they can be moved, the plant on which the eggs were deposited should be transplanted to a breeding tank. The eggs ordinarily hatch in three to six days at a temperature of 68 degrees. Since scores of eggs are involved, it is wise to save only those for which there is a use. The baby fish, or fry, require a half-dozen daily feedings of infusoria, a microscopic organism that is raised with a preparation available in pet shops. As they grow somewhat older, the fish will benefit from tropical fish food of a fine consistency, tiny bits of hard-cooked egg yolk, and dried daphnia.

TROPICAL FISH

A tropical fish is one whose habitat is in tropical or subtropical waters. In the United States, fish found at or below the latitude of the Carolinas are regarded as "tropical." However, tropical fish are captured all over the world. Others with tropical antecedents are bred in this country by both professionals and amateurs. For many hobbyists, breeding is one of the great appeals of raising tropical fish. Of equal satisfaction, however, are their remarkable colors, their great beauty, and the infinite adaptations they have made over millions of years to the special circumstances of their lives.

Types of Tropical Fish. The great majority of tropical fish raised by amateurs are fresh water varieties. These are discussed in this section. For salt water varieties, see the section Marine Life. Tropical fish also may be categorized as live bearers, fish whose eggs hatch inside them, or egg layers, fish whose eggs hatch externally.

Among the easiest tropicals to raise and breed are three colorful, prolific live bearers: guppies, swordtails, and platies. With a ten-gallon aquarium, you might acquire one or two of each and establish a small community tank. If you don't wish to breed the fish, purchase only one sex, preferably males since they are far more beautiful. If you do breed them and a female becomes pregnant, she should be removed to a separate tank to have her young, then returned to the community tank so that she doesn't eat them. The jet black mollies also are interesting live bearers. But they do better in a tank of their own in which the water has been treated with sodium bicarbonate (a teaspoon and a half per 10 gallons).

To these species one might add egg layers such as zebra fish, angel fish, the delicate pristella, and the tetras and gouramis. Breeding egg bearers is more difficult than breeding live bearers, but frequently it is more interesting. As described earlier, some egg layers hatch their eggs in nests of bubbles. Others do so in their mouths. Still others hang their eggs from plants by threads or hide them in the gravel. Herbert Axelrod's *Encyclopedia of Tropical Fishes* is an excellent guide to the particular techniques and problems in breeding the hundreds of varieties available.

Temperature. Most tropical fish thrive at a temperature of 75 degrees, although a range of 70 to 80 may be satisfactory. To maintain these temperatures, generally a water heater is needed, as discussed earlier.

Food. Most tropical fish will subsist on the dried foods available in pet shops, but they will benefit immeasurably (in terms of activity, color, and general health) if they also are provided with other foods. One of the most useful live foods is brine shrimp, which may be purchased freeze-dried or may be incubated from eggs. Another is tubifex worms, for which a special feeder is available. Daphnia and bits of earthworm, clam, and liver also may appeal to them. As noted earlier, dried or inanimate food should be consumed within five minutes, or what remains should be removed.

MARINE LIFE

A salt water aquarium provides an introduction to a world few of us know. It might house crabs, mussels, clams, pectens, or barnacles or varieties of minnows or a pair of seahorses or the brilliantly colored fish that inhabit the coral reefs. However, such a tank is more difficult to develop and maintain than other types. The reason is that sea life has a harder time adapting to a tank than many fresh water varieties which have been tank bred. But the results are well worth the effort.

Acquiring Specimens. If you live near the seashore, start by collecting local specimens. The time to search is at low tide. The best places are rocky areas, tide pools, and bays. It would be useful to have a hand net, a pinch bar, a pocket knife, and a few jars or plastic containers with covers. Wear sneakers and bring canvas gloves. For a first aquarium, try for two or three small crabs or a clam, a mussel, and a barnacle, or three or four minnows about the same size. In working a beach, check mud flats for clam holes, rocky sections and pilings for mollusks, and tide pools and bays for other specimens. Some aquarists also do their collecting off coral reefs, but this requires great skill.

Marine specimens also can be obtained through dealers in large cities and from professional collectors. One source is the Bio-Marine Supply Company, Box 285, Venice, California 90291. The Aquarium Club of America also sells marine life. See the section Organizations.

Water. It has become increasingly difficult to obtain sea

PLATE I *Lyretail black mollies* (*genus* Poecilia), *female at top.*

PLATE II   *Male guppy* (Poecilia reticulata).

PLATE III   *Black neon* (Hyphessobrycon herbertaxelrodi)

PLATE IV   *Zebra danios* (Brachydanio rerio), *male at top.*

PLATE V   *Green wagtail swordtails* (Xiphophorus helleri), *male at top.*

PLATE VI *Veiled lace angel fish* (Pterophyllum scalare).

water that is not polluted unless one journeys a distance from shore. When polluted water is placed in an aquarium, the concentration of pollutants is intensified to a point at which few creatures can survive. Instead of relying on natural salt water, purchase a quantity of ocean salts at a pet shop and mix your own. To assure that the result is satisfactory, you will need an inexpensive hydrometer, which measures the specific gravity of the water, and a salt water pH kit. If the specific gravity and the pH are not right, the health of your specimen could be seriously affected.

The specific gravity of the water is determined by the salt concentration. The ideal reading is 1.020, but a range from 1.017 to 1.022 is acceptable. Once the tank has been set up, mark the water level with a piece of tape. If evaporation occurs, thereby increasing the salt content, return the water to its original level by adding fresh soft water or distilled water. The pH, as discussed earlier, reflects relative acidity or alkalinity. The water should be slightly acid, with the recommended level at 8.3. If it drops, add small quantities of sodium carbonate until the reading is satisfactory.

Plants and Ornaments. Whether salt water vegetation can be successfully transplanted to a tank is questionable. Some aquarists say that common brown kelp will grow in a tank, but that other brown and red plants tend to poison the water. Another reports that sea lettuce will thrive in a tank. If a plant is attached to a stone, its chances of survival are better if at least portions of the stone are moved. There is general agreement that lovely white coral is a safe addition. It is useful in that it provides specimens with a place to hide. Seashells, on the other hand, are suspect because of the pollutants they may carry.

Setting Up a Tank. The capacity of a marine tank is roughly half that of a goldfish tank or about a half-inch of fish per gallon. As a result, you will need at least a 10- or 15-gallon tank. As discussed earlier, a tank should be free of metal, which corrodes in salt water. Instead purchase a plastic, fiberglass, or all-glass tank.

Cover the bottom with about an inch of finely packed beach sand. To be certain the sand is clean, place it in a plastic bucket and continuously run cold water on it at a slow enough rate so that the sand is not carried away. When the water that drains from the bucket is clear, the sand is clean. Sand is used instead of gravel so as to prevent the accumulation of debris. In fresh water aquaria the roots of plants absorb much of this accumulation. Since marine plants generally are not rooted in the same sense, all debris must be removed by the mechanical means described earlier. After the sand is in place, install the plants and any stones to which they are attached. Then slowly fill the tank, pouring the water on a saucer positioned in the sand. The tank also will need a cover, an aerator, a filter, and a thermometer.

Water Temperature. Marine life taken from northern waters requires a temperature of about 55 degrees. Maintaining this temperature during the summer months is difficult unless you are prepared to install a refrigeration unit or float plastic bags of ice cubes in the water. A more practical alternative is returning the specimens to their natural habitat and assembling a new collection when the weather becomes cooler.

Tropical reef fish require a temperature of about 70 degrees. To maintain this, you will need a thermostatically controlled heater described earlier.

Food. All of the following are beneficial: brine shrimp, tubifex worms, white worms, daphnia, and finely chopped raw fish, clams, and other mollusks. Food should be provided daily in small quantities. What is not eaten within five minutes should be removed. The only exceptions are live foods whose habitat is salt water. Live fresh water food such as tubifex worms will die within a few hours if not consumed and then should be promptly removed.

Health. Dealing with illness in salt water specimens is difficult because relatively little is known. As already noted, it is essential to keep specific gravity, the pH, and water temperature at the right level and to aerate the tank and keep it clean through filtration and other methods. Just as with fresh water specimens, marine life should be sterilized before being added to a community tank. Sterilization involves a two- or three-minute fresh water bath containing 25 milligrams of potassium permanganate per gallon. If a fish becomes ill despite these precautions, consult Herbert Axelrod's *Salt-Water Aquarium Fish.*

Breeding. This is another area where, at this writing, little is known and only limited success has been possible.

NATIVE FISHES AND AMPHIBIANS

You may find the inhabitants of lakes, ponds, and streams near your home as fascinating as specimens from more distant waters.

Since they cannot be purchased, however, they must be collected, which itself is an interesting pursuit.

Fishes. Native fishes that adapt well to aquarium life include dace, darters, sunfish, bluegills, catfish, crappies, suckers, perch, killies, chub, bass, and eels. Such fish may live together in reasonable harmony if they are under three inches long. Pickerel, pike, and sticklebacks also adapt to tank life but will not hesitate to attack and consume the rest of your collection. As a result, they need tanks of their own. This also is the case, as they grow larger, with bass, sunnies, and bluegills.

Small streams and ditches often are a good source of small fish. In such cases use a soup strainer to collect specimens. In larger bodies, use a fine-mesh nylon dip net. Some specimens also may be landed with standard fishing gear and barbless hooks. Save only the smallest fish you catch. If it is necessary to handle them, do so gently and make certain your hands are wet. Otherwise, you may inadvertently remove some of their scales. Transport the fish in plastic buckets filled with water from the pond or stream from which you took them. Slosh the water vigorously so that it is well oxygenated, place only a few fish in any one bucket, and cover with cheesecloth or screening. If you have difficulty identifying what you have caught, consult one of the standard guidebooks.

Water: Fill your tank with water from the pond or stream involved.

Plants: The rooted plants described in the section on goldfish are appropriate. It also is practical to use plants from the water a fish occupied.

Setting Up a Tank: For a community aquarium use a 15-gallon tank. With a larger species that requires a separate tank, use a 10-gallon unit. Position the tank so that it receives at least two hours a day of direct sunlight. Then arrange it as you would a tank for goldfish. You will need an aerator, a filter, and a thermometer. A cover and a light also would be useful. Keep the temperature of the water at about 65 degrees.

Food: Feed the fish tropical fish food of a medium or coarse consistency plus bits of chopped raw meat, fish, and earthworm. Some fishes also will eat insects of all types. Larger fish will eat live minnows, small frogs, and bits of earthworm. Inanimate foods which have not been consumed within five minutes should be removed.

Health: See the discussion Treating Illness in the section on fresh water fish.

Breeding. Few native fish will breed in captivity. Sunfish, stickle-

Sunfish (Lepomis gibbosus).

Catfish (Corydoras aeneus), *female at left.*

Barred Fantail Darter (Boleosoma).

Killifish (Jordanella floridae), *male at right.*

backs, and shiners occasionally may do so if a tank is large enough, there are sufficient plants, and other conditions are right. All three species construct nests in which the female deposits her eggs. Sunfish and shiners dig their nests in the gravel at the bottom of a tank. The stickleback builds its nest, which looks something like a bird's nest, in the foliage. When breeding begins, remove any fish not involved. After the eggs are hatched, remove the parents. Feed the young daphnia and tropical fish food of a fine consistency.

Amphibians. These include frogs, toads, salamanders, and newts, which are a variety of salamander. Each starts life as an egg, then hatches as a tadpole, which has gills and behaves like a fish. Then each loses its gills, acquires legs and lungs, and spends the remainder of its life both on land and in water. Frequently this metamorphosis takes a matter of weeks or months, but with a bullfrog at least two years are required.

It is possible at times to purchase tadpoles at pet shops and raise them to adulthood. But collecting the eggs yourself and observing the complete cycle is far more exciting. The time to start is in the early spring; the place is the edge of a pond or a marshy area. With any kind of luck you will find floating on the water jellylike clumps of eggs that look a little like tapioca pudding. These may be the eggs of frogs, salamanders, or newts. Or you may find eggs encased in elongated "worms" of jelly, which in turn are entwined in aquatic plants. These are toads' eggs.

To remove the eggs, you will need a plastic bucket or dishpan. Fill it with pond or marsh water and gently place the eggs inside. At home, keep the eggs in an aquarium or a fish bowl. Line the bottom with about an inch of sand, then fill halfway with the water in your bucket and carefully add the eggs. Position the aquarium so that it receives a moderate amount of warm sun for about two hours a day. If you have acquired toads' eggs, they may hatch in less than a week. In other cases several weeks may be required. If the eggs turn white, they either were not fertilized or they have died and should be removed immediately.

When the tadpoles emerge, feed them the slimy green algae that coats rocks in ponds and streams. If algae isn't available, they will be equally delighted with a lettuce leaf which has been boiled for at least an hour, then minced. After they achieve an inch or so of growth, also feed them bits of earthworm and raw beef. When they are about three inches long, transfer two or three to a fresh water community tank and return the others to their original habitat.

When their legs begin to appear, move those tadpoles you have kept to a separate aquarium. It should contain a number of stones which enable them to emerge from the water. When the tadpoles become adults, you may wish to free them or keep them in a terrarium for a period. In the latter case, sink a bowl of water at one end and screen the top.* Feed them live insects, bits of raw fish and beef, and dog-food pellets. However, roll the inanimate food toward them; otherwise they will ignore it.

ORGANIZATIONS

There are hundreds of aquarium societies throughout the United States and Canada which are a source of lectures, demonstrations, advice, and at times discounts on fishes and equipment. Some also sponsor competitions and shows and publish newsletters. To find such a group, check with a pet shop dealer, a museum of natural history, or the local newspaper. The Aquarium Club of America sells its members fishes and equipment at discount by mail. Its address is P.O. Box 157, Belpre, Ohio 45714.

BIBLIOGRAPHY

Books

Aquarium Book for Boys and Girls, Alfred Morgan, Charles Scribner's Sons, New York, 1959.

Beginner's Guide to Fresh-Water Life, Leon A. Housman, G. P. Putnam's Sons, New York, 1950.

Encyclopedia of Tropical Fishes, Herbert R. Axelrod, William Vorderwinkler, T. F. H. Publications, Jersey City, 1962. A guide to breeding fishes.

Exotic Aquarium Fishes, 19th Edition, William T. Innes, Pet Books, Inc., Maywood, N.J., 1966. A classic introduction.

Field Book of Fresh Water Fishes, Ray Shrenkeisen, G. P. Putnam's Sons, New York, 1963.

Field Book of Ponds and Streams, Ann H. Morgan, G. P. Putnam's Sons, New York, 1930.

* Terraria are discussed in Chapter 19, Plants.

Pets from the Pond, Margaret Waring Buck, Abingdon Press, New York, 1958.

Salt-Water Aquarium Fish, Herbert R. Axelrod, William Vorderwinkler, T. F. H. Publications, Jersey City, 1963.

The Sea Beach at Ebb Tide, Augusta F. Arnold, Dover Publications, New York, 1949.

The Book of Wild Pets, Clifford B. Moore, Charles T. Branford Co., Boston, 1954. A classic account of native fresh water fishes and amphibians.

Periodicals

The Aquarium, 87 Route 17, Maywood, N.J. 07607. Monthly.

Tropical Fish Hobbyist, 245 Cornelison Ave., Jersey City, N.J. 07302. Monthly.

17·FOSSILS

THE RANGE OF FOSSILS is enormous. There are impressions of leaves, footprints of dinosaurs, and the remains of countless forms of life so ancient their age is incomprehensible, so strange they often seem to bear no relationship to the world as we know it. Together they provide the evidence the paleontologist needs to reconstruct the history of the remote past.

The first fossils a beginner is likely to find are common varieties such as the trilobite, an ancestor of the crab and the lobster; the crinoid, a relative of the starfish that looks like a flowering plant; the brachiopod, an oysterlike animal that lived in a hinged shell; the pelecypod or clam; the endoceras, an elongated shell that once served as home to an octopuslike creature; and the cup coral, which looks a little like a cornucopia.

My thirteen-year-old son acquired a cup coral a number of years ago, but neither of us knew what it was until I began the research for this chapter and asked an expert to identify it. I learned that it had lived in the Devonian Period perhaps 400 million years ago. "It's a nice specimen," I was told, "but nothing to get excited about." Yet holding the remains of a creature that lived long before man evolved is an awesome experience.

Although an amateur's finds may be of interest to him and no one else, at times they have great significance. Not too many years ago a California plumber discovered a major fossil bed, dating from the Pleistocene Epoch, in the desert west of San Diego. Meanwhile, another amateur, working in North Bergen, N.J., almost within sight of Manhattan, found the remains of a gliding reptile of considerable scientific importance. A paleontologist I interviewed is convinced that any amateur who over the years pursues his hobby diligently and responsibly will make an original contribution to knowledge. Even if this is not the case, he may serve as a source of important leads for scientists whose numbers are too limited to do all the research that is needed. A few amateurs also work closely with paleontologists, assisting as volunteers in laboratories and even on expeditions. At times, in fact, an amateur becomes so intrigued with this science he becomes a paleontologist himself.

The general collector who maintains an interest in paleontology inevitably specializes. He may develop a comprehensive regional collection or focus on a broad category such as marine invertebrates or a narrow category such as one species and its varieties.

However, not all fossil hunters are interested in paleontology or in advancing knowledge. Their objective is to obtain souvenirs. There are certain classes of fossils so common they are of no interest to the scientist and little is lost if an amateur takes one or two specimens for his personal collection. But there also are many types of great importance that are being collected indiscriminately. In Utah, Montana, and elsewhere, greedy, ignorant collectors have vandalized important fossil beds, stripping them of the evidence they contain, even disrupting work in progress. When they make unusual finds, moreover, they are too lazy or too ignorant to report them to a museum or a university and too selfish to contribute them. Instead, these specimens become steppingstones in gardens or paperweights or are consigned to a shoe box in the basement and forgotten.

THE ORIGIN OF FOSSILS

"Fossil" means "dug up." Defined more broadly a fossil is any trace of an animal or plant that lived in the geologic past. A great many fossils are three-dimensional objects such as bones and shells. But a great many others, as noted earlier, are impressions of leaves or are footprints or even worm tracks. The most ancient fossils as yet discovered by man are microorganisms over 3 billion years old which were found in the fossilized remains of a fig tree in South Africa. The fossils amateurs are likely to encounter, and recognize, may range in age up to 600 million years. However, any remains over 12,000 years old are regarded officially as fossils.

Fossils typically are found in sedimentary rocks: those that were mud

$$\boxed{\text{G E O L O G I C \quad T I M E \quad S C A L E}}$$

Era	Period	Epoch	Beginning of Interval (Millions of Yrs.)	Important Events
Cenozoic (3%)	Quaternary	Recent	.01	Man becomes abundant
		Pleistocene	1.5-3 (?)	Many mammals vanish First man
	Tertiary	Pliocene	7	Mammals reach their maximum diversity
		Miocene	26	Grasslands – grazing mammals
		Oligocene	37-38	
		Eocene	53-54	Spread and diversification of mammals
		Paleocene	65	
Mesozoic (8%)	Cretaceous		136	Dinosaurs continue abundant, then vanish Flowering plants become dominant.
	Jurassic		190-195	First birds. Dinosaurs increasingly abundant and diverse First mammals
	Triassic		225	First dinosaurs Abundant cycads and conifers
Paleozoic (19%)	Permian		280	Extinction of many animals
	Carboniferous	Pennsylvanian	345	First reptiles. Great coal forests, conifers
		Mississippian		
	Devonian		395	First amphibians First insects
	Silurian		430-440	Fishes abundant First land life (plants and invertebrates)
	Ordovician		ca. 500	First fishes
	Cambrian		570	First abundant record of marine life, trilobites common
Pre-Cambrian (70% of the history of life)				First life – perhaps 3,000,000,000 years ago

and now are shale or those that were sand and now are sandstone or limestone.* Fossils of animals and plants frequently were formed in the mud of tropical lowlands. Montana was such a place 70 million years ago. When a creature died, it fell into the mud and was covered. Marine fossils formed when bodies became buried in the sand at the bottom of an ocean or an inland sea. In both situations the soft parts rotted away and the hard parts were filled with and often replaced by mineral matter. This also was the case with wood that was fossilized or petrified. At times a body completely rotted, leaving a natural mold in the sediment. In still other cases, all that remains is the impression of a leaf or a footprint or a worm track in what once was mud.

Sedimentary rocks typically exist in layers, each of which may represent a particular geologic period. Some layers are many feet thick and extend for hundreds of miles. Some of the sediments involved have resulted from the action of lakes or other bodies of fresh water. Much of the sedimentary rock, however, is the result of the periodic inundation of the mainland by vast seas. As a result, a great proportion of the fossils one finds are of marine origin, even those in locations far from existing oceans. Thus, in the Rocky Mountains one still may find the fossils of horseshoe crabs and corals. The particular layer of sediment in which a fossil is found indicates the geologic period in which it lived or first appeared.

Not all sediments were laid down in all places, of course. Because of geologic upheavals, moreover, sediments are not always found in an orderly chronological arrangement. However, each is a chapter in geologic history representing millions of years of life. The layers of sediments in a particular area make up what is known as a geologic column. The most dramatic column that is readily visible can be seen in the walls of the Grand Canyon in Arizona.

TYPES OF FOSSILS

Vertebrate Fossils. These are the remains of animals with an internal skeleton and a backbone. They include mammals, amphibians, and reptiles such as the dinosaur. Such fossils are relatively scarce and highly important. To the dismay of the paleontologist, it is these that fascinate amateurs most. A responsible amateur will not hunt for such specimens, nor will he remove them if he encounters any. In such cases

* See Chapter 20, Rocks, Minerals, and Gem Stones.

the best procedure is to inform a museum or a university of the find.

Invertebrate Fossils. These are the most widespread fossils and are available in the largest numbers. They are the remains of various forms of marine life and of worms, insects, and other animals with soft bodies. The fossils listed at the beginning of this chapter all were invertebrates. Others commonly found include jellyfish, sponges, lamp shells, starfish, and horseshoe crabs.

Plant Fossils. The most common variety is the fern. However, fossils of other plants and fossilized seeds, spores, and wood also are available.

Coral.

205

Pelecypod.

Bryozoa.

Crinoid.

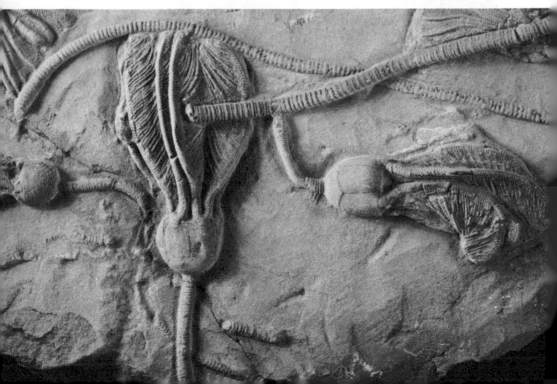

Trilobites.

Brachiopods.

GETTING STARTED

Books. The best introduction to fossil hunting is *The Fossil Book* by Carroll and Mildred Fenton. If you become deeply involved, you also may want to read a basic book on geology. *Essentials of Earth History* by William Lee Stokes, a college level introduction, should satisfy most of your needs. For these and other works, see the Bibliography. You also will want a guide to fossil locations in your area. The possibilities are discussed in the section Hunting Fossils.

Fossil Clubs and Other Sources of Guidance. Where fossil clubs exist, they sponsor field trips and provide instruction. Frequently these groups are organized as sections of larger mineralogical societies. For information on the nearest club, inquire at the paleontology or geology department of a natural history museum. If there isn't a club available, try to find an advanced amateur to talk with or consult a professional paleontologist associated with a museum, a university, or a public geological survey. In dealing with professionals, work hard to impress them with your sense of responsibility, or you may receive a cool reception.

One of the most useful experiences for a serious amateur is participating in a museum-sponsored field trip or expedition. Such opportunities do not occur often, but occasionally one of the smaller natural history museums is willing to include an amateur if he pays his own way and is willing to engage in hard labor and follow directions. The Science Museum at St. Paul, for example, has relied on the help of college and high school students on various occasions.

EQUIPMENT

In some locations fossils and fragments of fossils lie on the ground and all one needs are his hands and the ability to recognize a fossil when he sees one. When a fossil is embedded in sediment, some simple equipment also is needed.

Cutting and Digging Tools. In digging specimens out of hard sediment, use a geologist's pick with a chisel end or a carpenter's all-metal wood chisel together with a simple claw hammer. Cold chisels are too blunt for this purpose unless they are sharpened. In soft sediments, use a shoemaker's awl or a screwdriver that has been sharpened to a point. In removing plant specimens from between thin layers of shale, use an oyster knife or a paring knife, insinuating it between the layers as you might between the pages of a book. If you are working in loose sediment, often a trowel and a three-quarter-inch short-bristled paintbrush will be the most satisfactory tools. The paintbrush and a whisk broom also will be useful in cleaning soil or sand from a particular specimen prior to its removal.

Hand Lens. This will help you find small fossils in fossil-bearing sediment. As discussed later, it also will help you determine if an object is in fact a fossil.

Materials for Packing Fossils. Use rolls of toilet paper (with enough removed so that they can be flattened for inclusion in a knapsack), sheets of newspaper, paper bags of various sizes, masking tape, and rubber bands.

Miscellaneous Equipment. A notebook, a steel measuring tape, sharpened pencils, a camera, a knapsack.

HUNTING FOSSILS

Locations. Some regions are richer in fossils, or more fossiliferous, than others, but all the states and the Canadian provinces are likely to have some fossils. In fact, you probably are no more than a day's drive from a satisfactory location. The best-endowed states are the following:

Arizona, California, Illinois (particularly for plant fossils), Indiana, Kansas, Kentucky, Missouri, Montana, Nebraska, New Mexico, New York, Ohio, Oklahoma, Oregon, South Dakota, Texas, West Virginia (for plant fossils), and Wyoming.

Those with relatively poor hunting include Delaware, Hawaii, Louisiana, Michigan, Wyoming, and all of the New England states.

Frequently the number and kinds of fossils available will vary widely from one part of a state to another. New Jersey, the state where I live, is a good example. Deposits in the southern part of the state were laid down on a seabed 40 million years ago, in the Tertiary Period, and have been bared at various points by erosion. In this section, one finds the fossilized remains of snails, crabs, and clams, as well as the teeth of sea lizards and sharks. To the north, in a Triassic deposit over 200 million years old, there are dinosaur tracks. Still farther north, in a Silurian deposit over 400 million years old, there are fossil fish and trilobites.

At the outset rely on established locations where large numbers of fossils have been found. A fossil club or an experienced amateur would be an excellent source of such information. A governmental survey would be another source, as noted earlier. In addition, some government units and geological societies publish guides to fossil beds in their areas. For a national survey of leading locations, consult *Hunting for Fossils* by Marian Murray. If you are on good terms with a paleontologist, you also might ask him for advice. But some won't tell you where to look. "It's a little like the Mafia asking a jeweler for the combination to his safe," one explained.

In deciding where to find a particular fossil, experienced collectors may seek out new areas, relying on their knowledge of geology and paleontology and on topographic and geologic maps. Road cuts, quarries, and new excavations all are possible locations if they are in the right kind of rock. Whether public or private land is involved, it is necessary, of course, to obtain permission to hunt for fossils. The one exception is Federal public domain land which exists largely in the West.

Techniques. Before setting out, do some research. Learn what the location is like, how old the sediments are, and what kinds of fossils you are likely to find. Then study photographs or drawings so that you will recognize them. Of course, an intriguing aspect of paleontology is that one never really knows what he is going to find.

At the fossil location itself, the process involves looking for fully or partially exposed material. You may find complete fossils, or fragments, or nothing. If a cliff is involved, first check the accumulation of talus at the base. If you find fossils, examine the section of the cliff from where they presumably came. If the cliff happens to be an ancient coral reef, closely examine its face for embedded fossils, using a hand lens to search for the smallest ones. If there is a stream running through a bed, the eroding action of the water may have carried away softer sediments and exposed various fossils. If this is a possibility, put on tennis shoes and search the stream bed and also the banks of the stream and the area at the base of the banks. If it is a hot day, you will get nice and wet even if you don't find a thing.

In all cases beware of false fossils. One is a dendrite that looks like a fossilized fern, but actually is a design produced in or on a mineral by another mineral. Another is a stone shaped like a fossil. Examine such objects closely for the structural regularities which are characteristic of a living organism.

If you find a fossil embedded in sediment, use the tools discussed earlier to dislodge it. However, remove as little as possible of the sediment, or matrix. If a fossil is particularly fragile, it may be necessary to strengthen it with one or more coats of dope or shellac before removal. Vertebrate paleontologists use this method in removing the skeletal remains of larger fossils. If the object is too fragile or too large to move on your own, make a photograph of it, note the precise location on a map, cover it with soil, if possible, and seek expert advice. If you encounter footprints or other imprints, it may be more practical to make casts of the specimen than to remove it. For this purpose use a latex molding material available at art supply stores. Should you encounter a natural mold of the type described earlier, also use this material.

Assign to each fossil you remove a catalog number, then record in your notebook the type and age of the sediment (take a sample of the matrix if you are not sure); the position of the fossil in the sediment, including a photograph; its genus and species, if known; and the location of the site, including a sketch map with landmarks so that you can find it again.

Wrap each fossil in a generous quantity of toilet tissue, then wrap masking tape around the tissue so that it doesn't unravel, and place the fossil in a paper bag. Wrap large objects in newspaper, then secure the paper with tape or rubber bands and place in a bag. Label each bag with the catalog number that matches the one in your notebook.

If you can't identify a fossil, check the illustrations in the standard guides for your region. If this is not helpful, show your specimen to a paleontologist at a natural history museum. If you have found something unusual, offer it to the museum.

PREPARATION OF SPECIMENS

It is desirable to remove as much of the matrix as possible so that you can see as much of the fossil as possible. However, removing a matrix is a skill that comes with experience and is best learned under guidance. In doing such work, the experienced person uses small chisels, drilling tools, and dissecting needles. Where necessary he also devises new approaches and equipment. Repairing fossils and patching fragments together also requires instruction.

Washing the soil from specimens is desirable if it is feasible. If a fossil seems reasonably sturdy, use a soft toothbrush or a paintbrush and water. However, some fossils tend to break up and fall apart in water.

An imprint in shale is an example. If in doubt, experiment first with a sample of the sediment.

STORAGE AND DISPLAY

Initially store your acquisitions in cigar boxes or shoe boxes divided by strips of cardboard. Label each specimen with its catalog number. As your collection grows, you will want more durable, better-looking containers. The possibilities include clear plastic specimen boxes, specimen trays, compartmented collection boxes, individual plastic trays, and Riker mounts, all of which are available at low cost from biological supply houses and larger hobby shops. If you have difficulty finding a source, ask a geology or biology teacher at the local high school.

BIBLIOGRAPHY

Books

Essentials of Earth History, William Lee Stokes, Prentice-Hall, Inc., New York, 1965.

The Fossil Book, Carroll and Mildred Fenton, Doubleday & Co., New York, 1958.

Fossils, a Guide to Prehistoric Life, H. T. Rhodes, Herbert S. Zim, Paul R. Shaffer, Golden Press, Inc., New York, 1962.

Hunting for Fossils, Marian Murray, The Macmillan Co., New York, 1967.

Periodical

Earth Science, P.O. Box 550, Downers Grove, Illinois 60615. Monthly.

18·INSECTS

Most PEOPLE have little to do with insects. When an insect appears, the tendency is to retreat or to leap for the insecticide. Some insects clearly deserve this reaction. But actually only 1 per cent are harmful to humans or cause damage. If one can overcome his inhibitions, the world of insects is a fascinating place to explore. The life cycles of the insects, their appearance at each stage, the nests the various species construct, the sounds they make, how they move about, the social lives some have developed, and the migratory habits of a number are intriguing subjects for observation and study. What also is intriguing is the fact that insects are so ancient (some species are over 200 million years old), so numerous (throughout the world there are over 600,000 kinds), and so much a part of our lives, yet so poorly known.

There are several ways to learn about insects. The simplest is to seek them out in their habitats and observe them. Another is to capture a few, house them in cages, and rear them. A third is to build a collection of insect specimens. It is, of course, useful to learn something about insects at the outset. Although they are remarkably diverse, they share many characteristics. Their bodies typically consist of three parts: a head equipped with a pair of antennae, a thorax with three pairs of legs and often a pair of wings, and an abdomen. All insects go through a metamorphosis. If it is "complete," they proceed from egg to larva to pupa and finally to adult, a stage many achieve only to reproduce and die. If it is "incomplete" the progression is from egg to nymph to adult.

The vast majority of insects belong to one of four groups: the beetles or Coleoptera, which is the largest order with 250,000 species; the butterflies and moths or Lepidoptera; the ants, bees, and wasps, or Hymenoptera; and the flies, gnats, and mosquitoes, or Diptera. In exploring for insects, it is of particular importance to know just what the common varieties look like before setting out. All of the field guides in the Bibliography provide this information.

WHERE AND WHEN TO FIND INSECTS

Insects are found in and on flowers, in tall grass and weeds, on the leaves and bark of trees and shrubs, under rocks, logs, planks, and debris, in soil, and in puddles, streams, ponds, and lakes. Dark, dampish areas of a basement also afford good hunting. The spring and summer are the best time to find larvae and adults. The time to find eggs generally extends from the fall through the spring. Winter is the best period for hunting the cocoons of moths and the chrysalids of butterflies.

OBSERVING INSECTS

Searching a back yard or a small corner of a weed lot or park is a fine way to learn the common varieties of insects and something of their behavior. Literally hundreds of species inhabit such areas. The entomologist Frank Lutz once found 1402 kinds of insects in his back yard in a New Jersey suburb. Even the inexperienced amateur will easily find scores. In the process he can start a "life list" of the insects he has seen and identified.

All one needs for this activity is a hand lens, a notebook to record "finds" and comments, a sense of where to look, and patience. The amateur with an interest in sketching or photography also will want to bring his equipment, for the opportunities are fascinating. Once a back yard or weed lot has been explored, he can move on to a field of wild flowers, a quiet pond, a swift stream, a wooded glen, or a desert or mountain area. There are, of course, so many insects, no one person can hope to see them all. As a result, the amateur and the professional ultimately specialize in insects of a particular type.

Observation in the field, however, does have its limitations. Flying insects are not always willing to remain at rest while an observer stares at them through a hand lens. Moreover, the steps in a metamorphosis cannot easily be observed nor at times can feeding habits, mating, or other behavior. As a result, some amateurs rear insects in cages, which enables them to make observations, sketches, and photographs at their leisure. When they have learned all they wish to know, they either release their guests or preserve them as specimens, using the techniques described below. Housing and feeding insects is not complicated. Here are some of the possibilities.

Ants. To observe the social life of the ant, one needs an ant "house" and a colony of ants. Frequently both can be purchased through a hobby shop or a biological supply firm. However, it is not too difficult to build a nest and acquire some ants on your own.

There are many types of nests. One of the simplest is a vertical nest which includes a quantity of soil so that the tunnels the ants dig can be seen. It consists of a one-inch wooden frame 10″ × 14″ with window glass the same size taped securely to each side. The crosspiece at the top of the frame is removable. In addition, it contains two half-inch holes which provide access to the nest. One hole is used to supply the ants with food. The other is used to provide moisture through a sponge positioned at the point at which the hole opens into the cage. The sponge is held in place with tacks. Both holes are covered with thin pieces of wood which pivot on nails. A simple stand consists of three two-inch pieces of wood with deep cutouts to accompany the nest. To find ants, look for anthills in lawns, meadows, wooded areas, and on hillsides. Also look under stones. When you locate one, dig deeply into the hill with a trowel and transfer the ants and the soil to a shoe box. Collect at least 50 ants. If possible, include a few of the largest, since

A vertical ant nest.

one may be a queen or egg layer. Also include a number of pupae and larvae. Then remove the top of the nest frame and gently pour the colony inside. Feed the ants daily. They thrive on drops of sugar water or honey water and occasional bits of apple, cake, or chopped insect. Also be certain to keep the sponge damp.

When the ants are not being observed, the glass sides should be covered with cardboard to keep the interior dark. If red glass is used instead of the clear variety, the cardboard is not necessary.

Aquatic Insects. Insects of all descriptions are found in quiet ponds and lakes and may be caught rather easily with a kitchen sieve or a dip net. The possibilities include back swimmers, water striders, whirligig beetles and larvae of land-based insects such as dragonflies and damsel flies. Install specimens in an aquarium or in large jars. Add some pond water and sand, an algae-covered stone or two, and possibly a few plants of the type commonly used for fresh water aquaria, as suggested in Chapter 16. In every case, screens are essential. If there are larvae in your collection, at least one or two plants or stones should protrude from the water so that newly emergent adults can find a perch. Soon after they appear, they should be freed or moved to a dry cage. The algae and other plants will serve as food for many insects. For those that prefer meat, provide occasional servings of flies, mosquitoes, or daphnia, which may be purchased in pet shops.

Cockroaches. The best source of these ancient creatures is an exterminator, unless you are unfortunate enough to have a private supply. If you live in the Northeast, the likelihood is that you will acquire the German or Croton variety, which is so named because it was found when the Croton reservoir which serves New York was dug. On the West Coast the Oriental roach prevails. Elsewhere it is the American roach. Store specimens in a glass jar with a perforated lid. The bottom of the jar should be covered with damp sand or sawdust. Install a bottle cap in the sand as a source of water, a small branch on which to climb, and a piece of cardboard tilted against the wall of the jar as a place to hide. Roaches eat bits of lettuce, apple, and moist bread and dog biscuit. Except when they are being observed, they should be kept in the dark. Should they breed, remove the egg capsules to a separate jar for hatching.

Field Crickets. In ancient China, well-bred ladies found it pleasant to go cricket hunting, carrying tiny gold cages in which to keep the crickets they found. One of the appealing things about crickets is, of course, the "music" they make as they scrape one wing against another. Entomologists at the American Museum of Natural History say that cricket chirps are expertly rendered musical slurs that resemble the work of a violinist. However, what also appealed to the Chinese was the cricket's ability as a fighter, particularly when other crickets were involved. Over the centuries cricket fighting became a national sport in China, marked by elaborate competitions, betting, and even cricket trainers.

Crickets are frequently found under logs, stones, and planks, and on damp ground. A chimney globe makes an excellent cage. Simply insert it in a flowerpot filled with soil or sand and cover the opening with cheesecloth or screening. A large jar or a small terrarium also will serve. So will a length of wire screening rolled into a cylinder and secured at the top and bottom with caps from half-gallon ice cream containers. In each case install a bottle cap in the soil as a water source and a small piece of damp cardboard as a hiding place. Crickets eat small pieces of lettuce, fresh fruit and moist dog biscuit and bread. They also like honey. Baby crickets eat grass seed.

Grasshoppers. Any of the cricket cages described above would be appropriate for a grasshopper. However, use damp sod instead of soil as a base. Since grasshoppers tend to leap about quite a bit, as much as 30 inches at a leap, be sure to screen the top. Feed grasshoppers bits of lettuce, clover, and fresh fruit.

Moths and Butterflies. The moth and the butterfly offer the best and the most dramatic opportunity to observe at least one or two of the steps in a metamorphosis. You might find the eggs of one of these insects on a leaf and attempt to follow the cycle from that point. More often, however, you will find a caterpillar, a cocoon, or a chrysalid and start there.

Eggs and Caterpillars: Caterpillars have specialized tastes in plant food, and it is to the plants they favor that one looks for caterpillars and the eggs from which they emerge. A few of the possibilities are described below. For others, consult one of the detailed guides in the Bibliography.

Moths—ailanthus tree, cynthia moth; deciduous trees, cecropia, polyphemus; fruit trees, polyphemus; grasses, tiger; hickory and walnut, luna; royal walnut, sassafras and spicebush, promethea; willow tree, polyphemus.

Butterflies—elm tree, angel wing, mourning cloak; milkweed, mon-

217

arch; poplar, mourning cloak; sassafras and spicebush, spicebush swallowtail; violets, fritillaries; wild cherry, tiger swallowtail; wild carrot and wild parsley, black swallowtail; willow tree, mourning cloak, redspotted purple.

Should you find eggs, store the leaf on which they rest in an airtight jar in a cool environment. Make a note of the plant so that you can return to it for fresh leaves if caterpillars emerge. If they do, it may take but a few days or several months. If the eggs hatch, place the caterpillars in a tank or a large jar with loose soil on the bottom, and screen the top. Each day add twigs with fresh leaves from the appropriate plant. If the plant is small enough to grow in a flowerpot, transplant it. Then enclose it with a chimney lamp, add the caterpillars, and cover with a screen or cheesecloth. After changing its skin, or molting, several times over a period of weeks, a caterpillar spins its cocoon or chrysalid.

Since a caterpillar lives out of doors, it is desirable, although not essential, to leave its cage on a porch or in a back yard. If you find one feeding, it can be caged where you find it. Enclose that portion of the plant with a generous sleeve of cheesecloth or flexible window screen tied shut at both ends. If the caterpillar eats everything available inside its cage, permit it to move to another section of the plant, then recage it.

Cocoons and Chrysalids: To find cocoons and chrysalids, look on trees or other plants which are food sources. They may be secured to branches, bark, or leaves. At times they are found under these plants or on fence posts or windowsills, or in outbuildings, or even in the soil. Although cocoons and chrysalids are created throughout the year, the best time to look for them is in the late fall and the winter, when foliage is at a minimum.

Finding a cocoon does not assure that it contains a living pupa. The weight of the cocoon will be one indication, since a living pupa is heavier than a dead one. Gently shaking a cocoon also may provide an answer, since a living pupa may respond by moving a bit after you stop moving its container. If there are small holes in the cocoon, the pupa may have been attacked by another insect that then laid its eggs inside. If it seems that a cocoon contains a living pupa, handle it gently. If it must be transported any distance, pack it in a box. If it is attached to a branch, remove several inches of the branch with it.

A cocoon found out of doors should be placed in an empty tank or a large jar with an inch of loose soil on the bottom and a piece of screening across the top. A cocoon created by a caterpillar you have reared should be left in its cage. Both containers should have a twig on which the adult can perch when it emerges.

If a pupa is kept in a warm room, it may take about ten weeks to mature, varying with the species. If it is kept out of doors, the process takes longer. It is practical to store a cocoon between a window and a storm window or to place its cage on a porch. With an indoor cage, sprinkle the pupa and the soil with water once a week. With an outdoor cage, this is not necessary. Unless you know which species you are rearing, it is difficult to know just when a moth or a butterfly will emerge. Two or three days beforehand you may hear or see some movement. In any case it is well to check the cocoon every day, for the emergence of an adult is a remarkable sight.

If the adult you have reared is a female, it may be possible to observe two other steps in the cycle. One is mating; the other is the laying of eggs. Place her out of doors in her cage. If there are any males in the vicinity, it is likely her scent will attract them. If you can catch one of the right species, put it in the cage with her and arrange several leaves from the appropriate food plant on the bottom on which the eggs can be laid. Afterwards release the adults. Should you wish to keep the eggs, follow the procedure described earlier.

Praying Mantis. A screened terrarium lined with sod is a good home for this insect. Feed the mantis live insects or bits of hamburger meat impaled on a toothpick that you move in front of it. If you encounter a mantis case, which looks something like a cocoon on a twig, place it in a separate cage. In due course you will be endowed with hundreds of mantids. Those you wish to keep should be fed aphids until they grow somewhat larger. However, be sure to provide generous servings; for if they are hungry, they will eat one another.

Other Insects. A great many insects can be kept for a period in a screened jar or tank with an inch or so of damp, loose soil. In taking them from their natural environment, however, you assume an obligation to determine what kind of insect you have found and what its needs are. First check a field guide. If this isn't helpful, contact a nature center or an entomology department at a museum or university.

COLLECTING INSECT SPECIMENS

There are many persons who derive great pleasure from capturing, preserving, and mounting insects. Some seek as broad a representation as possible. Indeed, one of the great attractions is finding new species, since there are large numbers of unidentified insects. Other collectors restrict their collections to a particular species such as butterflies, moths, or aquatic insects.

Field Equipment. A collector will need a pair of forceps; a nylon mesh insect net, which he can buy or readily make; a number of killing jars, which may be purchased or easily prepared at home; envelopes for temporary storage of large insects; medicine vials and small boxes for small insects; and a knapsack. Collecting kits are available.

Collecting Techniques. Some insects may be picked by hand or with forceps from the ground, trees, or flowers. The exceedingly small insects found in leaf mold and flower blossoms are captured with a specialized device called an aspirator which sucks them into a screened tube. "Sweeping" fields of grasses and wild flowers with a net is still another technique. The collector proceeds through a field in a zigzag fashion, swinging the net first to the left and from that point to the right.

"Beating" and "sieving" are two other possibilities. In beating, the collector beats the branches of trees and shrubs with a heavy stick in the hope of releasing a shower of insects. He places a white cloth about a yard square or a formal beating sheet under the foliage so that he can readily see the insects when they fall, then captures them with a forceps or an aspirator. Sieves are used to search samples of soil and leaf mold for the insects they contain. There are commercially made insect sieves, but the kitchen variety will serve. As noted earlier, a kitchen sieve also may be used to capture aquatic specimens, although a specially designed aquatic net is more efficient. If a collector has a standard sweeping net, it may be possible to install an aquatic bag on the frame.

The most exciting technique is "air netting," which is used in taking butterflies and other flying insects. The experienced collector waits quietly at plants to which the insects he is seeking typically are attracted. When one settles down to eat, he makes his move. The recommended technique is to bring the net in sideways. If the insect is caught, flip the net over so that the opening is closed. Some collectors also do their netting through the open window of a slowly moving car, stopping every few minutes to remove and store their specimens.

Attracting Insects: Collectors sometimes use lights, "sugaring," and ground traps to obtain insects. Porch lights, car lights, or a lantern set on a stump or a rock often will attract a great many moths and other night fliers. One collector I know makes use of a gasoline lantern and a washtub filled with water. He places a few bricks in the water, then positions the lantern on top of the bricks. The insects that are attracted eventually fall in the water and drown.

"Sugaring" also attracts night fliers. It requires warm weather and a sticky sweet fermenting fruit pulp. When the pulp is dabbed on a tree the moths may appear in significant numbers. There are many recipes for preparing a sugaring pulp. One requires that stale beer, brown sugar, and molasses be mixed and aged in a warm place for several days. Another calls for overripe bananas or apricots which are mixed in white sugar and left to ferment. Apply the sugared pulp during the day, then return that night and again the next day to check the results.

A ground trap is used to attract crawling insects. It consists of a can or a jar which is baited with a sugar-water or honey-water mixture and sunk in the soil so that its rim is at ground level. The insects attracted by the bait fall in and drown. It is necessary to wash the sugar off, or the insects will attract still other insects.

Killing Specimens. After an insect is captured, it is placed in a "killing jar," where it is exposed to fumes that kill it, ordinarily within an hour. Professional entomologists use cyanide killing jars, which operate with great efficiency, but a beginner will find that nonpoisonous killing jars he prepares himself are highly satisfactory. He will need at least two narrow-mouthed screw-top jars for small insects and two wide-mouthed jars for large insects. A large piece of absorbent cotton is placed at the bottom of a jar and moistened with carbon tetrachloride. It is then covered with blotting paper cut to fit the interior of the jar, a piece of untreated cotton, and another piece of blotting paper.

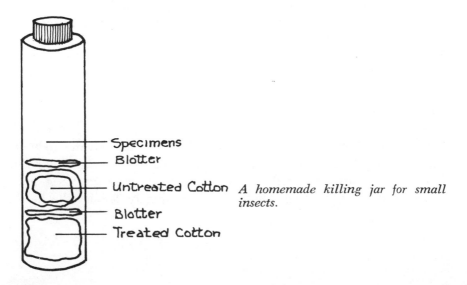

Specimens
Blotter
Untreated Cotton
Blotter
Treated Cotton

A homemade killing jar for small insects.

The jar should be wrapped with strips of plastic, paper, or adhesive tape to minimize shattering if it is dropped.

Insects obtained by hand or with forceps are dropped gently into the jar, which is then tightly closed. Insects attracted by sugaring often fall in of their own accord if the jar is held directly under them. If a number of relatively small insects have been netted, the portion of the net they occupy is placed in a jar and the cap is closed. When these insects are sufficiently groggy, they can be removed from the net and put back in the jar by hand or with forceps. If a butterfly is netted, the collector reaches inside the net and grasps the insect by its thorax. With the other hand he places a killing jar in the net directly under the butterfly, drops the insect in, and tightens the lid.

Temporary Storage. Insects usually are removed from killing jars with forceps. Larger species should be placed in cellophane envelopes until they are prepared for mounting. Smaller varieties should be stored in vials or cardboard boxes.

Relaxing. Ideally, insects should be mounted soon after they are taken; otherwise the wing muscles, particularly with larger insects, stiffen to a point at which the wings cannot be properly spread. If this occurs, it is necessary to place the insects affected in a relaxing jar. Place a damp sponge or a large wad of moist cotton or blotting paper at the bottom of a jar and cover it with a paper towel or fine window screening. Keep the insect in the jar for twenty-four hours while the moist air does its work. Then place the insect on a spreading board and extend its wings, using strips of paper to hold them in position. The specimen should be dry and ready for mounting within a week.

Mounting and Storage. Soon after an insect is killed, its soft parts decay. All that remains is its hard external skeleton. It is these skeletons and their wings which compose insect collections. In mounting insects, you will need special non-rusting mounting pins of various sizes, paper points for the smallest insects, labels either fashioned at home or purchased, and storage boxes. These include a variety of wooden and cardboard models with glass or solid covers. However, cigar boxes will serve as adequate containers. Paint the interior black or white and glue a pinning surface of fiberboard or corrugated paper to the bottom.

In mounting an insect, insert the pin vertically through the body of the specimen; then position the body about a half-inch below the head of the pin. Beetles traditionally are pinned through the right wing, butterflies and moths through the thorax immediately behind the head, and other insects immediately behind and slightly to the right of the head. Large insects may be strengthened with the insertion of an additional pin through the length of their bodies. The smallest insects generally are glued to the tip of triangular paper points. A standard pin is then inserted through the point.

When the insect is in position, the pin is also inserted through one or more tiny labels arranged at different levels below the specimen. The top label includes the scientific name of the insect and data on where, when, and by whom the insect was found. The label just below describes the insect's habitat. Some collectors use a third label near the bottom of the pin for its scientific name. "Pinning blocks" assure that all specimens and labels in a case are at a uniform height. When a display is arranged, sprinkle moth flakes throughout the container so that other insects do not eat the specimens. Once specimens have been mounted, they should not be handled. If they must be moved, do so with a pinning forceps.

ASSISTING MUSEUMS

The entomology departments at some natural history museums welcome the assistance of an advanced amateur who wishes to collect in their behalf. At times smaller museums also are interested in volunteers who wish to help with pinning and labeling.

ORGANIZATIONS

Entomological clubs are usually associated with natural history museums or nature centers. In addition, some naturalists' clubs have entomological sections.

BIBLIOGRAPHY

General

Exploring the Insect World, Edwin Way Teale, Grosset & Dunlap, New York, 1944.

Familiar Insects of North America, Will Barker, Harper & Bros., New York, 1960.

Field Book of Insects, Frank E. Lutz, G. P. Putnam's Sons, New York, 1948.

Field Book of Ponds and Streams, Ann H. Morgan, G. P. Putnam's Sons, New York, 1930.

A Guide to Familiar American Insects, Herbert S. Zim, Clarence Cottam, Simon and Schuster, New York, 1951.

How to Know the Insects, H. E. Jaques, William C. Brown Co., Dubuque, 1951.

The Insect Guide, Ralph B. Swain, Doubleday & Co., Garden City, N.Y., 1948.

The Insect World of J. Henri Fabre, introduction by Edwin Way Teale, Dodd, Mead & Co., New York, 1949.

The Insects, Peter Farb, Time, Inc., New York, 1962.

Introduction to the Study of Insects, Donald J. Boror, Dwight M. De-Long, Holt, Rinehart & Winston, New York, 1954.

The Junior Book of Insects, Edwin Way Teale, E. P. Dutton & Co., New York, 1953. A book for young people.

Silent Spring, Rachel Carson, Houghton Mifflin Co., Boston, 1962.

Collecting Techniques

The Book of Wild Pets, Clifford B. Moore, Charles T. Branford Co., Boston, 1954. Part III.

Collecting Cocoons, Lois J. Hussey, Catherine Pessino, Thomas Y. Crowell Co., New York, 1953. A book for young people.

Collecting, Preparing, and Preserving Insects, Department of Agriculture, Ottawa, 1955.

Collecting, Preserving, and Studying Insects, Harold Oldroyd, The Macmillan Co., New York, 1959.

Collection and Preservation of Insects (M601), Superintendent of Documents, Washington, D.C. 20402.

Field Book of Nature Activities and Conservation, William Hillcourt, G. P. Putnam's Sons, New York, 1961. Chapter 6.

Particular Insects

Ants, Wilhelm Goetsch, University of Michigan Press, Ann Arbor, 1957.

Beetles, Ewald Reitter, G. P. Putnam's Sons, New York, 1961.

The Butterfly Book, W. J. Holland, Doubleday & Co., New York, 1930.

A Field Guide to the Butterflies, Alexander B. Klots, Houghton Mifflin Co., Boston, 1951.

How to Know the Beetles, H. E. Jaques, William C. Brown Co., Dubuque, 1947.

How to Know the Butterflies, Paul R. Erlich, Anne H. Erlich, William
C. Brown Co., Dubuque, 1961.

The Moth Book, W. J. Holland, Dover Publications, New York. Paperback reprint of a classic work published in 1930.

Natural History of Mosquitoes, Marston Bates, The Macmillan Co.,
New York, 1949.

Wings in the Meadow, Jo Brewer, Houghton Mifflin Co., Boston, 1967.

19·PLANTS

Plants are so commonplace we tend to take them for granted. However, we overlook a remarkably diverse world that is not only exciting to explore but crucial to our existence. It is from plants that we obtain most of the oxygen we breathe, much of the moisture we need, and, directly or indirectly, all the food we eat. The plants are, moreover, the most numerous of all living things. There are in all over 375,000 separate species, ranging in size and complexity from redwood trees as tall as a 30-story building to the one-celled blue-green algae that form a slimy scum on ponds, a plant that first appeared two billion years ago. To these add the other trees, the other algae (including one 200 feet long), the bacteria, and the seemingly limitless varieties of shrubs, grasses, ferns, wild flowers, horsetails, lichens, liverworts, mosses, mushrooms, and molds. It is this extraordinary diversity, reflecting the continuing struggle to adapt to the circumstances of life, that makes the study of plants so intriguing.

ACTIVITIES

Many persons spend their free time simply exploring for plants, learning to identify them, and enjoying them for their colors, shapes, and intricacy. Some carry with them a notebook and a sketch pad or camera to record what they find. Some also take specimens that they dry and mount for herbarium collections, transplant to gardens or terraria, or use to make prints or dried arrangements. Still others combine an interest in nature study with an interest in food, seeking out certain mushrooms and other wild plants to enhance their meals.

One finds plants virtually everywhere—in woods, fields, marshes, and bogs, along roads, at beaches, in the water, even on other plants.

Despite their great numbers, some are scarce and others are becoming so. It is important, therefore, to use discretion in collecting. For a sense of what should not be picked contact the relevant organization listed below.

EQUIPMENT AND SUPPLIES

For studying plants in the field you will need a 5x to 10x hand lens with a case or with a lanyard which will permit you to hang the glass from your neck; a primer on botany, a general field guide, and, as your interests develop, specialized guides (see Bibliography); a notebook to record what you find; insect repellent; and a knapsack. For collecting specimens you will need a trowel and a sharp knife. If you intend to dry and mount specimens, you will need a herbarium press or a reasonable substitute, several of which are discussed in the section Trees. You also will need a quantity of plastic bags for specimens you intend to transplant and small boxes and vials for seeds, pods, and twigs. For mounting specimens use herbarium mounting sheets; for storing them use a portfolio or a loose-leaf binder. To display particularly lovely or unusual specimens use botanical Riker mounts. If botanical supplies are difficult to obtain, ask the biology department at your local high school for advice.

ORGANIZATIONS

The amateur botanist may find sources of guidance and others with his interests in local naturalists' clubs, garden clubs, botanical societies, Audubon groups, or mushroom hunting or mycological clubs. In addition, the National Audubon Society maintains nature centers in a number of localities and operates residential summer workshops in Connecticut, Maine, Wisconsin, and Wyoming; some of the programs offered carry college credit. For information write Audubon Camp Department, 613 Riversville Road, Greenwich, Connecticut 06830. The following groups may be sources of useful printed materials: The National Audubon Society, 1130 Fifth Avenue, New York, N.Y. 10028; Garden Club of America, 598 Madison Avenue, New York, N.Y. 10022; Superintendent of Documents, Washington, D.C. 20402; major natural history museums; and large botanical societies. Write for a list of available publications.

TREES

There are in the United States and Canada over a thousand varieties of trees. At least a hundred varieties grow within a few miles of your home, even if you live in the heart of a city. It is likely that all or almost all are members of two vast families: the broad-leafed deciduous trees and the needle-leafed conifers or evergreens. You also may encounter two families which consist of but a single species each: the ginkgo, or maidenhair, and the fernlike cycad, which is found in subtropical regions of the United States. Both are closely related to the conifer. In fact, the three were the first trees to evolve and also the first seed-bearing plants. Unlike the deciduous trees, they have neither flowers nor fruit. Instead they bear cones or other primitive arrangements in which their seeds lie exposed. Most keep their needles, or leaves, throughout the year. Deciduous trees, of course, lose theirs every fall.

Learning about Trees. To understand trees, it is important to understand their structure, how they get their food, and how they grow. Many of the books listed in the Bibliography provide this information. One of the most useful is *An Introduction to Trees* by John Kieran. Once you have done some reading, concentrate on learning to identify the trees in your area. The easiest method is identifying leaves, but it also is interesting to learn the characteristic shapes of various trees and to distinguish their bark, twigs, and seed carriers. Developing a collection of leaves and other specimens, as discussed below, is an enjoyable way to do this.

It also is interesting to adopt a tree. Keep a diary for much of a year in which you record the changes that occur, such as budding, flowering, seed formation, and storm damage. Also record which insects, birds, and other plants make use of the tree. Photographs, sketches, and mounted specimens will enhance the record. In fact, after a while you will come to regard the tree as a friend.

Leaf Collections. The possibilities include leaves of all species in your area, leaves of all colors, leaves of a particular group of trees, such as fruit trees and timber trees, and leaves selected to illustrate the life cycle of a particular tree. For the latter collection use a deciduous tree. Obtain a bud and one of the first leaves, then acquire additional specimens every three or four days until the leaves have reached maturity. Complete your collection with a colored leaf and a faded leaf. Also include one or two specimens on which insects have fed.

Some collectors assemble single leaves, but the most satisfactory specimens for a herbarium collection consist of two leaves and a portion of the twig from which they grew. Using a sharp knife or clippers, cut the twig from the tree just above a bud or a leaf. If you do not have a herbarium press to take into the field, you easily can make one. You will need two pieces of plywood each about a foot square, a quantity of blotters or pulpy paper to use between the two boards, and a pair of book straps or heavy rubber bands to hold everything in place under pressure. Place the leaves between the blotters and adjust the straps. You also can store specimens in a loose-leaf binder between blotters or newsprint cut to size. At home, change the blotters every other day. If you don't have a press, weight them with bricks or heavy books.

Once the leaves have dried, coat them with natural shoe polish or wax to preserve their colors. To apply wax, place a leaf between two sheets of wax paper and press with a warm iron. As the wax melts, it transfers to the leaf. Mount each specimen on herbarium paper or a heavy card, using glue or cellophane tape to hold it in place. In the lower right corner, letter the specimen's common and scientific names, the place and date of acquisition, a description of where the specimen was taken, and the name of the collector. Then cover with a sheet of clear acetate.

Other Collections. Winter twigs: The twigs on deciduous trees bear buds during the winter months which contain the leaves, stems, and flowers that emerge the following spring. Since each species has a distinctive bud, a twig collection can be as varied as a leaf collection. Each twig also has distinctive scars which show where leaves once grew and where buds developed earlier in its history. By studying the bud scars, one can determine how much a twig has grown each year. In removing twigs, cut them as described above and mount on heavy cards with glue or cellophane tape.

Seeds and Seed Carriers: Every species also has distinctive seeds and seed carriers. Most specimens should be dried in a relatively warm place, then mounted. Pine cones should be washed with a detergent to remove any pitch, sprayed with a clear plastic, and stored in boxes or on shelves.

Seedlings: A miniature forest grown from various tree seeds is a fascinating possession. When the seedlings are several inches in height, they can be pressed, mounted, and preserved. An empty aquarium is a good place to plant tree seeds. The National Audubon Society suggests the following procedures. Cover the bottom of the aquarium with peb-

229

bles and add a two-inch layer of garden soil mixed with sand. After soaking the seeds overnight, plant them at a depth of about a half-inch. Keep the soil damp but not wet and make certain the seedlings are fully exposed to sunlight. Identify each seed by writing its species on a Popsicle stick inserted in the soil next to it. If a seed doesn't sprout, it may require a period of freezing or "wintering over." Place the seeds of such species in a freezer for the winter, then try again in the spring.

Crafts. Leaves are so lovely and diverse they frequently are used for decorative purposes. Here are several approaches. Place freshly picked leaves of different species between two pieces of glass, then tape the panes together (which seals out air) and display the leaves on a table or mantel. Display a selection of leaves through a windowpane, holding them in place with a sheet of clear Contact paper, a plastic shelving material. Encase several leaves between two sheets of Contact paper; display them on walls or use them to decorate wastepaper baskets or lampshades.

Making leaf prints also is intriguing. The prints may serve as decorations or as the basis of a collection. One technique involves transfer printing. Printer's ink is applied to the face of a leaf. The leaf is then brought in contact with a sheet of soft paper or a piece of fabric which is gently rubbed with the bowl of a wooden spoon. This method is described in Chapter 3, Making Prints. Rubbing is another traditional technique. A leaf is covered with a soft piece of paper which in turn is rubbed with a soft pencil or with the side of a crayon from which the wrapping has been stripped. An image of the leaf soon emerges. There also is spatter printing. A leaf is positioned on a sheet of soft paper and water color is spattered on the sheet. When the leaf is removed, a silhouette appears. To apply the color, you will need a square of window screen and an old toothbrush. Hold the screen over the leaf, dip the brush in the paint, and move it briskly across the screen in outward strokes.

Research. A good deal of research on tree development and tree diseases is in progress at agricultural and forestry schools of many state universities. A postal card or telephone call will determine if a researcher is in need of volunteers to collect specimens or make observations.

WILD FLOWERS

The most common, the hardiest, and the most prolific wild flowers are European immigrants that arrived over the years in packing straw, loads of grain, and other conveyances and established themselves by happenstance. They include Queen Anne's lace, burdock, yarrow, goldenrod, sticktight, and dozens of other species. They flourish in roadsides, meadows, and vacant lots, and virtually anywhere else there is a minimum of water and sunlight. In the process they serve as pioneer plants, aerating and enriching barren soil and thereby helping other species to establish themselves. When they appear in our gardens, however, we regard them as "weeds" and run for the hoe.

Native wild flowers—the "Americans" as they sometimes are called—generally are more delicate, less numerous, and harder to find. Many grow deep in wooded areas or in bogs or marshes, often half hidden by leaves and grass. Some are moderately plentiful, but others, because they produce few seeds and require a special environment, are rare. Many spring flowers are in this category and so are some orchids and lilies. However, rarity also may be a sectional matter. The amateur in search of specimens first should determine the status of the species in his area. The best sources of information are the local nature clubs already cited, natural history museums, agricultural and forestry colleges, and state conservation departments. Some make available lists of wild flowers that should not be picked, that may be picked in moderation, and that may be picked freely.

When rare flowers are involved, a responsible collector contents himself with photographs, sketches, or simply a close examination and the pleasure of adding such species to a list of flowers he has seen. With the "Europeans" and other plentiful varieties, there are opportunities to build herbarium collections and also collections of seeds and seed carriers. As noted earlier, some collectors also gather plants they use in dried arrangements, and others, with an interest in cookery, seek out the edible plants.

Identifying Wild Flowers. A field guide is essential. Since color is the best aid in identification, such books generally are organized with the white flowers in one section and the greens, yellows, reds, blues, and intermediate shades in others. Habitat and period of bloom also are provided. It also is important to understand the structure of a flower, since the arrangement and number of stamens, pistils, and other parts may be crucial to an identification. There are 18 families of wild flowers. The most common is the composite family which includes most of the European varieties. All species in this group have what appears to be a single flower but actually is a cluster of many tiny blooms. Other major families include mint, mustard, parsley, orchid, and pulse.

Observation. Observing the same wild plants over an extended period may be as intriguing as looking for species you haven't seen before. One possibility involves adopting a single plant for a season of growth and keeping an illustrated record of its experiences. A more ambitious effort involves a square yard of a garden, a weed lot, or a park which is checked weekly to determine the current number of plants, their species, their status, and any unusual occurrences since the last census. If possible, mark the section with stones or with stakes and string.

Edible Plants. Many wild plants are a source of interesting things to eat. The tender leaves of the young skunk cabbage are tasty if they are boiled in two or three changes of water and served with butter. Boiled and buttered cattail spikes also are good to eat, but the spikes must be picked shortly before the pollen appears. For guidance on the many opportunities, consult the Bibliography.

Gardening. It is not difficult to establish a wild flower garden, even in a window box or a collection of flowerpots. At times wild flower stock may be purchased from a nursery. In addition, composites may be transplanted after they have bloomed. Several hours in advance, wet the soil to which they are to be moved. Then cut the plants back to about eight inches in height and dig them out with a sizable quantity of soil. After they have been transplanted, partially shade them with large flowerpots for a few days and water regularly. Wild flower seeds also may be used to start a garden. Collect these in the fall, sprinkle in loose soil, water, and cover with peat moss.

A Terrarium. If you own an empty aquarium or fish bowl, you can create a wooded glen of miniature wild plants. Place an inch or two of clean coarse gravel or sand on the bottom of the tank. Then add about two inches of rich soil, varying the terrain somewhat. Next transplant the glen. The possibilities include small specimens of winterberry, partridgeberry, checkerberry, ferns, and creeping evergreens. A few tree seedlings also would be appropriate. So would a moss- or lichen-covered stone or a rotting stick with a fungus. After everything is in place, add a large quantity of water, but not so much that any is left standing. Use either pond water or tap water stirred vigorously to incorporate air. Then cover the terrarium with a sheet of glass. Every three weeks thereafter, wet the plants with a spray. Do so more frequently if the soil becomes dry.

Dried and Preserved Specimens. To obtain herbarium specimens, use the techniques described earlier for pressing and mounting leaves. Small wild flowers also make beautiful wall decorations when pressed and mounted as bouquets and framed under glass. In addition, many collectors use dried composites for table arrangements, planters, wreaths, and other decorative objects. Frequently they incorporate berries, bark, weathered wood, pine needles, and other natural materials. Some also enjoy creating seed mosaics. A good deal of what is needed for these projects is available in gardens or nearby fields and woods. As a hobbyist becomes more skilled, he may grow what he cannot readily obtain or turn to commercial sources.

Drying and Preserving: Most of what is collected during the fall and winter already is dry. When artificial drying is needed, there are several techniques. One involves hanging bunches of plants heads down from hooks in a dry, dark attic for a week or more, varying with the species. Another involves immersion in silica gel. A third requires the use of clean fine sand or a mixture of sand and borax in which flower heads are buried for several days. Flowers and grasses are preserved in their natural state by placing their stems in a solution of one part glycerin and two parts water. The intricacies of these techniques are covered in detail in the manuals listed in the Bibliography.

A Seed Mosaic: This is an easy yet interesting project for a beginner. The result can be framed and used as a wall hanging. The materials include a sheet of heavy cardboard or plywood, a pair of tweezers, clear glue, and a large quantity of dried seeds of various colors and sizes. Arrange the seeds in piles. Then sketch the design, indicating the types of seeds for each section, and transfer it to the cardboard or plywood. Butterflies, birds, flowers, faces, and abstractions are some of the possibilities. Apply the glue to a small area and add enough seeds so that the background does not show through. If necessary, maneuver the seeds into position with the tweezers. When the mosaic is dry, spray it with a liquid plastic.

Other Activities. Children usually like these.

Milking the Dandelion: The milk in the root resembles the juice of the rubber tree and when rubbed between two fingers produces a kind of rubber.

Exploring the Milkweed: Watch the monarch butterfly feed or use the milk of the milkweed as a kind of glue; or, in the fall, blow on the pods to free their high-flying seeds. The silky hairs the seeds trail also can be woven into string.

GRASSES

To most of us, grass is grass. If you set your mind to it, however, you probably can find from 50 to 100 varieties in your city or town. Throughout the country there are over a thousand different grasses. They are almost everywhere: in weed lots, roadsides, lawns, meadows, pastures, farmers' fields (as corn, other cereals, and sugar cane), woods, and salt marshes, and on hillsides and ocean beaches. With their tapering blades, subtle coloring, and tiny intricate blossoms, they are truly lovely plants. From the arrival of sweet vernal in the early spring to the departure of the beard grasses in the fall, they grow, blossom, and reseed in infinite numbers.

Identifying Grasses. It is easy enough to tell corn from sugar cane, but with other species it is useful to have a clear knowledge of habitat, season of bloom, and structural differences, all of which a good field guide provides. It is particularly helpful to have a hand lens, since structural differences may be important and at times are difficult to see with the unaided eye. In fact, some blossoms are so small an entire field might be in bloom and you would not know it unless you knew the grasses.

Grass stems generally are hollow and the sheaths from which the leaves grow are partially opened. The leaves occur first on one side of a stem, then on the other side in what is called "two-ranked growth." The blossoms vary in appearance, but typically consist of tiny clusters of minuscule spikelets. When these are restricted to a single stem, they are called "spikes." When they grow on divided branches, they are known as "panicles." Like the blossoms of other plants, they have stamens and pistils to distribute and receive pollen. The structure differs somewhat, however, because grasses are fertilized by wind-borne pollen, while many other plants rely for pollination on insects. The grass blossoms do not have petals and sepals; instead they possess tiny scales, or glumes, of various shapes and arrangements.

Bermuda Grass (Cynodon dactylon), *Pepper Sauce Canyon, Oracle, Arizona.*

Mat Grama (Bouteloua simplex), *Mogollon Mountains, Socorro County, New Mexico.*

Italian Rye Grass (Lolium multiflorum), *Westchester County, New York.*

Annual Bluegrass (Poa annua), *Washington State.*

236

Sedges and rushes often are confused with grasses. The sedges differ in that their stems are solid and frequently triangular and their leaves are "three-ranked" rather than "two-ranked." The rushes differ in the structure of their blossoms.

Collections. Herbarium specimens generally are organized by family, habitat, or region. They also may be organized by use. The cereals make an interesting collection, for example. Specimens should be collected when they are in bloom and mounted as described in the section Trees.

Crafts

Printing: Grasses, sedges, and rushes yield beautiful transfer prints, but inking can be difficult when clusters of blades are involved. See Chapter 3, Making Prints.

Weaving and Plaiting: If one has patience and a sufficient quantity of long-bladed grass, he can make place mats or rope. If he has access to rush, he can create baskets, chair seats, even hats.

Papermaking: See Chapter 2, Making Paper.

Arrangements. The different sizes, shapes, textures, and colors of fresh grasses lend themselves to beautiful displays. Store them in water in vases, glass bowls, and other containers.

NON-FLOWERING PLANTS

Two-thirds of the plants bear flowers and seeds. The deciduous trees, the wild flowers, and the grasses discussed above are in this group. So are the shrubs, vines and cacti. The coniferous trees, the ginkgoes, and the cycads also have seeds, but do not have true flowers. The remainder have neither flowers nor seeds. These include algae, bacteria, ferns, horsetails, lichens, liverworts, and mosses, as well as the molds, mushrooms, and other fungi. They are a more primitive and a more ancient group than the flowering plants and in several respects are more interesting. Lacking flowers and seeds, they rely on a variety of means to reproduce. Some distribute powdery spores from which new plants grow. Others use their spores to create tiny intermediate plants. These contain an egg cell and a sperm which must unite before the parent plant is reproduced. Others rely on cell division or, as with lichens, simply break apart, blow away, and if the conditions are right continue growing elsewhere. Moreover, many of these plants have neither roots nor stems nor leaves. Although they are less numerous than other varieties, they are more widespread. They are found not only in wooded areas but in the barren reaches of the Arctic, on mountain-tops, in oceans and in ponds, in farmers' fields, even in your home.

Algae. The single-celled blue-green algae is the oldest known form of life and the source from which many other plants descended. The earliest remains scientists have found are over 2 billion years old. Today the algae (Latin for seaweed) are the principal aquatic plants in both salt and fresh water, the chief food on which fish rely, and a crucial link in the chain of life. They range in size from species visible only through a microscope to a variety of kelp 200 feet long. The microscopic varieties are by far the most numerous. They form clusters, chains, or threads, or float alone, or even swim as in the case of two "plant-animals," the euglenoids in fresh water and the dinoflagellates in salt water. One of the best-known products of microscopic algae is pond scum, the green slime found on stagnant water and in aquariums. However, another is plankton, which holds the promise of meeting the world's anticipated food shortage. The larger varieties of algae possess a fascinating array of shapes, colors, and names, including devil's apron, Irish moss, and mermaid's wine glass. A few species also are found on land. Two varieties are responsible for the green stain on trees that often is confused with moss. An alga also joins with a fungus to produce another kind of plant, the lichen.

There are 40,000 species of algae, but they consist of relatively few families. These include the blue-green algae, which is the most primitive; the green algae, which takes in primitive and more advanced varieties; the red and the brown algae, which are found along beaches and rocky coastlines as seaweeds; the euglenoids, which live in quiet fresh water pools; the golden algae, of which fresh water plankton consists; and the dinoflagellates and the diatoms, which make up salt water plankton.

Collecting Algae: Seaweeds and other large varieties may be dried as herbarium specimens or preserved in jars of rubbing alcohol. In collecting specimens, you will need a sharp knife and several sizable containers, such as plastic bags or buckets. If you are after marine species, wear sneakers to avoid cutting your feet in rocky areas. The microscopic varieties can be collected by taking small samples of water, but distinguishing among the thousands of species involved requires a good deal of knowledge.

To mount the large varieties, you will need a deep pan and heavy herbarium mounting sheets. Float a specimen in the pan, slip a mounting sheet into the water under it, and raise the sheet until the alga rests on it. Then lift the mounting sheet and the plant from the water, place them on newspaper, and cover with muslin or cheesecloth and additional paper. When the specimen is dry, it should adhere to the mounting sheet. If it doesn't, use small pieces of plastic tape to hold it in place.

Horsetails, Club Mosses, and Ferns. When the horsetails and club mosses appeared some 400 million years ago, they were the first plants with stems. When the ferns appeared some 30 or 40 million years later, they were the first plants with true leaves. For tens of millions of years thereafter these plants were the predominant growth on earth, achieving as much as a hundred feet in height in lush, widespread forests. When these forests began to disappear some 350 million years ago, they began their slow conversion to the coal on which we still rely. But some species managed to survive.

The ferns, club mosses, and horsetails we know today are far smaller than their primordial ancestors, but otherwise have changed little in appearance. In the United States they are most plentiful in the damp subtropical areas. However, there also are many varieties in the temperate regions, particularly in damp woods, along streams and ponds, and in boggy soil. There also are species that prefer a drier habitat such as a meadow. There also are ferns that live in water or grow in trees.

Identifying Ferns: If one is to know the ferns, he first must understand their structure and the terminology used to describe it. A fern's leaves are called "fronds." Most ferns have compounded leaves that consist of several leaflets each. The leaflets are called "pinnae." In some species they are subdivided into subleaflets called "pinnules." Depending on the number of subleaflets, a leaf is a pinnate, bipinnate, or tripinnate. A few species have simple leaves which are not divided into leaflets. The edges of a leaf are called "margins." If the edges are smooth, they are "entire" margins. Otherwise they are "toothed" or, if deeply separated, they are "lobed."

A fern's spores generally are stored on the undersides of its fronds in tiny sacs called "sporangia." These are clustered in what appear to be brown dots or streaks called "sori." A fern's stem usually grows underground in a horizontal position from which stalks and fronds grow vertically. The most common fern is the bracken or brake fern, which has large triangular fronds. The largest of the fern families is the polypody.

Identifying Club Mosses and Horsetails: Today's club mosses are creeping evergreens from six inches to a foot in height. Several species that resemble miniature hemlocks are called "ground pine" or "ground cedar." The horsetails are tall and thin and look like miniature towers. Their stems are hollow and marked with ridges and, in most species, are crowned with a cone of spores. Their foliage consists of small coils of narrow leaves that look a little like pipe cleaners. Some species are less than a foot tall. Others reach a height of six feet. The field horsetail is the most common in the United States and Canada. However, the most useful is the rough horsetail or "scouring rush" whose five-foot stem includes so much silica that frontiersmen used it to scrub out pots and pans.

Collecting Specimens: It is likely that some ferns in your area are rare. Before removing specimens, check with the local garden club or one of the other organizations listed in the section Wild Flowers. In preparing herbarium displays, follow the directions for pressing and mounting leaves. Since club mosses and horsetails are difficult to mount, they are best left where you find them.

Crafts: Ferns yield beautiful transfer prints. See Chapter 3, Making Prints.

Gardening: If ferns are plentiful and you have a garden, consider starting a fernery by transplanting several varieties. Select the smallest specimens you can find; if possible, remove the entire stem and root-stock plus a sizable quantity of soil. Establish your fernery in a shaded location. Prepare the soil and wet it thoroughly several hours before the transplanting, then water lightly immediately afterward. Tiny ferns also make an excellent addition to a terrarium. See the section Wild Flowers.

Lichens. A lichen actually consists of two tiny plants growing together for their mutual benefit. In almost all cases the partners are a fungus and a blue-green or a green alga. The fungus contributes moisture, the protection of a threadlike skin it weaves around its partner, and minerals it takes from the surface to which it clings. The alga contributes food, primarily carbohydrates.

The plant that results takes many forms. Some appear as hard crusts on rocks and tree trunks. These are the "crustose" varieties. Others, the "foliose," are flat but leaflike in appearance. Still others, the "fruticose," branch upward as much as two or three inches. Lichens also differ in texture—they may be rippled, folded, warty, smooth—and in color, which ranges from a dull gray-green to soft yellows, golds, and reds. After a rain, when their muted colors come alive, they are a lovely sight.

The lichen grows in temperate regions in cool wooded areas and on rocks, but it is so hardy it is the dominant plant, frequently the only plant, in the far reaches of the Arctic, on mountaintops, and in other barren areas. In such cases it serves often as a pioneer plant, breaking rock into a rudimentary soil that will support other simple growth. Since lichens require clean air, however, one rarely finds them in cities.

Collecting Lichens: You will need a hand lens to examine specimens, a sharp knife to remove them, and a supply of plastic sandwich bags to hold them. Be certain to check all fallen trees, since you may find lichens in upper branches you otherwise could not reach. Dry your specimens in the sun or press them lightly between sheets of pulpy paper or blotters, using the technique described in the section Trees. Some lichens are easy to identify, but others require examination through a microscope. A microscope also is necessary if you wish to see the alga beneath the skin. Keep lichens in small envelopes, with the collection data entered on the front. Store the envelopes in a shoe box or narrow drawer.

Gardening: Lichens are another plant that does well in a terrarium. See Wild Flowers.

Mosses and Liverworts. These minuscule plants have a great deal in common. They were the first green land plants. They have neither roots nor stems nor leaves in the accepted sense. To reproduce, they rely not only on spores but on sperms and egg cells, using a primitive method already described. They also inhabit the same damp, shaded places, although mosses tend to be more widespread. Moreover, they look a good deal alike. In fact, you probably have mistaken liverworts (and *their* close relatives the hornworts) for mosses. A basic difference is that the mosses grow upright, while the liverworts tend to lie flat against the rocks, soil, or logs on which they are growing. In most cases, however, even the mosses are no more than two inches high. Woodsmen may be interested in one other fact. The moss they seek on the north sides of trees when they are lost isn't moss at all. It's algae.

Identification: Since these plants are so small, often a hand lens is needed to identify a particular species. The chief means of identification are the structure of their "leaves," the capsules in which spores are stored, the number of teeth the capsules have, and the length of the stalks from which they grow.

Collections: Mosses and liverworts may be pressed and mounted on herbarium sheets. For techniques, see the section Trees.

Terraria: Both plants adapt to life in a terrarium. See Wild Flowers.

Molds, Mushrooms, and Other Fungi. Every green plant from the tree to the alga manufactures its own food. It converts inorganic water, carbon dioxide, and minerals to organic proteins, carbohydrates, and fats. The key to this miracle is chlorophyll, a remarkable green pigment which enables a plant to harness the energy of the sun. The only plants without chlorophyll and the only ones that do not create their own food are the fungi. They rely on the green plants for nourishment.

Most fungi consist of a spore-producing organ, such as the cap and stem of a mushroom, and a mycelium, a mass of threadlike hairs that carry out the life processes. Typically the mycelium either buries itself in the ground or in leaf litter, where it feeds on organic matter, or it infiltrates a rotting log or stump. When it invades a dead plant, it secretes an enzyme which enables it to digest the food it encounters. When a fungus has completed its work, often all that remains is humus. In the process it has met one of nature's essential needs: returning the dead to the soil. In fact, without the fungi and the closely related bacteria, organic matter would not decay.

The fungi also serve in other ways. They are a source of antibiotics and vitamins and are essential to the production of bread and alcoholic beverages. They also convert rather ordinary cheese to the delicious Camembert and Roquefort. In addition, the best known fungus, the mushroom, is an extraordinary food in its own right. But the fungi also have another face. They cause disease and death in plants, in animals, and occasionally in humans. They also are responsible for food spoilage and for the destruction of clothing through mildew and of buildings through rot.

The 250,000 kinds of fungi are an intriguing confusion of shapes, sizes, colors, and behavior. The algaelike varieties include various molds, mildews, and blights. The sac types take in the yeasts and the delicious morels and truffles. The basidium family includes most of the mushrooms as well as rust and smut. A miscellaneous group are responsible for athlete's foot, ringworm, and other diseases. Frequently the bacteria and the slime molds also are classified as fungi. For the beginner, the slime molds and the mushrooms offer the most interesting possibilities for exploration.

Slime Molds. The slime mold is one of the most unusual creatures on earth. In its animal stage it is a small, slimy, jellylike mass of protoplasm which might be red, yellow, brown, or white. It generally grows on damp soil or decaying logs, particularly the underside of a log. One of the fascinating things about the slime mold is that it moves. Creeping forward imperceptibly, it engulfs, then consumes the food it needs. In its reproductive stage the slime mold sends up tiny spore cases just as a fungus does. These rarely are over a quarter of an inch in height, but a number are exquisitely detailed. There is one, for example, produced by the basket slime mold, that looks like an enclosed woven basket. Some of the spore cases grow on stems, but others develop directly on the host. To find them, it is necessary to closely examine decaying logs, fallen trees, and dead leaves with a magnifying glass.

Collections: The spore cases make interesting collections. Remove them with a portion of the surface on which they are growing, dry them in the sun, and store in small plastic boxes or botanical Riker mounts. Should you encounter the animal stage, remove it and the surface on which it is resting to a dish, place a wet piece of absorbent cotton next to the dish to keep the air moist, then cover the dish and the cotton with a clean jar. If your luck holds, you may see the mold enter its reproductive stage and send forth spore cases. The mold itself can be dried in the sun and stored in a small plastic box.

Mushrooms. There are several thousand varieties of mushrooms. Some are delicious (although not nutritious), others are poisonous in varying degrees, and others are neither. However, most are beautiful and all are remarkable for their shape and coloration. Strictly speaking, a mushroom is a gill fungus. It has a stem and an umbrella or cone-shaped cap with gills on the underside. However, most members of the basidium family may be regarded as mushrooms, including the puffball, which looks like it sounds, and the pore or bracket fungus, which grows shelflike from the sides of trees. The morels and truffles, which belong to the sac family, also should be included in this classification. Poisonous and other inedible varieties are sometimes called "toadstools," but there is no scientific basis for this term.

Mushrooms frequently grow in damp, cool wooded areas, although some prefer wet, cold climates and others thrive under wet, warm conditions. Typically they are found in the litter that covers a forest floor and on logs, stumps, and dead trees. In fact, some prefer particular types of trees. A good field guide will give you all this information.

If there is a club of mushroom hunters or mycologists in your area, it would be useful to join. Other members can guide you to locations where you are likely to find mushrooms and help you to identify them. Since many edible species are easily confused with poisonous varieties, a beginner is playing a dangerous game if he cannot identify with assurance what he decides to eat.

Herbarium Specimens: Some mushrooms will be virtually dry when you collect them, but others must be dried in the sun for several days before they can be stored. Some collectors place them on trays; others hang them from the branch of a tree. Place each specimen in a separate box with moth flakes to protect it against hungry insects.

Spore Prints: The spores of a common mushroom are contained in its gills on the underside of the cap. The color of the spores and the pattern of the gills vary with the species. As a result, mycologists sometimes rely on spore prints in making identifications. But the prints are so beautiful and varied, they are interesting to collect in their own right.

To make a spore print, position a mushroom cap with its gills facing down on a piece of paper. Place a small wad of wet paper toweling next to it. Then cover both with a clean jar. Remove the jar after three or four hours and carefully raise the cap. If all has gone well, the quiet moist air will have induced millions of spores to fall to the paper, revealing the pattern of the gills. To keep the print from smearing, spray it with a fixative; then label. The only difficulty you should encounter involves selecting the color of the paper. Spores may be white, yellow, brown, pink, violet, green, or black. Unless you know your fungi, you can only guess as to the color to use to achieve a good contrast. To be certain of an attractive result, collect two or three specimens and make prints of each on paper of different colors.

BIBLIOGRAPHY
General
Adventures in Living Plants, E. B. Kurtz, Jr., Chris Allen, University of Arizona Press, Tempe, 1965. For children.

The Amateur Naturalist's Handbook, Vinson Brown, Little, Brown & Co., Boston, 1948.

Botany, Carl L. Wilson, Walter E. Loomis, Holt, Rinehart & Winston, New York, 1962.

Field Book of Nature Activities and Conservation, William Hillcourt, G. P. Putnam's Sons, New York, 1961.

Introductory Botany, Arthur Cronquist, Harper & Bros., New York, 1961.

The Plants, Frits W. Went, Time, Inc., New York, 1963.

Plants: An Introduction to Modern Botany, Victor A. Gruelach et al., John Wiley & Sons, New York, 1962.

Trees

The Complete Guide to North American Trees, Carlton C. Curtis, S. C. Bausor, New Home Library, New York, 1943.

A Field Guide to Trees and Shrubs, George A. Petrides, Houghton Mifflin Co., Boston, 1958.

First Book of Tree Identification, Matilda Rogers, Random House, New York, 1951.

An Introduction to Trees, John Kieran, Hanover House, Garden City, N.Y., 1954.

Manual of Trees of North America, Charles S. Sargent, Houghton Mifflin Co., Boston, 1933. For advanced amateurs.

North American Trees, Richard J. Preston, Jr., Iowa State University Press, Ames, 1962.

The Story of Trees for Audubon Juniors, Shirley Miller, National Audubon Society, 1130 Fifth Avenue, New York, N.Y. 10028.

Trees, Shrubs, and Woody Vines of the Southwest, R. H. Vines, University of Texas Press, Austin, 1960.

Wild Flowers

Beginner's Guide to Wild Flowers, Ethel H. Hausman, G. P. Putnam's Sons, New York, 1955.

Field Book for Boys and Men, Boy Scouts of America, North Brunswick, N.J., 1967.

Field Book of American Wild Flowers, F. Schuyler Matthews, Norman Taylor, G. P. Putnam's Sons, New York, 1955. Eastern United States.

Field Book of Rocky Mountain Wildflowers, John J. Craighead et al., Houghton Mifflin Co., Boston, 1963.

Field Book of Western Wild Flowers, Margaret Armstrong, G. P. Putnam's Sons, New York, 1915.

Field Guide to Edible and Useful Wild Plants, Myron C. Chase, Nature Study Aids, Inc., Red Wing, Minnesota, 1965.

A Field Guide to the Wildflowers, Roger Tory Peterson, Margaret McKenny, Houghton Mifflin Co., Boston, 1968. Northeastern, north-central United States.

The First Book of Wild Flowers, Betty Cavanna, Franklin Watts, New York, 1961. For children.

How to Know the Wild Flowers, Mrs. William Dana Starr, Dover Publications, New York, 1963. Reprint of an early classic.

An Introduction to Wild Flowers, John Kieran, Doubleday & Co., New York, 1952.

Weeds, Dorothy C. Hogner, Thomas Y. Crowell Co., New York, 1968. For children.

Weeds of Northeastern United States and Canada, Frederick H. Montgomery, Frederick Warne & Co., New York, 1964.

Wild Flowers and How to Grow Them, Edwin F. Steffek, Crown Publishers, New York, 1954.

The Wild Flowers of California, Mary E. Parsons, Dover Publications, New York. Reprint of 1907 edition.

Drying and Preserving Plants

Creative Decorations with Dried Flowers, Dorothy S. Thompson, Hearthside Press, New York, 1965.

Decorating with Pods and Cones, Eleanor Van Rensselaer, Van Nostrand-Reinhold Co., New York, 1957.

Decorating with Seed Mosaics, Chipped Glass, and Plant Materials, Eleanor Van Rensselaer, Van Nostrand-Reinhold Co., New York, 1960.

Design for Flower Arrangers, Dorothy Riester, Van Nostrand-Reinhold Co., New York, 1959.

The Dried-Flower Book, Nita C. Carico, Jane C. Guynn, Doubleday & Co., New York, 1962. A primer.

Dried Flowers with a Fresh Look, Eleanor Reed Bolton, Van Nostrand-Reinhold Co., New York, 1958.

Edible Plants

Free for the Eating, Bradford Angier, Stackpole Books, Harrisburg, 1960.

Stalking the Wild Asparagus, Euell Gibbons, David McKay Co., New York, 1962.

Terraria

The Book of Wild Pets, Clifford B. Moore, Charles T. Branford Co., Boston, 1954. Part II.

Grasses

The American Grass Book, S. G. Archer, C. E. Bunch, University of Oklahoma Press, Norman, 1953.

The Book of Grasses, Mary E. Francis, Doubleday, Page & Co., New York, 1912.

Grass: The Yearbook of Agriculture, Superintendent of Documents, Washington, D.C., 1948.

How to Know the Grasses, Richard W. Pohl, William C. Brown Co., Dubuque, 1958.

Manual of the Grasses of the United States, A. S. Hitchcock, Dover Publications, New York. Reprint of 1950 Edition.

Non-Flowering Plants

Non-Flowering Plants, F. S. Shuttleworth, Herbert S. Zim, Golden Press, New York, 1967.

Plants Without Leaves, Ross E. Hutchins, Dodd Mead & Co., New York, 1966.

Algae

Algae, the Grass of Many Waters, Lewis H. Tiffany, Charles C Thomas, Publisher, Springfield, Ill., 1968.

The Fresh Water Algae of the United States, G. M. Smith, McGraw-Hill Book Co., New York, 1950.

How to Know the Fresh Water Algae, Gerald W. Prescott, W. C. Brown, Dubuque, 1954.

Marine Algae of the Northeastern Coast of North America, W. R. Taylor, University of Michigan Press, Ann Arbor, 1957.
Also see Non-Flowering Plants above.

Ferns

The Fern Guide, Edgar T. Wherry, Doubleday & Co., New York, 1961. Eastern, central United States.

Ferns of the Eastern Central States, J. M. Shaver, Dover Publications, New York. Reprint of 1954 edition.

Ferns of the Northwest, T. C. Frye, Binfords & Mort, Portland, Oregon, 1956.

A Field Guide to the Ferns and Their Related Families, Boughton Cobb, Houghton Mifflin Co., Boston, 1956.

How to Know the Ferns, F. T. Parsons, Dover Publications, New York, 1961.

The Southern Fern Guide, Edgar T. Wherry, Doubleday & Co., New York, 1964.
Also see Non-Flowering Plants above.

Lichens

How to Know the Lichens, M. E. Hale, Jr., William C. Brown Co., Dubuque, 1968.

The Lichen Book, G. G. Nearing, Eric Lundberg, Ashton, 1962.

The Lichen Flora of the United States, Bruce Fink, University of Michigan Press, Ann Arbor, 1960.

Lichen Handbook, M. E. Hale, Jr., Smithsonian Institution, Washington, D.C., 1961.

The Observer's Book of Lichens, K. A. Alvin, K. A. Kershaw, Frederick Warne & Co., New York, 1963.
Also see Non-Flowering Plants above.

Mosses and Liverworts

How to Know the Mosses and Liverworts, Henry S. Conrad, W. C. Brown, Dubuque, 1956.

Mosses with a Hand Lens, A. J. Grout, published by the author, Newfane, Vermont, 1947.
Also see Non-Flowering Plants above.

Mushrooms and Other Fungi

Common Edible Mushrooms, Clyde M. Christensen, Charles T. Banford, New Center, Mass., 1943.

Common Fleshy Fungi, Clyde M. Christensen, Burgess Publishing Co., Minneapolis, 1965.

The Field Book of Common Mushrooms, William S. Thomas, G. P. Putnam's Sons, New York, 1948.

Illustrated Genera of Wood Decay Fungi, C. J. Fergus, Burgess Publishing Co., Minneapolis, 1963.

The Mushroom Handbook, Louis C. C. Krieger, Dover Publications, New York. Reprint of 1936 edition.

The Mushroom Hunter's Field Guide, Alexander H. Smith, University of Michigan Press, Ann Arbor, 1963. The best of its type.

Mushrooms and Toadstools, John Ramsbottom, Collins, London, 1959.

Mushrooms of the Great Lakes Region, V. O. Graham, Dover Publications, New York. Reprint of 1944 edition.

The Savory Wild Mushroom, Margaret McKenney, University of Washington Press, Seattle, 1962. A cookbook.

20·ROCKS, MINERALS, AND GEM STONES

A ROCK IS A MASS of stony material that consists of one or more minerals. A mineral is a chemical element or a chemical compound that consists of a unique structure of crystals. Feldspar, quartz, and mica are three of the most common minerals. There are, in all, over 2000 known varieties, and virtually every year new ones are discovered, at times by amateurs. To the uninitiated, rocks are drab objects hardly worth a second glance. However, the "rockhound," or amateur mineralogist, knows better.

For many amateurs, the fascination of mineralogy lies in roaming the countryside, finding minerals, identifying them, and displaying them. Some spend their weekends and even their vacations in search of colorful new specimens. "I had never realized," one rockhound told me, "that there could be anything on earth so beautiful as a mineral."

Frequently the emphasis is on a general collection or on minerals of a particular region or on those of a particular type, such as metallic ores, radioactive minerals, and fluorescent minerals that glow in a most extraordinary way when exposed to ultraviolet light. A number of advanced amateurs also are intrigued by the chemistry of minerals and maintain laboratories to do analyses. Others are involved with crystallography, a science that deals with the forms, structures, and mathematics of crystals.

Still other hobbyists in this field have quite a different set of interests. Some practice lapidary art, converting semi-precious and precious gem stones to jewels. Others, as discussed in Chapter 17, hunt in the rocks not for minerals but for fossils.

GETTING STARTED

There are several steps to take no matter what your particular interest. They include reading, visiting a museum, and joining a club.

Books. The best primer on mineralogy is *A Field Guide to Rocks and Minerals* by Frederick H. Pough, which is listed in the Bibliography. You also will need a guide to mineral locations in your area. Such publications are covered in the section Collecting Minerals.

Museums. Virtually every natural history museum has an extensive collection of minerals which it would be useful for a beginner to inspect. Pay particular attention to the specimens from your area and from where they were taken. Eventually you might find similar ones.

Clubs. Not all amateurs belong to a mineralogical club, but joining one is quite helpful to a beginner. There are over a thousand such clubs throughout the United States and Canada. They conduct field trips, offer lectures and workshops, and may issue publications and sponsor mineralogical "shows." The largest clubs are divided into sections concerned with mineral collecting, lapidary work, and fossil hunting.

Frequently such groups are associated with a natural history museum. If this is not the case in your area, a rocks and minerals dealer may be able to refer you to a club. Otherwise, contact the American Federation of Mineralogical Societies. The addresses of its regional units are as follows:

California Federation of Mineralogical Societies, Juanita Curtis, 609 W. 36th Street, Long Beach, California 90806.

Eastern Federation, Carl Krotki, 140 West End Avenue, New York, N.Y. 10023.

Midwest Federation, Jean Reynolds, 107 Tuttle, Clarendon Hills, Illinois 60514.

Northwest Federation, Lee Kendall, P.O. Box 5, Glenwood, Oregon 97120.

Rocky Mountain Federation, Hardy Jenkinson, 8364 Powell Avenue, Magna, Utah 84044.

Texas Federation, Mignon Wagner, 611 Clifford Drive, Austin, Texas 78745.

In Canada, write: Mineralogical Association of Canada, c/o Mines Branch, 555 Booth Street, Ottawa, Ontario.

In getting started you also will need at least a rudimentary knowledge of the types of rocks and minerals and where to look for them and how to proceed when you find them.

TYPES OF ROCKS

There are three categories of rocks in which you will be collecting. They are organized by origin.

Igneous. *Ignis* is Latin for "fire." Rocks in this category originally were fiery molten magma that cooled, hardened, and crystallized. The more slowly the magma cooled, the larger the crystals and the coarser the rock that resulted. Granite, diorite, pegmatite, and gabbro are such rocks. The more rapidly the magma cooled, the finer the crystals and the smoother and glassier the surface. Obsidian, felsite, and basalt (traprock) are examples. Igneous rocks are the primary sources of the exceedingly hard minerals used for gem stones.

Sedimentary. These rocks are literally sediment. They consist of grains of sand, calcite, or weathered igneous rock carried to a particular location by moving water or left behind by swamps, lakes, and shallow seas as they slowly dried. As the sediment dried, it solidified. One of the most common sedimentary rocks is sandstone. In some specimens one even finds ripple marks left by the receding water. Two other common varieties are limestone, which consists of calcite, or calcium carbonate, from the shells of ancient shellfish; and shale, which originally was a muddy clay. In fact, wet a piece of shale and it will smell like mud. Sedimentary rocks typically are layered or stratified. As discussed in Chapter 17, these rocks are a primary source of fossils and fossil impressions. However, few gem stones are found in such rock. Two exceptions are jasper and agate, for which the Oregon coast is famous.

Metamorphic. This is "changed" rock. Under enormous heat and pressure, shale, for example, became slate, limestone became marble, granite became gneiss, and sandstone, one of the softest stones, became quartzite, one of the hardest. In changing from igneous rocks, metamorphic rocks acquired a new crystal structure. Before, crystals occurred at random; afterward, they appeared in bands or layers. In changing from sedimentary rock, metamorphic varieties acquired a smoother, more crystalline structure and became considerably harder. There are many metamorphic rocks which yield gems.

TYPES OF MINERALS

Of the 2000 known minerals, about 30 are found over and over again in rocks. Some of the most common include the following:

Feldspar. This is one of the most widespread minerals. It is a principal element of igneous rocks such as granite, gneiss, and basalt. When it decomposes, the result often is clay. It generally is white or pink but also may be green, gray, or yellow. It may be transparent, translucent, or opaque.

Quartz. This is another mineral that is distributed extensively and is a major constituent of igneous rocks. In addition, beach sand and the white pebbles one finds on beaches usually are quartz. It occurs in white, smoky white, rose, and yellow and ranges from transparent to opaque.

Mica and Hornblende. Mica commonly occurs in sheets which can be peeled apart. They are so thin they once were used as window glass or isinglass. A colorless variety, called "muscovite," is found in granite, gneiss, and pegmatite. Other varieties are black, white, yellow, brown, and green. Hornblende is still another constituent of granite. It is dark green or black in color.

Calcite. Limestone, marble, chalk, marl, and travertine consist primarily of calcite. Ordinarily it is colorless or white, but it also occurs in reds, yellows, and browns. It ranges from transparent to opaque. Dolomite looks a great deal like calcite; however, calcite bubbles when it comes in contact with vinegar or soda pop.

About a hundred minerals are suitable for use as gems. Another hundred are fluorescent. A basic collection of common minerals, or a starter set, may be purchased for about $5. It is a useful tool in learning to recognize specimens in the field.

WHERE TO FIND MINERALS

Most amateurs do their collecting in established locations that are known for their mineral deposits. There probably is at least one such site no more than a few hours' journey from your home. One of the best sources of information on where to look is mineralogy clubs. You also may obtain information from a government agency such as a geological survey or from a geology department at a university or a natural history museum. Dealers in mineralogical and lapidary supplies also may be helpful. In addition, they may sell detailed guides to local mineral resources. These are preferable to publications which undertake to cover the entire country, since they provide more detailed information.

Sources of minerals typically include quarries, road cuts, railroad cuts, fresh excavations, river banks, stream beds, and other sites where rock has been bared. Stony fields, beaches after a storm, and old mine dumps also may be fruitful. In fact, three of the world's richest and most diverse mineral locations are in the United States. They are at Franklin, New Jersey, where over 200 different minerals have been found, including many fluorescent varieties; at Calcite and Galena in the Ozark Mountains; and at Bisbee, Arizona, a copper mining center since the 1880's. As mineral hunting has grown in popularity, an increasing number of sites are operated by business firms which charge rockhounds a fee for the use of the land. These sites include old quarries and mines and even diamond fields.

As amateurs grow more experienced, however, they also may rely on a growing knowledge of geology and on geologic and topographic maps to seek out the unusual and the rare on their own.* Some who become particularly knowledgeable leave the beaten track to explore desolate canyons and other wilderness areas in their search.

CLOTHING AND EQUIPMENT

Clothing, Tools. You will need stout boots, canvas gloves for handling jagged rocks, and a hard hat if you are working in a quarry or at the base of a cliff. A shovel or trenching tool is needed for digging in stream beds and for removing an overburden to reach what you suspect lies underneath. Some hobbyists also rely on a Geiger counter in searching for radioactive minerals and on a portable ultraviolet lamp for finding fluorescent varieties. However, learning to identify such minerals may be sufficient. For trimming specimens to a manageable size, use a 9-inch chisel.

Identification Kits. Relative hardness is a key factor in identifying a mineral. Either purchase a kit for making such measurements or as-

---

* Such maps are sold at low cost by the United States Geological Survey. For information on maps available write U. S. G. S. Map Information Center, Washington, D.C. (areas east of the Mississippi River) and U. S. G. S., Federal Center, Denver, Colorado 80225 (areas west of the Mississippi).

semble your own, as described below in the section Collecting Minerals. A basic collection of common minerals already has been mentioned.

Knapsack.

COLLECTING MINERALS

It is important to know in advance which minerals you are likely to find at a particular location and what they look like. A good field guide will describe the possibilities in considerable detail. It also may have photographs of the minerals involved. If not, study the specimens at a museum or a mineral dealer's. Of course, if you have acquired a starter set that is relevant, study those specimens.

It is important to avoid trespassing. Before using either public or private property, be certain to ask permission. With private property it is appropriate to provide the owner with a waiver of responsibility in the event there is an accident. In all cases avoid destruction, fill in holes you dig, and clean up any litter before you leave. There also is a question of how many specimens to take. Usually only a few are needed, but some rockhounds are so greedy they have come to be called "rock hogs." In fact, the bad manners of such persons at times have caused quarries and other interesting sites to be closed to all collectors.

In working a site, safety is a factor. In a quarry and at the base of a cliff it is wise to wear a hard hat as protection against the possibility of falling rock. In many sections the most dangerous period for rock falls is the early spring when freezing and thawing cause extensive cracking and breakage. Quarries offer another potential hazard. It is the possibility of inadvertently activating an old blasting cap. For such reasons children should not be brought to these sites. In addition, caves and the interiors of old mines should be shunned, fascinating as they may be, unless you have truly experienced leadership. If you are prospecting in desert areas, avoid making camp in dry stream beds, since they are particularly susceptible to flash floods.

Finding Minerals. Most amateurs start as surface collectors, picking up what attracts them in a rocky field or in a stream bed or on a beach or at the base of a cliff or some other outcropping. What they find at times are rock fragments with minerals partially exposed. To obtain specimens of particular minerals, however, often it is necessary to break into the kinds of rocks that are likely to contain them, using a pick, a hammer, or a prying tool. In searching for tourmaline or aquamarine, for example, a collector would turn to pegmatite, a large granitelike formation with huge crystals that also is a source of quartz, feldspar, and other varieties. In looking for flint, he first would find limestone or chalk. In breaking into a rock, however, beware of flying fragments. With the exception of outstanding specimens, trim what you find to standard sizes: roughly 1″ × 2″ × 1″ or 3″ × 4″ × 1″.

Identifying Minerals. Some minerals may be identified on the basis of experience or through photographs in a field guide. But it may be necessary to subject a specimen to one or more tests and close examination before you can be certain of what you have. Even then the opinion of another amateur or a professional mineralogist or geologist may be required.

One of the important characteristics of a mineral is its hardness. All known minerals have been assigned a number which indicates their relative hardness. A complete field guide will contain these designations. They are derived from Mohs' scale, a 150-year-old system of measurement which is based on the ability of a mineral to scratch or to be scratched by objects of a known hardness. Collectors use a kit of minerals or other objects of known hardnesses to test the minerals they find. An advanced amateur I interviewed uses a penknife, a penny, a piece of glass, and a piece of quartz in making his determinations. An adaptation of Mohs' scale incorporating these objects is shown below.

Hardness
Number
1 Scratched readily by a fingernail. Talc is such a mineral. A fingernail has a hardness of 2½.
2 Scratched less readily by a fingernail. Gypsum and alabaster are examples.
3 Scratched by a penny. Calcite and malachite are examples. A penny has a hardness of 3½.
4 Scratched readily by a penknife. Fluorite is an example. The hardness of a standard knife blade is 5½.
5 Scratched less readily by a penknife. Apatite and serpentine are examples.
6 A mineral that can scratch glass if pressure is applied. Feldspar, obsidian, and orthoclase are examples. The hardness of glass is 5½.
7 A mineral that readily scratches glass. Agate, tourmaline, and flint are examples.

PLATE VII   *Amethyst, Reel's Farm, Iron Station, Lincoln County, North Carolina.*

PLATE VIII   *Barite, Cleveland County, Oklahoma.*

PLATE IX   *Prehnite, Lower New Street Quarry, Paterson, New Jersey.*

PLATE X   *Dolomite, Corydon Stone Quarry, Corydon, Indiana.*

PLATE XI   *Agate, Jefferson County, Oregon.*

PLATE XII   *Sand Calcite, Pine Ridge, Badlands, South Dakota.*

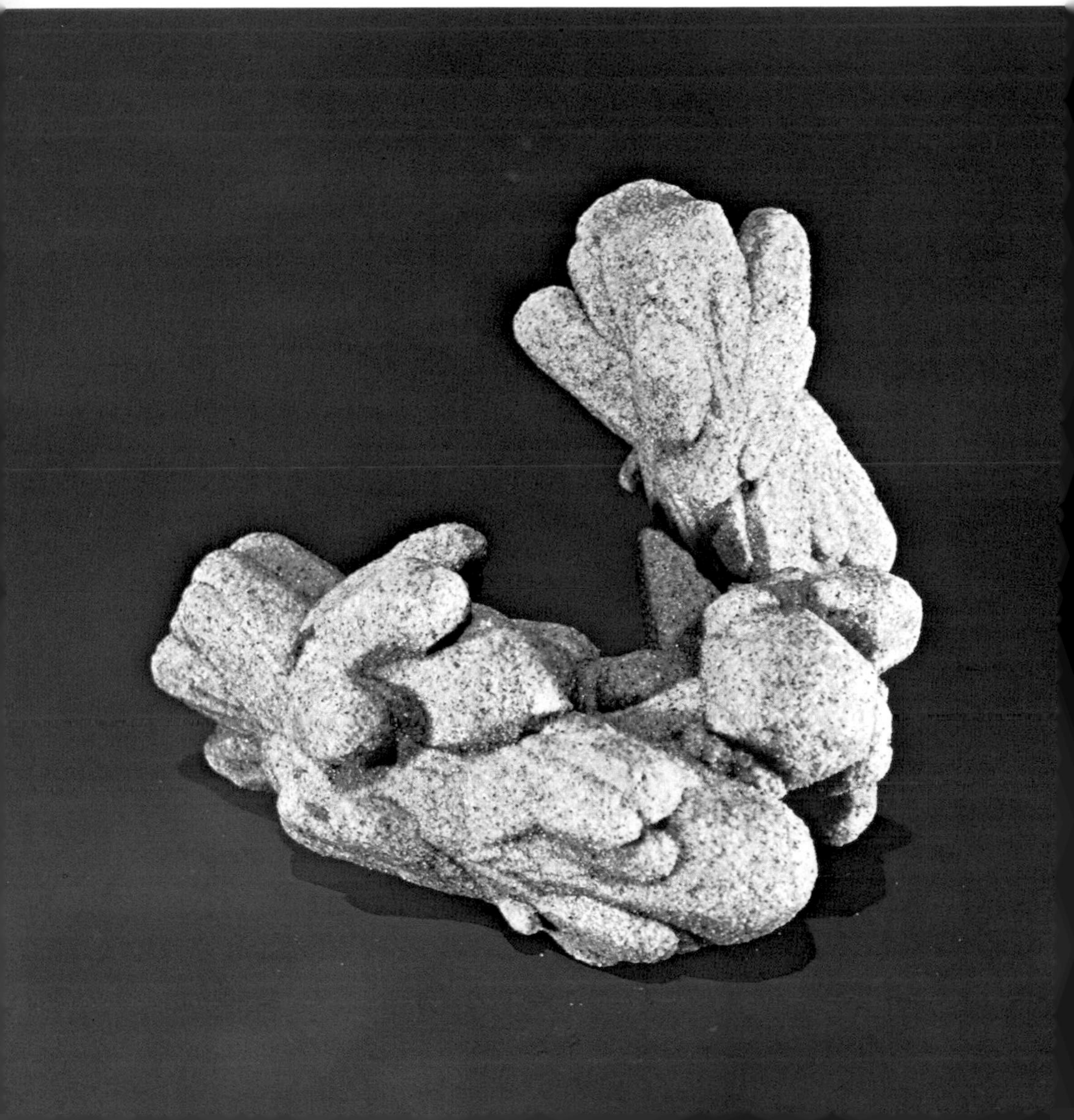

8 A mineral that can scratch quartz. Beryl, emerald, and topaz are examples. Quartz has a hardness of 7.

9 A mineral that can scratch topaz. Corundum, ruby, and sapphire are examples. Topaz has a hardness of 8.

10 A diamond, the hardest of all minerals.

Those minerals with a hardness of 7 or higher are semi-precious or precious stones.

In making identifications, collectors also may test for streak, the color of a mark a mineral will make on a piece of unglazed white tile. The color of the mineral itself also is of consequence. So are its characteristic pattern, its luster, relative transparency, and relative weight, and the way it cleaves or splits when broken.

Catalog Data. When you acquire a new mineral, assign it a catalog number. The number should be inscribed on a small label and attached to the specimen. It also should be entered in your notebook with the following data: identification; where the specimen was found; whether it was loose or had to be removed from a larger rock; if so, the layer from which it was removed; and other rocks and minerals nearby. In addition, describe the specimen in terms of the characteristics cited above. Its chemical formula, crystal form, and any commercial uses also would be relevant.

Packing Specimens. Wrap each specimen in newspaper, secure the paper with masking tape, and place in a bag. Store the smallest specimens in plastic vials or the boxes adhesive bandages come in. Transport your finds in a knapsack.

CLEANING, STORAGE, DISPLAY

Cleaning. New specimens should be cleaned before being stored or displayed. Most can be washed with a fingernail brush or a toothbrush and soap. However, soft minerals like talc, gypsum and selenite cannot be washed. Gently remove whatever dirt you can with a short-bristled paintbrush.

Storage and Display. It is practical to store your first specimens in cigar boxes and shoe boxes. But as your collection grows in size and beauty, you may want to acquire better-looking, more efficient containers. The possibilities include compartmented specimen boxes, clear plastic boxes, glass-topped boxes, and Riker mounts for individual specimens. Some hobbyists display their prize items in bookcases with glass doors. To display fluorescent minerals, you will need a special unit incorporating ultraviolet light. It can be assembled in a home workshop by installing one or more argon bulbs in a housing. Various units are also available from a minerals dealer or a scientific supply house.

GEM STONES

Lapis is Latin for "stone." From it comes the term "lapidary." Mineral collectors who become lapidaries do not spend their time with just any stone, as suggested earlier. They seek only those minerals whose color and other qualities endow them with great beauty and whose hardness enables them to be cut efficiently. Some lapidaries collect their own gem stones, then grind and polish them. However, many become so intrigued with lapidary work, they give up collecting and buy the raw materials they need from other amateurs or from dealers. The polished stones they create may be displayed as they are or used in rings, bracelets, or other jewelry or may serve as lamp bases, bookends, or even tabletops. A number have used their hobby to establish a part-time business through which they sell the objects they make.

Getting Started. If possible, join a lapidary society or a mineralogical club with a lapidary section. Also do some reading. The books of John Sinkankas are the best in this field, with *Gem Stones and Minerals* and *Gem Cutting* of particular interest. *The Lapidary Journal* also is useful to the beginner. See the Bibliography.

Acquiring Gem Stones. A large proportion of the minerals capable of being cut and polished are members of the quartz and feldspar families. The varieties of quartz, for example, include amethyst, aventurine, chalcedony, citrine, rose quartz, and smoky quartz. In turn, chalcedony includes agate, carnelian, flint, and jasper. The western regions are the most fruitful sources of gem stones in the United States and Canada, but suitable minerals, including diamonds, are found in most areas. The field guides mentioned earlier can be of great help in locating good sites, as can the advice of an experienced amateur. If gem stones are purchased in the rough, their price ranges from a dollar to seven or eight dollars a pound. Rare stones are sold by the carat, gram, or ounce.

Cabochons and Facets. A cabochon is a gem stone which has

been ground into a particular shape and polished. A facet is a face cut in a gem stone. When several facets are cut, the brilliance of the stone is greatly enhanced. A beginner usually concentrates on cabochons, since preparing them requires less skill. Jasper, agates, and other translucent or opaque stones are used in this process. Ordinarily the stones are sawed into slabs, marked with the desired shape, then ground and polished.

A growing number of lapidaries assign much of the work of grinding and polishing to a tumbling device. They rough out a number of stones with a grinding and polishing wheel, or select those of the size they need, then place them in a rotating tumbler with an abrasive and water. As the tumbler rotates, the stones and the abrasives do the grinding on their own. At various points, progressively finer abrasives are used and ultimately a polishing agent is added. There is less work involved in this method, but there also is less of a challenge and the process takes longer. As much as a month may be involved.

The raw material of the faceter is a transparent stone as free as possible from flaws. Faceters may work with any one of dozens of minerals. However, few use diamonds, since it takes a great deal of time to cut them. The process involves shaping the stone, then cutting facets in its surface at angles dictated by its crystalline structure. The result can be a stone of fiery beauty. When a faceter has overcome all of the standard challenges, he may try his hand at materials which for various reasons have never been faceted.

Equipment. Lapidary equipment is costly. A moderately priced grinding and polishing unit with a slabbing saw might come to $250 or more. A tumbler might cost $200 or more. However, there is a secondhand market in such equipment. In addition, some lapidary societies own equipment their members can use.

BIBLIOGRAPHY
Rocks and Minerals

Books:

Dana's System of Mineralogy, 7th Edition, Edward S. Dana, John Wiley & Sons, New York, 1962. Advanced.

A Field Guide to Rocks and Minerals, F. H. Pough, Houghton Mifflin Co., Boston, 1953.

How to Know the Rocks and Minerals, Richard M. Pearl, McGraw-Hill
  Book Co., New York, 1955.
The Mineral Kingdom, Paul E. Desautels, Grosset & Dunlap, New
  York, 1968.
Mineralogy for Amateurs, John Sinkankas, Van Nostrand-Reinhold Co.,
  New York, 1964.
The Rock Book, Carroll and Mildred Fenton, Doubleday & Co., New
  York, 1956.
The Rock Hunter's Field Manual, D. K. Fritzen, Harper & Row, New
  York, 1959.
The Rock Hunter's Range Guide, Jay Ellis Ransom, Harper & Row,
  New York, 1962.
The Story of Rocks, Dorothy E. Shuttleworth, Doubleday & Co., New
  York, 1956. For children.

Periodicals:
The Canadian Rockhound, P.O. Box 194, Station "A," Vancouver 1,
  B.C., Canada. Monthly.
Earth Science, P.O. Box 550, Downers Grove, Illinois 60515. Monthly.
Gems and Minerals, P.O. Box 687, Mentone, California 92539. Monthly.
Rock and Minerals, P.O. Box 29, Peekskill, N.Y. 10566. Monthly.

Gem Stones
Books:
Gem Cutting, John Sinkankas, Van Nostrand-Reinhold Co., New York,
  1962.
Gem Hunter's Guide, Russell P. McFall, Thomas Y. Crowell Co., New
  York, 1963.
Gem Stones and Minerals, John Sinkankas, Van Nostrand-Reinhold Co.,
  1961.
Gem Stones of North America, John Sinkankas, Van Nostrand-Reinhold
  Co., 1959.

Periodicals:
Gems and Minerals. See above.
The Lapidary Journal, Box 2369, San Diego, California 92112. Monthly.
  A valuable "Buyer's Guide" is published each year.

21·SEA SHELLS

THE EXTRAORDINARY THING about shells is their variety. Some are as small as grains of sugar, others as large as bathtubs. They come in every conceivable color and tint and in combinations and brilliances of awesome beauty. They may be smooth, polished, ribbed, turreted, knobby, or spiny. Some are shaped like horns. Others look like balls, wings, spiral staircases, volcanoes, buttons, canoes, and cones. There is even one—the carrier shell—that changes its shape by adding other shells to its back.

In every case, a shell serves, or has served, as the protective external skeleton of a mollusk, one of the oldest, largest, and most curious of the animal families. Since the mollusk's first appearance 500 million years ago about 100,000 species have evolved. Their shells have served man as money, jewelry, sacred objects, badges of honor, and raw material for buttons. They also have inspired artists and fascinated legions of collectors.

Shells consist of a thin outer layer, a heavy middle layer, and a shiny inner layer. They are created from lime and a hardening agent secreted by a fleshy pad called a "mantle" which lines the inside of a shell. Their colorful patterns are the work of a pattern of pigment-producing cells that are part of the mantle.

Collectors seek out shells for all sorts of reasons. Their unusual variety and beauty are strong appeals. Some also become fascinated with the mollusks themselves: how they feed, function, grow, survive, and reproduce. There also is a chance through collecting to make a contribution to science since a great deal remains to be learned about mollusks and their shells. Of course, there also is the pleasure of carrying out one's search on a warm, sunny beach beside a lovely blue ocean.

KINDS OF SHELLS

There are five categories of shells. The most numerous and the most important are the gastropods, or univalves, and the pelecypods, or bivalves. The others are interesting, but there are far fewer of them. They are the amphineura, the cephalopoda, and the scaphopoda.

Gastropods. This group includes the great snail family: the conch, the periwinkle, the murex, the limpet, the whelk, and some 80,000 other varieties. They are called "gastropods," which is Greek for "belly foot," because they move about with the aid of a large saclike muscle that emerges from the bottom of the shell. They are called "univalves" because their shell consists of but one piece.

The gastropods inside the shells are rather peculiar looking. They have a head, eyes, feelers, and a mouth. The mouth is positioned either under the feelers or, if the gastropod is a meat eater, at the end of a long, flexible tubelike snout, the proboscis. The mouth is equipped with a thin elongated "tongue," called a "radula," which is covered with tiny sharp teeth. In addition, most gastropods have a retractable siphon which they use for breathing when they are under water. When a gastropod becomes frightened and withdraws into its shell, it retracts its siphon and closes the opening with a piece of shell attached to its foot, much as it might close a trap door. This is called an "operculum"; frequently it is as beautiful as a shell itself.

Most gastropods build their shells with the same architectural features. Ordinarily there is a central column, a columella, which extends the length of the shell. The shell coils around the column as a spiral staircase might. As the shell grows, new coils, or whorls, are added. Most gastropod shells are "right-handed." If you hold the shell with the opening toward you, the shell coils from left to right. An occasional variety coils in the opposite direction. However, there also are various limpets and a New England mollusk, the mandarin hat, that do not coil.

Some gastropods are vegetarians, but others, as noted above, are meat eaters. These freely attack other mollusks, including their own species. They either use their proboscis to force their way into a closed shell, gaining entrance through the operculum, or they "drill" a new entryway with drops of acid they secrete.

Gastropod shells found on North American beaches include the following families:

Abalone: This is a large ear-shaped shell with a multicolored pearllike lining. It also is known as a "sea ear," an "ear shell," an "aurora," and a "rainbow shell." Typically it is found on Pacific beaches.

Carrier: The carrier shell actually is shaped like a top. However, one would never know it without dismantling the accumulation of old shells it cements to its back as camouflage. The American carrier occurs off the southeast coast.

Conch: The heavy spiral-shaped queen conch has the largest shell in American waters. Some are over a foot in length. It is surmounted by a crown of spires. Its colors include pink, red, and white. Using its claw-like operculum as an aid, it jumps and leaps about rather than creeping as do other gastropods. Like many other conches, its habitat is the shallow waters off the south coast of Florida.

Cowrie: The shells of the cowries are highly polished and beautifully marked, often with a measleslike assortment of brown spots. The upper surface is rounded; the lower surface has a flattened appearance. The cowrie is found off both the Florida and Southern California coasts.

Cones: Some members of the cone family are cone-shaped, but others have a squat quality or spires. They occur in many colors, markings, and patterns. Because they are so lovely, they are exceedingly popular. However, a few live cones are poisonous. Cones are found in warmer waters.

Limpet: This gastropod looks a little like a dunce cap. It is found on virtually every beach, but its greens and grays make it somewhat difficult to spot among seaweed and rocks. Usually it is less than four inches long. One of the most interesting varieties is the keyhole limpet, which has an opening through which ocean currents may pass.

Murex: There are several varieties of this killer snail, all of which are found off the southeast coast. They include the spiny murex, which is pink; the brown and white murex; and the white lace murex.

Periwinkle: The conical shell of this small creature is frequently less than an inch long. It is found on rocky seashores between the high- and low-water marks on both the Atlantic and Pacific coasts. The common shore periwinkle, a European immigrant that occurs on the Eastern seaboard, ranges from brown to gray in color with brown or red spiral bands. "Periwinkle" is a corruption of "petty winkle" or small whelk.

Volute: This family is found in the Caribbean, the Gulf of Mexico, and the warmer waters of the East Coast. Its handsome shells are among the most difficult to find and therefore among the most sought after. Most volutes frequent deep waters and are brought to the surface by dredging or storm action. One of the rarest American shells is Juno's Volute or the Junonia, which may bring more than $250. It is a pink shell with rows of chocolate-colored spots that is found at times on the beaches of Sanibel Island off Florida's Gulf Coast.

Whelk: With their thick, knobby spiral shells, members of this family sometimes are mistaken for the conch. Like the conch, the whelk has a large shell and is a meat eater. It occurs along the Gulf Coast and the Atlantic Coast south of Cape Cod. The egg cases of the whelk—strings of pale, disc-shaped containers—are found frequently on beaches.

Pelecypods. This class of mollusks shares two characteristics. One is a hatchet-shaped foot which it uses for moving about and digging and from which its name derives. The other is the form of its shell. Every pelecypod has two half-shells or valves which it opens and closes with an adductor muscle. Thus, the term "bivalve." The animals inside these shells have soft round bodies without heads. Most of them lack eyes. The exception is the pecten, or scallop, whose mantle includes over a hundred sparkling blue eyes. Clams and mussels are equipped with a pair of siphons with which they breathe and eat. Other varieties use their mantles for this purpose.

Most members of this class are easy prey for their enemies. Although they quickly close their shells when disturbed, there is little else they can do. Mussels and oysters are sedentary creatures that spend their lives attached to rocks and pilings and move about very little. Some clams burrow in wet sand or mud. Only the pecten can swim away, which it does by opening and closing its valves with its powerful, and delicious, adductor muscle.

There are some 15,000 species of pelecypods. The principal varieties include the following:

Clams: Clams occur in virtually all waters. A hard-shell clam is found from Canada to Texas. In New England it is known by its Indian name "quahog"; in the South it is called a "round clam." It is also called a "hard clam." When it is young, it may be known as a "cherrystone" or a "littleneck." Indians used the shells of this clam as wampum. There is a soft-shell clam, or long clam, which is plentiful on the Pacific Coast. One of the most intriguing of the clams is the razor variety, which is shaped like a straight razor. It swims and burrows into the sand at astonishing speed and also leaps great distances, all in an effort to escape its enemies. It is found on both the Atlantic and Pacific coasts. The largest of the shellfish is a giant clam whose habitat is the South Pacific. When it is fully grown, its valves are three or four feet across and weigh 150 pounds each.

Mussels: The marine variety have small dark shells and are found on all coasts. They cluster in beds on rocks and on pilings and wharves, anchoring themselves with a byssus, a group of strong black threads they spin. Although mussels do move about, it is a complicated procedure. First they must cast off the existing byssus, then make their way to a new location with the aid of their hatchet-shaped foot, then reanchor themselves. The common shiny orange or yellow jingle shells are members of the mussel family. There also are fresh water mussels.

Oysters: Members of this family also are sedentary, attaching themselves with a byssus to rocks and other objects. The domestic varieties range in size up to six inches and are found on all coasts. The Delaware and Chesapeake bays and the waters around Long Island in New York have been famous sources of oysters. The pearl-bearing oyster is found primarily in warmer waters. This variety is lined with mother-of-pearl, or nacre, which frequently is used for buttons and other ornamentation. A pearl is formed when a grain of sand, a parasite, or some other object lodges inside the shell. To protect itself the oyster coats the intruder with layer after layer of nacre. Pearls also are produced by the abalones, fresh water mussels, conches, and hard-shell clams, but these have little or no value.

Pectens: Since one of its valves is scalloped, this bivalve is called a scallop. Pectens are found in many waters but are most common along the Atlantic coast. They may be black, brown, bright orange, or pink. In addition, some are marked with irregular streaks of color and others have a cross-hatching that resembles calico. The reddish lion's paw is among the most spectacular and desirable of the scallops.

Amphineura. The only members of this class are the chitons, small primitive creatures which have changed little since they first appeared. Their shell consists of eight overlapping plates held together with a kind of girdle. It frequently is called a coat-of-mail shell. Typically a chiton is grayish black with occasional streaks of white. The underside of its shell is white with streaks of aqua, blue, or pink. It lives under rocks and in crevices, clinging to its perch with such determination it may be necessary to use a knife or a chisel to remove one.

Cephalopoda. The octopus, the squid, and the cuttlefish all are members of this class, but they have outgrown the need for a shell. The only species which has not is the celebrated pearly or chambered

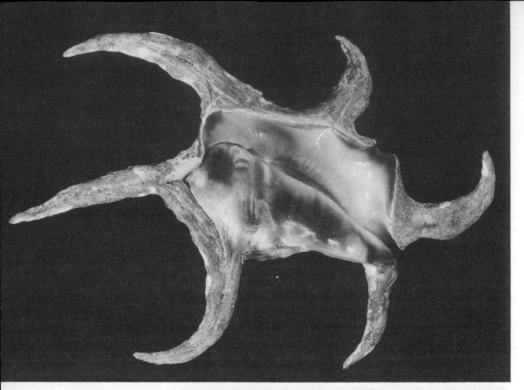

[ABOVE]
Spider Conch.

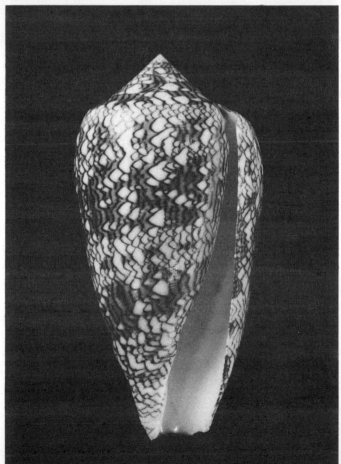

Cone.

266

Murex.

[BELOW]
Limpet.

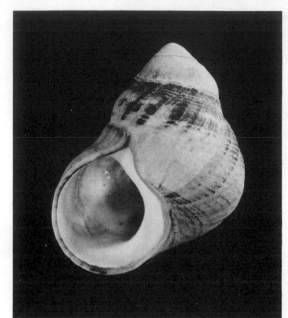

Periwinkle.

[BELOW] *Cowry.*

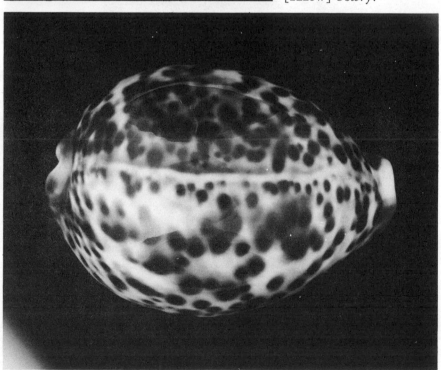

Pecten.

nautilus with its hundred arms and piercing eyes. The nautilus constructs a shell of many rooms. In a quiet period it occupies a large outer room. When trouble looms, it retreats to a smaller, less accessible chamber. It is found in the South Pacific and Indian oceans and in museums.

Scaphopoda. Members of this class occupy shells shaped somewhat like the tusk of an elephant. As a result, they are called "tusk" or "tooth" shells. Since the mollusk occupies only the lower portion, the shells are largely hollow. Ordinarily they are white and range in size from less than an inch to five inches. They are found buried in sand or mud with only the tip in view. Northwest Indians used tusk shells as wampum.

269

COLLECTING SHELLS

If they lie empty on the sands of a beach, shells are categorized as "dead." If they are occupied by a living mollusk, they are "alive." Since many dead shells are faded and broken, they serve best as learning materials which help the beginner increase his knowledge. Specimens worthy of collecting either are the freshly dead shells of mollusks that died just a short while before or those of mollusks taken alive and killed.

Where to Find Shells. An ocean beach offers many opportunities, particularly the zone between the high- and low-tide marks. In this area, explore the beach itself and any mud flats. Also look in seaweed, under driftwood and rocks, under wharves and pilings, and in tidal pools. Since there are mollusks underground, also look for the small mounds or holes that indicate where they might be. The protective coloration of a shell adds to the challenge. The primitive chitons look like the rocks to which they cling. Other shells look like lumps of sand. Many gastropods and pelecypods, moreover, are covered with a dark fibrous "skin" called a "periostracum" which makes them look like dirty pieces of sponge.

Exploring in the shallows also may be fruitful. With a glass-bottomed bucket or a fishscope you can extend your search into deeper water. Push the bucket ahead of you, peering into it as you move. The black interior walls sharply reduce the shadows and rippling effect, giving the water surprising clarity. Strong swimmers explore even farther from shore, using face masks and other underwater gear. For collecting in the water you also will need a container to hold your finds. Some amateurs rig an inflated inner tube with a bushel basket for this purpose. They then tie the tube to their waists with a long line.

Still others in search of pectens row through known pecten beds trailing a line behind them. When the line makes contact with a pecten, it snaps at it and hangs on. Occasionally collectors resort to dredging. They either rent a small dredge and attach it to a boat or engage a professional dredger who explores the ocean bottom in their behalf at a distance from shore.

When to Collect. Since collecting is unpredictable, you may have good fortune at any time. But generally the best conditions are at low tide, particularly after a storm. Most newspapers in coastal communities carry tide tables. In addition, a complete schedule for a particular area can be obtained from the United States National Ocean Survey, National Oceanic and Atmospheric Administration, Rockville, Maryland 20852. The habits of mollusks also should be taken into account in planning a field trip. Some species, like cowries, are most easily found at night, when they move about in search of food. There also are seasonal differences. In Florida, for example, the best periods for collecting shells are the winter and the spring. During the rest of the year many mollusks seek cooler waters.

EQUIPMENT

If you confine your activities to a beach, it will be useful to have at least some of the following equipment: a trowel, a small shovel, or a clam rake for digging; a pair of heavy gloves and a prying tool for overturning rocks; a sharp knife, a hammer, and a chisel for rock-clinging specimens; a non-rusting bucket for live specimens and the sea water they require; one or two smaller containers for smaller live specimens; a basket or a sack and newspaper for packing dead or freshly killed specimens. If you are collecting in the water, you also will need a pair of sneakers and the equipment mentioned earlier. In either case you should have a notebook, a pencil, and adhesive labels.

IDENTIFYING SHELLS

The best way to learn the shells is to work with a field guide. The best of these are *American Sea Shells* by R. Tucker Abbott and two guides by Percy A. Morris: *A Field Guide to the Shells of Our Atlantic and Gulf Coasts* and *A Field Guide to the Shells of the Pacific and Hawaii*. There are also a number of useful regional guides. All are listed in the Bibliography.

At times the popular name of a shell will be useful in identifying it. Thus, mandarin hat, turkey wing, and bleeding tooth look quite a bit like their names. On the other hand, a popular name can be a source of confusion. There is, for example, a sunrise tellin that also is known as a "sunrayed tellin" and a "rising sun shell." In addition, several different shells all are known as "star shells." A number of others are called "coffee bean shells." As a result, it is wise to learn a shell's Latin name. This usually consists of two or three words. The first is the genus. The second is the name of the shell. If there is a third, it provides infor-

271

mation on where the shell was found, who its discoverer was, or what it looks like.

If you have difficulty identifying a shell, the specialists at a natural history museum usually will be pleased to help you. But you should know where and when the specimen was found. They may be less co-operative if you arrive with a large number of specimens you need help with. On the other hand, a museum might be pleased to have part of a collection to assist in its research. Some advanced collectors regularly share their finds in this way.

PACKING AND TRANSPORTING SHELLS

Each specimen should be labeled with a small piece of numbered adhesive. The number should then be entered in a notebook with the following data: Latin and popular name of the shell, condition of the shell (dead, freshly dead, alive), other characteristics, name of the collector, date of the find, location of the find with any relevant landmarks.

Dead shells should be wrapped individually in newspaper. If the distance to your home is short, live shells should be transported in ocean water. If the distance is great, they should be cleaned soon after they are caught.

CLEANING SHELLS

Live Shells. Place the shells in a kettle of fresh water, slowly bring the water to a boil, and cook for several minutes. This will kill the mollusks and cause any pelecypods to open. Let the water cool. Then remove the bodies.

With the pelecypods this involves cutting the flesh away without scratching the shell. If the valves are to be displayed separately, also cut the muscle that holds them. If they are to be displayed together, place a drop or two of glycerin on the muscle to keep it pliant.

With gastropods the procedure is more complicated. First cut off the operculum, glue it to a tuft of absorbent cotton, and set it aside. Then insert a crochet hook inside the shell, embed it in the animal, twist slowly in the direction of the shell, and pull gently. If part of the body remains behind, soak the shell in fresh water for several days, changing the water each day. When the remains finally decay, flush them out with a vigorous stream of water. Some gastropods will be too small to accept a hook. These should be soaked in fresh water as described above or stored in formaldehyde. The shells that have been soaked should be dried out of doors in a cool shaded location. Then insert the operculum and wipe the shell with mineral oil.

Surfaces. Use the following procedures to clean the surface of a shell.

Algae: Place in fresh water and scrub with a toothbrush.

Barnacles: Soak in a 10 per cent bleach solution for a week.

Periostracum: Place in fresh water and scrub with a toothbrush. If this is not successful, soak for a day in a 15 per cent bleach solution. Some collectors prefer to keep the periostracum, since it reflects the natural condition of the shell. A number try to obtain two specimens: one with a periostracum and one without.

After you have cleaned a shell, wipe it with mineral oil.

EXCHANGING SHELLS

There are shell collectors throughout the world who are interested in exchanging shells from their areas for shells from yours. A directory listed in the Bibliography contains the names of many. You will learn of others in your collecting forays, at club meetings and conventions, and from museum scientists. In arranging for an exchange, describe your shells as accurately as possible, or you may have them returned. Provide their Latin names, describe their condition, and indicate if they were taken alive or freshly dead, if they are hinged, if they have operculums, and so on.

BUYING SHELLS

It is best to shape the dimensions of your collection with your own material before buying shells. If you cannot find a particular shell or it is impractical to travel a great distance to obtain it, there are dealers in many cities. *Van Nostrand's Standard Catalog of Shells* provides a list of such merchants and a guide to shell values.

STORING SHELLS

Collectors arrange their shells by regions or by families. In storing shells, consider the suggestions for storing fossils (Chapter 17)

273

and rocks and minerals (Chapter 20). However, keep your specimens out of sunlight or their color may fade.

ORGANIZATIONS
There are a growing number of shell clubs, many of which are associated with natural history museums. For a current list, write: Mrs. Marion Hubbard, Secretary, American Malacological Society, 3957 Marlow Court, Seaford, N.Y. 11783.*

BIBLIOGRAPHY
Introductions
Collecting Sea Shells, Kathleen Y. Johnstone, Grosset & Dunlap, New York, 1969.
Introducing Sea Shells, R. Tucker Abbott, Van Nostrand-Reinhold Co., New York, 1955.
Sea Treasure, Kathleen Y. Johnstone, Houghton Mifflin Co., Boston, 1957.

Field Guides
American Sea Shells, R. Tucker Abbott, Van Nostrand-Reinhold Co., New York, 1955.
Canadian Atlantic Shells, E. L. Bousfield, National Museum of Canada, Ottawa, 1960.
Field Book of Seashore Life, R. W. Miner, G. P. Putnam's Sons, New York, 1950.
A Field Guide to the Shells of Our Atlantic and Gulf Coasts, Percy A. Morris, Houghton Mifflin Co., Boston, 1951.
A Field Guide to the Shells of the Pacific and Hawaii, Percy A. Morris, Houghton Mifflin Co., Boston, 1966.
Florida Marine Shells, Curtis N. Vilas and N. R. Vilas, Bobbs-Merrill Co., Indianapolis, 1952.
The Sea-Beach at Ebb-Tide, Augusta F. Arnold, Dover Publications, Inc., New York, 1949.

* The secretary of this organization changes every three years, but mail is forwarded.

274

Seashells of Tropical West America, Myra Keen, Stanford University Press, Palo Alto, 1958.

Sea Shells of the World, R. Tucker Abbott, Golden Press, New York, 1962.

The Shell Book, Julia E. Rogers, Charles T. Branford Co., Boston, 1960. An updated reprint of a 1908 edition.

Shells of the New York City Area, W. K. Emerson and M. K. Jacobson, Citadel Press, New York, 1961.

Van Nostrand's Standard Catalog of Shells, R. Tucker Abbott and R. J. L. Wagner, Van Nostrand-Reinhold Co., New York, 1967.

West Coast Shells, Josiah Keep and J. L. Bailey, Jr., Stanford University Press, Palo Alto, 1935.

General

The Edge of the Sea, Rachel Carson, Houghton Mifflin Co., Boston, 1955.

How to Collect Shells, a symposium, American Malacological Union, Route 2, P.O. Box 318, Marinette, Wisconsin 54143. $2. Order direct.

The Romance of Shells in Nature and Art, L. A. Travers, M. Barrows Co., New York, 1962.

The Sea Around Us, Rachel Carson, Oxford University Press, New York, 1951.

Shell Collecting, an Illustrated History, S. Peter Dance, University of California Press, Berkeley, 1966.

The Shells: Five Hundred Million Years of Inspired Design, R. Tucker Abbott, Hugh and Margaret Stix, Harry N. Abrams, Inc., New York, 1968.

Skin and Scuba Diving, The Athletic Institute, Merchandise Mart, Room 805, Chicago, Illinois 60654. 50 cents. Order direct.

Booklets

Sources of Information on Mollusks, Division of Mollusks, Museum of Natural History, Smithsonian Institution, Washington, D.C. 20560. Free.

Books for Young People

The Adventure Book of Shells, Eva K. Evans, Capitol Publishing Co., Irvington, N.Y., 1955.

275

Beginner's Guide to Seashore Life, L. A. Hausman, G. P. Putnam's Sons, New York, 1949.

Sea Shells, Ruth H. Dudley, Thomas Y. Crowell Co., New York, 1953.

Seashores, Herbert S. Zim and Lester Ingle, Simon & Schuster, New York, 1955.

PART IV

SCIENCE AND COMMUNI- CATION

ARCHAEOLOGY
ASTRONOMY
RADIO
WEATHER FORECASTING

22·ARCHAEOLOGY

AN ARTIFACT is evidence of a previous civilization. However, only when it is studied in the context in which it is found does it become meaningful. In fact, the story of a site only can emerge when it is systematically excavated and mapped and exhaustive records are compiled. Even this work does not become fully useful until it is interpreted and then published in a professional journal for other archaeologists to share. A person who merely digs for souvenirs he displays in his living room or stores in a box in his basement and who does not keep records or inform others of his work literally destroys part of the past.

"Pot hunter" is a term professional archaeologists use for the amateur whose interest in archaeology is limited to arrowheads and other souvenirs he can find. If a pot hunter is fortunate enough to find a fruitful site, he keeps the information to himself for fear that someone else might take "his" artifacts. If such a person were told he is irresponsible, he probably would be offended. Yet at times the charge is justifiable.

There are amateurs, however, who are helping to preserve the past. In a few cases they have acquired the knowledge and expertise to do so on their own. More typically they pursue their interest through amateur archaeological societies. Such groups usually are associated with a history or a natural history museum or have an informal relationship with a professional archaeologist who guides them.

Usually they explore sites that were occupied by prehistoric Indians or early settlers. When this was written, one society in my state was excavating the foundations of a fort used during the Revolutionary War. Another was attempting to unearth an ancient Indian settlement in the outskirts of a nearby city. In addition to excavating, members of these groups clean, restore, and catalog the artifacts they find, prepare reports for publication, develop displays, talk to school children about their activities, and hunt for new sites.

Most amateurs start with little knowledge of archaeology. They learn the basic techniques from advanced amateurs and professionals and through reading. However, all beginners know how to dig. Moreover, some have other skills a society can use, such as the ability to survey a site, create a map, make photographs or drawings, or write reports.

FINDING SITES

In many sections, finding sites to excavate is not too difficult. At times there are traditional well-established sites to which amateurs turn. In addition, a government agency, a museum, or a university often will have done research on prehistoric Indian sites or obscure historical sites and will have published a description of at least their general location. In such cases the task for the members of an amateur society comes down to finding a precise location in which to excavate. Typically they first explore the area delineated in the research for streams or other bodies of water, since it is in such locations that settlements usually occur. They then look for plowed fields nearby, since these are relatively easy places to spot chips from the stones Indians converted to spear points, knife blades, and other implements. The chips, in turn, may indicate the remains of a settlement below.

Where there has been no research, a society must do its own to determine who the early peoples in the area were, what they were like, and where they might have lived. If the interest is in prehistoric Indians, a search will be based at least in part on inference drawn from previous experience. Tribes in the hunting and gathering stage of development, for example, would seek a source of fish, game, and berries in deciding where to settle. Typically they selected a wooded area along a watercourse. The point at which a stream entered a lake or a river was a favorite location. If they were in the agricultural stage, fertile reasonably level terrain also was an important consideration.

In searching out such features, sophisticated amateurs often study topographical maps, then obtain permission to examine promising locations. Typically they also check with farmers in the area to determine if they have turned up artifacts with their plows. Unearthing evidence of early colonial settlements may be less of a challenge. In such cases there may be documents, records, and even maps at local historical societies on which to base a search.

EXCAVATING A SITE

If permission to excavate a site can be obtained, test pits are dug. If the results are promising, the site is divided into a grid of five-foot squares. Each is staked and numbered and assigned to a member of the excavation team. His principal tools usually are a trowel and a probe. Working with great care, he digs down six inches at a time. If he makes contact with a solid object, he gently removes the surrounding soil with a paintbrush. If it turns out to be an artifact, he probes gently to determine if there is anything else nearby. If an Indian site is involved, he might find, along with arrowheads and spear points, hammerstones, pestles, ax heads, thumb scrapers, net sinkers (for fishing), and pots of stone or clay. Fragments of pottery are called shards. In dry climates artifacts also may include baskets and other objects woven from vegetable matter. At times animal bones or human skeletons are uncovered.

Frequently an excavator will encounter "features" before he finds artifacts. A feature might be the remains of a hearth or a rubbish pit, which would be indicated by a round or rectangular patch of dark soil. This, in turn, might be a source of artifacts. Post molds are another common feature. These are small dark, round sections of soil which are the rotted remains of wooden posts that served as fences or supports for tents or lodges. By plotting the features and artifacts found at a particu-

AMERICAN INDIAN ARTIFACTS

pottery shards.

Small spearhead of flint or jasper.

Stone ax head.

Fish net sinkers.

lar level, a picture of the settlement begins to emerge. Each level may be photographed with the remains in place. The artifacts from a particular square and level then are assigned a field number and stored in a bag. The type of artifact and the color of the soil in which it is found indicate the age of a site. To make certain that small artifacts are not overlooked, the soil is put through a strainer as it is removed.

Excavators typically dig down 30 to 36 inches before leaving a pit. Occasionally they find artifacts 5000 years old or more at this level. On the other hand, they may find nothing. In either case, all the soil is then replaced.

ORGANIZATIONS
For information on any amateur groups in your area, contact a state or provincial museum, a historical society, or the anthropology department of a university. If you live in eastern United States or Canada, another source of information is the Eastern States Archaeological Federation, c/o New Jersey State Museum, Trenton, N.J. 08625. If there are no archaeological societies nearby, there is always the possibility of organizing one. In such cases a museum or historical society might be helpful.

BIBLIOGRAPHY
Handbooks

The Amateur Archaeologist's Handbook, Maurice Robbins, Mary B. Irving, Thomas Y. Crowell Co., New York, 1965.

Archaeological Techniques for Amateurs, Philip C. Hammond, Van Nostrand-Reinhold Co., New York, 1963.

Beginning in Archaeology, Kathleen M. Kenyon, Frederick A. Praeger, New York, 1961.

History Under the Sea: A Manual for Underwater Exploration, Mendel Peterson, Smithsonian Institution Press, Washington, D.C., 1969.

Regional Studies

Archaeology of the Eastern United States, James B. Griffin, editor, University of Chicago Press, Chicago, 1952.

Introduction to the Study of Southwestern Archaeology, Alfred V. Kidder, Yale University Press, New Haven, 1962.

Prehistoric Man on the Great Plains, Waldo R. Wedel, University of Oklahoma Press, Norman, 1961.

General

Ancient Man in North America, W. H. Wormington, Denver Museum of Natural History, Denver, 1957.

Historical Archaeology, Ivor Noel Hume, Alfred Knopf, New York, 1968.

23·ASTRONOMY

MOST OF US ARE astronomers at heart. On a clear night we look up in wonder at a universe so vast and beautiful it seems impossible to comprehend. To explore the sky, however, is even more interesting.

GETTING STARTED

Read two books at the outset. One is a paperback, *The New Handbook of the Heavens*, which probably is the best of the many introductions to astronomy. The other is a children's book, *The Constellations*. Both are listed in the Bibliography. To identify stars, you also will need a star wheel or a set of seasonal star maps. If the moon fascinates you, also buy a moon map. All these materials can be purchased at low cost at a science museum or planetarium or from a scientific supply house.

Also join an astronomy club. One of the major advantages of a membership is that it enables you to learn faster. Large clubs frequently are divided into sections which reflect a member's experience or interests. For example, some groups may specialize in lunar or solar observations; others may be concerned with comets or planets or the craft of telescope making. Most clubs also offer a continuing series of lectures on astronomy. To find a club, inquire at the nearest science museum or planetarium. Also consider taking a course in astronomy. These are offered from time to time at YMCA's and at the evening adult schools many communities sponsor.

EQUIPMENT

Binoculars. If you own a pair of binoculars, initially use these for stargazing. A seven-power instrument will provide surprisingly good views of the moon. It also will enable you to resolve, or examine individually, tightly grouped stars like the famous cluster the Pleiades. If you have a more powerful instrument, mount it on a tripod. Its higher magnification produces a smaller field of vision, and the slightest movement would cause you to lose sight of an object.

Telescopes. A beginner often wastes his money by spending too little for a telescope. He acquires a poor lens, an unstable mount, or both, with the result that the equipment is difficult and frustrating to use. Ultimately he deposits it in a closet, where it languishes along with his interest in astronomy. To obtain a satisfactory telescope, it is necessary to spend at least $60. There are two types to consider: a refractor and a reflector. Both gather the light reflected from a distant object, bring it to a focus, then magnify it.

The refractor is in effect an oversize spyglass. It gathers light with a complicated double convex lens which is at the "sky end" of the tube. The light then travels to another lens at the viewing end, where it is magnified. The reflector uses an aluminum-coated mirror to gather light. However, the mirror is at the bottom of an open tube. It reflects the light it receives to a small mirror set at a 45-degree angle near the top of the tube. The mirror in turn directs the light to a lens, or eyepiece, through which the viewer peers. The larger the convex lens or mirror, the more light it gathers and the more detail it provides. In the language of the astronomer, a light-gathering lens or a mirror is an "objective." The diameter of the objective determines the size of the telescope.

The refractor's big disadvantage is its cost. If one were to invest the same amount of money in a reflector, he would obtain a considerably larger light-gathering surface. A satisfactory two-inch refractor, for example, costs about $75. A three-inch reflector of similar quality costs about $60. The reason is that a refractor requires an objective made from high quality optical glass. The reflector's mirror, on the other hand, is a relatively inexpensive item.

Despite the higher cost, amateurs and dealers I interviewed recommended a two-inch refractor as a first telescope. They base this on several considerations. A refractor is easier to handle than a reflector. In looking through a refractor, a viewer faces what he is observing. With a reflector, he points his instrument in the right direction, then looks down into it. A refractor also is a sturdier instrument, an important consideration if children are involved. It also is somewhat more compact and therefore easier to carry about.

Power: The amount of magnification a telescope provides is described in terms of its power. A telescope with a power of 25, for example, brings an object twenty-five times closer to a viewer than it actually is. In their advertising, manufacturers place great stress on the power their telescopes achieve, but this can be misleading. For general viewing a power of 25 to 40 often is sufficient. In fact, too much magnification interferes with good viewing. For special purposes and differing atmospheric conditions, two higher degrees of magnification also are needed. These usually are in the range of 60 to 120 and 180 to 240. They are achieved through the use of interchangeable eyepieces. Ordinarily a telescope can make use, for different purposes, of a power of 50 to 60 per inch. Thus, a 4-inch model could handle a magnification of up to 240.

Mounts. A proper mount permits a telescope to move effortlessly in any direction. This ability is of particular importance in tracking stars. Since the earth is in constant motion, a star will rapidly drift out of your field of vision unless you move the telescope to keep up with it. Stability also is essential in a mount. The cheapest telescopes often are equipped with a pillar and claw mount, which provides movement from side to side and up and down but is hard to operate efficiently. An azimuth-type mount is more satisfactory. Its movement is similar to that of the pillar and claw but is more responsive. Advanced amateurs may rely on a more costly equatorial mount, which requires one instead of two motions for tracking stars. This characteristic makes it ideal for taking photographs through a telescope. For most photography, however, a mount should include a small clock drive. This device makes it possible to automatically track a star or other object for the long periods of exposure ordinarily required.

Buying a Telescope. Scientific supply houses, camera stores, optical centers, hobby shops, and department stores sell telescopes. A few manufacturers also sell them by mail. The leading brands include Unitron and Pasco for refractors, and Dynascope for reflectors. Be certain a manufacturer or a dealer clearly states the limits of a telescope's performance in terms of what you can and cannot see. Also be sure to obtain a guarantee. There also is a market in secondhand equipment. The Star Gazers Exchange in the magazine *Sky and Telescope* is one source of leads. Members of an astronomy club may be another. After you have acquired your equipment, have an expert check it. Members of the teaching staff at a planetarium sometimes provide this service. A friendly amateur may be willing to help.

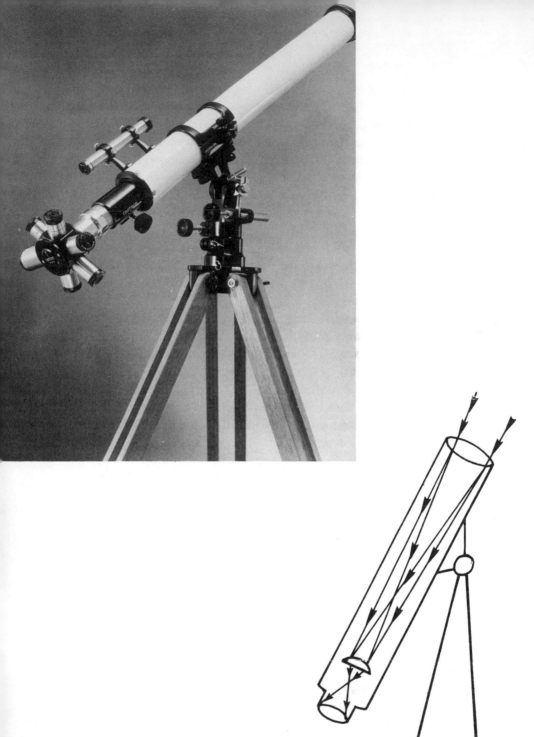

Refracting telescope.

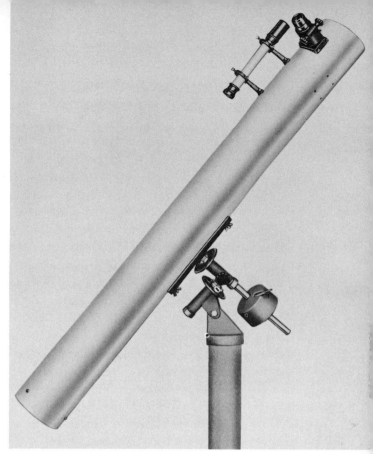

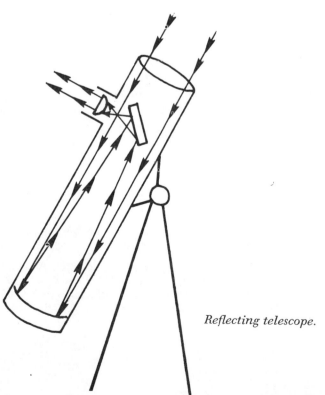

Reflecting telescope.

USING A TELESCOPE

The most practical time to learn the basic techniques is during the day. First learn how to move a telescope. Next master the technique of capturing an object in the small finder scope on top, then shifting to the telescope itself for a detailed view. Focus on trees, buildings, cars, and signs. But don't look in anybody's window. Even though what you see will be upside down, your neighbor might call the police.

When you have learned how to operate your instrument and have studied a star wheel or a map, practice at night. Set up your telescope in the darkest place you can find. Bring along your map and a flashlight with a red bulb with which to read it. Then wait until your eyes adjust to the dark, a process that usually takes about 20 minutes, and begin your explorations.

In selecting an eyepiece of the appropriate power, take into account the kind of observation involved. Under normal conditions a low-power unit is most effective in examining clusters of stars, individual stars, and the moon. In addition, a mid-power unit is most useful for planetary observation and when more detail is desired in lunar observations.

How well you see, however, depends on several factors. One is the clarity of the atmosphere. If there is haze or smoke, this will, of course, reduce the light from a celestial body and make it more difficult to see. Under such circumstances it may be helpful to use an eyepiece with a higher magnification. Start with the lowest power and increase it until distortion occurs. Another factor is the quality of the "scene," a term that refers to the steadiness of the atmosphere. Frequently atmospheric conditions create turbulence in the air, which in turn bends and refracts the light so that stars and other objects seem to boil, shimmer, or twinkle. In such cases reduce the power of the telescope; otherwise, the distortion is magnified.

EXPLORING THE SKY

With a telescope of the type recommended you will be able to see stars as dim as those of the fifth magnitude.* You will also be able

---

* Those of the first magnitude are 2½ times brighter than those of the second, which are 2½ times brighter than those of the third, and so on. The bowl of the Little Dipper offers a sense of the differences. Each of its four stars is of a different magnitude, ranging from the second to the fifth.

to see double stars that appear to the unaided eye like single stars, variable stars whose brightness regularly varies, open clusters such as the Pleiades, and luminous clouds of gas called "nebula." In addition, there are four planets that readily can be observed (Jupiter, Saturn, Venus, and Mars), and there are comets and meteors to study and artificial satellites to track. Ultimately many amateurs specialize in one aspect of astronomy. But at the beginning it is wise to simply explore. However, do not expect to see objects in the spectacular detail you find in published photographs. These usually are made at observatories and are the product of fine equipment, long exposures, and expert enlargement.

It is logical to concentrate first on the constellations and related stars, since they will be useful in finding your way around the sky. Then turn to the moon and the planets and finally to more distant bodies. As noted earlier, it is necessary to use a star wheel or star map as a guide. Bear in mind that, because of the rotation of the earth, there are continuing changes in the apparent position of celestial bodies and that not all are visible at all times. The maps take these changes into account.

In your first observations pay particular attention to the polar constellations. These seem to circle continuously in a counterclockwise motion around Polaris, the North Star. In the northern hemisphere they are in view throughout the year. At the North Pole Polaris is directly overhead. In southern Canada and the northern regions of the United States it is halfway up in the sky. As one proceeds still farther south, it drops still closer to the horizon. Polaris is part of the constellation Ursa Minor, the Little Bear, which includes the Little Dipper. It is the star at the end of the handle. However, to find Polaris, look first for the Big Dipper. The two stars that form the outside of its bowl are Merak and Duhbe, the Pointers. Continue for five lengths beyond the line they form and you will come to Polaris.

En route you will encounter the tip of the tail of Draco the Dragon. Beyond Polaris you will find Cepheus, a constellation which represents a mythical king of Ethiopia. Nearby is Cassiopeia, which represents Cepheus' wife. Depending on the season, it forms a "W" or an "M." Also nearby is the constellation Andromeda, named for the daughter of Cassiopeia and Cepheus, who was rescued from a hungry monster by Perseus, who, of course, married her. The constellation Pegasus, representing a mythological flying horse, also is in this area.

In the southern sky you will find the zodiac, a belt of 12 constellations which seemingly are clustered along the path of the sun. The four planets visible through your telescope also are in this region.

Of course, each constellation represents a vast section of the sky and includes many more stars than the few we perceive as a winged horse, a dragon, or a dipper. Its brightest stars are indicated on a map by the Greek letter alpha, the second brightest by the letter beta, and so on.

By learning the constellations and their relative positions, you readily can move from one section of the sky to another. In the same way you can move within a constellation from one star to another. This sometimes is called "star hopping." There also are more precise and more complex methods of finding your way which you may use as you grow more experienced. Standard handbooks describe these techniques.

Solar Observation. Observing sun spots also is highly interesting, but it involves a potential hazard and a need for special equipment. If you attempt to examine the sun directly through your telescope, the magnified light will seriously injure your viewing eye. Therefore, it is essential to equip your instrument with either a Herschel wedge, which eliminates all but a small portion of the light, or a small screen on which the sun's image is projected as it emerges from the lens. A variety of filters also are available, but most are susceptible to cracking and therefore may not be completely safe.

Photography. There also are exciting opportunities for amateur photographers who wish to photograph celestial bodies. Basic techniques are discussed in the general handbooks on astronomy. For a more detailed introduction, consult *Outer Space Photography for the Amateur*, which is listed in the Bibliography.

MAKING TELESCOPES

Good telescopes are expensive. With patience and the appropriate guidance, however, an amateur can make a fine reflecting telescope for a relatively small investment. There are several books that describe the techniques. In addition, planetariums and clubs frequently offer courses in telescope making. Anyone over 14 may enroll in the course offered at the Franklin Institute in Philadelphia. The student purchases a glass blank and the material needed to convert it into a light-gathering mirror. Then under guidance he grinds his mirror by hand, a process which may take from 20 to 80 hours, depending on how fast he works. If a mechanical grinder is available, less time would be required. When the mirror is ready, a housing, a mounting, and other equipment are purchased. The telescope that results costs $60 or $70 and may compare favorably with a commercial model that sells for five times that amount.

RESEARCH

A number of professional societies rely on amateurs to gather data for ongoing research projects. For information write to the following organizations:

American Meteor Society, 521 N. Wynnewood Avenue, Narbeth, Pennsylvania 19072.

Association of Lunar and Planetary Observers, Box A.Z., University Park, N.M. 88070.

Association of Variable Star Observers, 4 Brattle Street, Cambridge, Massachusetts 02138.

BIBLIOGRAPHY

Guide Books

Earth, Moon, and Planets, Fred L. Shipple, Harvard University Press, Cambridge, 1963.

Field Book of the Skies, William T. Olcott, G. P. Putnam's Sons, New York, 1959.

A Field Guide to the Stars and Planets, Donald H. Menzel, Houghton Mifflin Co., Boston, 1963.

Golden Book of Astronomy, Rose Wyler, G. Ames, Golden Press, New York, 1959.

New Handbook of the Heavens, Hubert J. Bernhard et al., McGraw-Hill Book Co., New York, 1941. Also available in a Signet paperback edition.

Stars, Herbert S. Zim, Robert H. Baker, Golden Press, New York, 1951.

Books on Telescopes, Binoculars

Amateur Astronomer and His Telescope, Gunther D. Roth, Van Nostrand-Reinhold Co., New York, 1963.

Amateur Telescope Making, Book I, Albert G. Ingalls, editor, Scientific American, New York, 1957. Books II, III are for advanced amateurs.

Exploring the Moon Through Binoculars, E. H. Cherrington, Jr., Mc-Graw-Hill Book Co., New York, 1969.

How to Use Your Telescope, Sam Brown, Edmund Scientific Co., Barrington, N.J. 08007. Order direct. An excellent introduction.

Outer Space Photography for the Amateur, Henry E. Paul, Chilton Co., Philadelphia, 1967.

Seasonal Star Charts, James S. Sweeney, Jr., Hubbard Scientific Co., Northbrook, Ill., 1962.

Books for Young People

Experiments in Sky Watching, Franklyn M. Branley, Thomas Y. Crowell Co., New York, 1959.

Find the Constellations, H. A. Rey, Houghton Mifflin Co., Boston, 1954.

The Stars, H. A. Rey, Houghton Mifflin Co., Boston, 1967.

The Stars, a New Way to See Them, H. A. Rey, Houghton Mifflin Co., Boston, 1962.

Catalogs

Edmund Scientific Co., Barrington, N.J. 08007. Telescopes, other astronomical equipment, books. Free.

Sky Publishing Corp., 49-51 Bay State Road, Cambridge, Massachusetts 02138. Star atlases, moon and sky maps, observation aids, books. Free.

Periodical

Sky and Telescope, 49-51 Bay State Road, Cambridge, Massachusetts 02138. Monthly.

24·RADIO

THERE ARE SOME 300,000 amateur radio operators in the United States and Canada. Elsewhere there are perhaps 100,000 more. Together they make up the fraternity of the "ham," a group with a special language and code of behavior and a deep commitment to public service.* In the United States, Canada, and many other countries, amateur radio is the only hobby licensed and regulated by the government. It also is regulated by treaty, the International Telecommunications Convention, which 80 nations have signed.

One of the great appeals of "hamming" is the opportunity to talk, using Morse code or one's own natural voice, to persons all over the world. In fact, when a ham announces with his CQ signal that he would like to chew the rag, he never knows who will answer. Hams also derive great pleasure from their equipment, even those who were not technically oriented to start. It is possible to acquire a basic transmitter and receiver for relatively little. Yet many amateurs spend large sums of money in developing rigs of exquisite complexity and sensitivity. A good number also spend much of their free time attempting to improve their equipment. As one ham explained, hamming is an infection.

The infection dates to 1895, when the Italian physicist Guglielmo Marconi managed to send a telegraphic signal without wires. It traveled somewhat over a mile. Six years later in St. Johns, Newfoundland, he received the first transatlantic signal sent by radio. It was the letter "S" transmitted from his research station in Cornwall, England. With Marconi's work as their inspiration, the first amateur radio operators began to appear.

---

* No one is certain how the term "ham" originated or precisely what it means. One theory is that it derives from "ham-fisted amateur," which reflected the feelings of the professional telegrapher years ago. Another is that it is a cockney English corruption of amateur.

In those first years they used the long waves.* With the growing needs of commercial broadcasters, maritime operators, and the military, the amateurs soon were restricted by the government to the higher frequencies and shorter waves. Perhaps "banished" is a better word, for it had been demonstrated mathematically that the short waves were worthless for communication. But a decade of experimentation by amateur operators showed that this was incorrect. In 1923 a group of hams succeeded in sending a message across the Atlantic on a short-wave length of 110 meters. In the years that followed, they succeeded in using still shorter waves. The government eventually reserved these for other purposes, but in recognition of their accomplishment American hams were assigned segments of a number of wave lengths for their exclusive use.

Hams have continued to experiment. In recent years they have bounced radio signals off the moon and have tracked artificial satellites. They also have made use of communications satellites which they designed and built and which the U.S. Air Force placed in orbit. When this was written, there were four such satellites aloft. They share the name OSCAR, for Orbiting Satellite Carrying Amateur Radio.

Although a number of hams are persons with technical training, many have none. However, the idea of communicating by radio fascinates them. Boys and girls as young as 8 have become ham operators. So have handicapped persons, blind persons, and men and women in their eighties. At times members of a family jointly operate a ham station. In fact, it is not unlikely that a ham lives in your neighborhood. In doing the research for this chapter, I found two that lived within a few blocks of my home.

Persons with citizen-band radios, however, are not ham operators. Theirs is low-power equipment designed for the exchange of brief messages over short distances. Although a citizen-band operator must be licensed, he does not need specialized knowledge or technical skill. To become an amateur radio operator, on the other hand, one must pass a series of examinations and undergo a period of apprenticeship.

---

* Sound is transmitted over electromagnetic waves. These compose a spectrum ranging from long waves with low frequencies to short waves with high frequencies. Commercial broadcasting in the United States and Canada is done in the low frequencies, ranging from 550 to 1600 kilocycles. Those frequencies above 1600 kilocycles, or the short waves, are used primarily for long-distance communication.

GETTING STARTED

The wisest first step is to determine just how interested you are. It would be helpful to read the set of introductory booklets published by the American Radio Relay League, the major organization of radio amateurs. These are listed in the Bibliography. If your library doesn't have them, they can be purchased at a radio equipment store or directly from the league. It also would be useful to talk with a ham radio operator and attend a meeting of a local radio club. If you have difficulty finding an operator or a club, the league should be able to help. Its address is Newington, Connecticut 06111.

BASIC EQUIPMENT

The next step is to acquire a receiver with which you can monitor amateur transmissions. In listening in, you become what the hams call an SWL, a short-wave listener. Aside from the fascinating party line it offers, a receiver is useful at this stage for two reasons. It provides an introduction to the operating procedures hams use. It also offers an opportunity to practice Morse code, which is one of the licensing requirements. This is discussed below.

There are two kinds of receivers. One picks up only ham transmissions. The other provides broader coverage, including most of the ham bands, fire, police, marine, and airline communication, and standard domestic and foreign broadcast bands. This type is not as sensitive, or selective, as a ham receiver, but it may be a more practical investment. If you get your license, you can trade it for a specialized piece of equipment. If hamming loses its appeal, it can serve as a general radio.

A satisfactory receiver costs upwards of $100. You can save money, and also learn a good deal, by building a receiver from a commercially prepared kit. You can save even more by making one with parts you buy separately. The Relay League publication *How to Become a Radio Amateur* has directions for a simple three-transistor receiver which is assembled in this way. Secondhand receivers and surplus military equipment also are available. But in buying such items, rely on the guidance of an experienced person. Be sure that the instruction book originally provided with the equipment is available. With military equipment, determine if modifications are required before it can be used in your home. Frequently the power supply must be altered.

You also will need two other pieces of equipment. One is a headset which makes it possible to pick up signals more clearly and with greater privacy. The other is an antenna. Ultimately you might decide to spend several hundred dollars for one. At the outset, however, all you need is a length of antenna wire, which should be hung out a window, hooked to a downspout, or extended between a house and a tree. Established amateurs convert a room or part of a basement into a radio shack. Initially a sturdy table and a quiet corner should suffice.

After you have worked with a receiver for several months, consider assembling a simple transmitter. You won't be able to use it until you obtain a license, but putting it together will help prepare you for the questions relating to apparatus in the licensing examinations. The booklet *How to Become a Radio Amateur* includes directions for making a basic two-tube transmitter.

Local radio equipment dealers are listed in the classified sections of your telephone directory. An experienced amateur can tell you which are the most reliable. There also are a number of regional and national chains to consider. These issue free catalogs which can be used in ordering equipment and supplies by mail. They include the following:

Allied Radio, 100 Northwestern Avenue, Chicago, Illinois 60680.
Heath Company, Benton Harbor, Michigan 49022.
Lafayette Radio Electronics, 111 Jericho Turnpike, Syosset, N.Y. 11791.
Radio Shack, 730 Commonwealth Avenue, Boston, Massachusetts 02215.
World Radio Laboratories, Inc., 3415 West Broadway, Council Bluffs, Iowa 51501.

OBTAINING A LICENSE

United States. Amateur radio is regulated by the Federal Communications Commission (FCC) in Washington, D.C. There are six different classes of operation with distinct privileges and restrictions. Each requires a license obtained through an examination. There are no restrictions as to the age of an applicant. The classes are as follows:

Novice. For beginners.
General. For established amateurs.

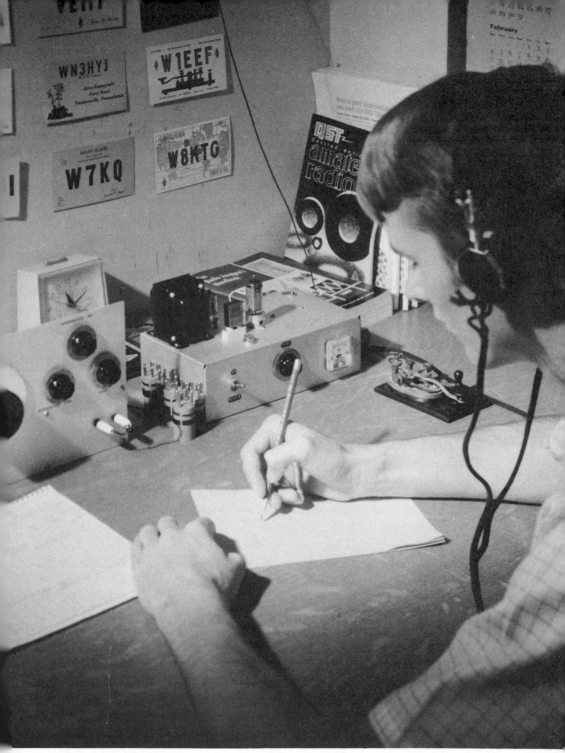

A simple radio shack.

Advanced. For advanced amateurs.

Extra. For top-ranked amateurs.

Technician. For amateurs with an interest in technical experimentation.

Conditional. For amateurs who cannot appear for an examination and are tested by mail.

An amateur operator first must obtain a novice license. Typically he then tries for a general license and later may seek an advanced license. Each examination covers the ability to transmit and receive Morse code as well as FCC regulations, construction and operation of equipment, and the theory of electricity. The examination for the novice class is, of course, the easiest. An applicant must send and receive code at the rate of at least five words a minute and pass a brief written examination. It consists of 20 questions such as the following:

When may an amateur radio station be used by a person who does not hold a valid license?

At what intervals must an amateur station be identified by the transmission of its call sign?

What are the rules and regulations regarding the purity and stability of emissions?

What is the purpose of a modulator, an amplifier, a rectifier, a filter?

What is the relationship between a cycle, a kilocycle, and a megacycle?

The examination for a novice class license is supervised by a volunteer examiner in the community where an applicant lives. The license is good for one year, restricts the operator to certain frequencies and modes of operation, and cannot be renewed. To continue as a radio amateur, he must try for a license of a higher class. The general and advanced licenses require sending and receiving code at a minimum rate of 13 words a minute. For an extra class license the minimum is 20 words a minute. With the exception of the novice and conditional classes, all examinations are conducted by a government examiner at a regional FCC office and are renewable after five years.

Canada. The regulatory agency is the Department of Transportation (DOT) in Ottawa. There are two primary classes of operation: amateur radio operator and advanced radio operator. Conditional licenses are issued when an applicant lives at too great a distance from a regional office. An applicant must be at least 15 years of age. The examination for amateur radio operator requires a minimum of 10 words a minute in Morse code. In addition, there are oral and written questions on technical and regulatory matters. The advanced license requires 15 words a minute and greater technical knowledge.

Preparing for an Examination. Two booklets provide a detailed picture of licensing requirements and examinations. In the United States, applicants should read *The Radio Amateur's License Manual*, a Relay League publication. In Canada, applicants should read *The Radio Amateur Licensing Handbook* by Jim Kitchin. Both are listed in the Bibliography.

The major hurdle for most beginners is learning the Morse code. Several types of instruction are available. One of the best is the classes local radio clubs sometimes offer. Courses of instruction are also provided on long-playing records and prerecorded tape. Regularly scheduled code practice transmissions are offered nightly by the Relay League's radio station, W1AW. The schedule is available on request. Decoding messages monitored in standard transmissions by other amateurs also offers excellent practice. For practice in sending code, you will need a telegrapher's key. A particularly useful model is battery-operated and enables you to hear your transmissions over an AM radio.

A great many applicants do not pass a licensing examination the first time they take it. However, one can take the examination again after 30 days. When you finally earn your license and call letters, you join a select group.

ADDITIONAL EQUIPMENT

After you are licensed to go on the air, you will need a simple transmitter if you don't already have one. As discussed earlier, it is not too difficult to build such a unit. Kits are available starting at under $50. Ready-built models start at under $100. You also will need a logbook to record your activity as required by the FCC; maps of the United States, Canada, and the world; a world clock or a standard clock and conversion tables so that you may calculate the time elsewhere; and a supply of pencils and scratch pads for receiving messages. Traditionally hams who converse with one another by radio also exchange QSL cards, which carry their station letters, names, and addresses. They then display those they receive. To participate, it will be necessary to design a card and have a quantity printed.

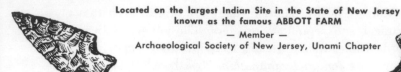

Located on the largest Indian Site in the State of New Jersey
known as the famous ABBOTT FARM
— Member —
Archaeological Society of New Jersey, Unami Chapter

RARE
INDIAN
RELICS

W2RIR

RHODE
ISLAND
RED

MATTHEW J. HORVATH
209 LAKE AVENUE ... TRENTON, NEW JERSEY 08610
MERCER COUNTY

ZONE
#5

HUNGARIAN
NET

SSB
#5388

Abbott Zoned
Incised Pottery

WAC
WAS

DXCC
WAZ

A QSL card used by a "ham" who is also an amateur archaeologist.

When you earn a permanent license, you also may wish to obtain more advanced equipment. There is no limit to what you can spend. Over the years the average amateur invests more than $700 in his shack. The ham with a fat wallet may spend thousands of dollars.

ORGANIZATIONS

At the time you acquire your first license, join a local radio club, both for the advice you undoubtedly will need and the fun it affords. Many hams also join the American Radio Relay League, which provides technical advice, issues a fine magazine, functions as a lobbyist for the radio amateur, and provides a multitude of other services.

ON THE AIR

Many hams enjoy talking just for the fun of it. Often only two will be involved, but at times there will be three or more. Fre-

quently the same hams form a network, or net, to hold regularly scheduled conversations. In the Philadelphia suburbs, for example, there is
a group of commuters who converse from mobile radio equipment in
their cars on the way to work each morning. They call their group the
Orange Juice Circuit. More often than not hams talk about their equipment, their families, and, of course, the weather. To find someone to
talk to, the ham issues a general call, or a CQ call, as it is known. It
might sound like this: "Calling CQ, CQ, CQ. Calling CQ. This is W2CB.
Calling CQ. Hello, CQ, CQ."

If there is someone listening who feels like talking, he will establish
contact. If someone else is listening and has something to say, he may
wait for a pause in the conversation, then interject, "Break, break." One
of the original participants then will say, "We have a breaker, if he'll
identify himself," and another person joins the conversation.

Good talk is regarded as of such importance that the Relay League
has established a Rag Chewers' Club. A ham qualifies for membership,
and a certificate, if he chews the rag with another ham for at least a
half-hour. If he "works a station" in every state, he becomes eligible
for a WAS (Worked All States) certificate. If he makes contact with a
ham on each of the continents, he can acquire a WAC certificate. If he
makes contacts in at least 100 countries, he joins the exclusive DX Century Club. Although most transmissions are made from a basement or
a study, a growing number come from mobile stations in cars, on boats,
and in aircraft.

It is estimated that about 60 per cent of transmission is by voice or
"phone," with the remainder in Morse code. However, in all cases hams
use an intriguing shorthand. Male hams are known as OM or old man.
Unmarried females are YL's, no matter what their age. Married women
are X-YL's or OW's. A newcomer to amateur radio is a YS, for "young
squirt." When hams refer to one another by name, it usually is by first
name only; seldom do they ask what their friend's last name is. They
may start a conversation with GE, for "good evening," and conclude
with CUL, for "see you later," BCNU, for "be seeing you," 73, for
"signing off" or 88, for "love and kisses."

Public Service. Not all transmissions are small talk. Hams
traditionally have volunteered their time to serve the public. Their
most dramatic contributions have been made during disasters such as
earthquakes and floods in providing communication where otherwise
there would be none. Some also are on permanent standby as members

of the American Red Cross Disaster Service, the Radio Amateur Civil Defense Service, and the Air Radio Emergency Corps.

Another group devotes its time to "message handling." Some relay messages via radio from servicemen abroad to their families and friends at home. Others are members of a National Traffic System which relays messages without charge for anyone who wishes to make use of this service. A number are concerned with specialized messages. There is one group that relays information on human eyes needed for transplant purposes. Another broadcasts medical advice from the Duke University Medical Center in North Carolina to physicians in Latin America and Africa.

BIBLIOGRAPHY

Books and Booklets

How to Become a Radio Amateur, American Radio Relay League, Newington, Connecticut 06111.

Learning the Radiotelegraph Code, American Radio Relay League, Newington, Connecticut 06111.

The Radio Amateur Licensing Handbook, Jim Kitchin, R. Mack & Co., 1485 S.W. Marine Drive, Vancouver 14, B.C., Canada. For Canadian amateurs.

The Radio Amateur's License Manual, American Radio Relay League, Newington, Connecticut 06111.

Understanding Amateur Radio, American Radio Relay League, Newington, Connecticut 06111. An introduction to electronics and radio circuitry with information on how to build low-cost equipment.

Periodicals

CQ, 14 Vanderventer Avenue, Port Washington, N.Y. 11050. Monthly.

QST, American Radio Relay League, Newington, Connecticut 06111. Monthly.

73, *73*, Peterborough, N.H. 03458. Monthly.

25·WEATHER FORECASTING

PREDICTING THE WEATHER is a time-honored pursuit. Practically everyone tries his hand, but alas not everyone succeeds. The professional meteorologist is right about 85 per cent of the time. The layman usually doesn't do as well, but with less at stake he probably has more fun.

Some amateur weathermen rely for their forecasts on the behavior of birds, the presence of a halo around the moon, or the severity of their aches and pains. Those with a more serious interest in meteorology make daily observations of local conditions, maintain records, and even do research on weather patterns. A number assist meteorologists at TV stations or function as weathermen for local newspapers. Others, primarily in rural areas, serve the federal government as volunteer observers, providing daily readings the Weather Service otherwise would not have.

The weather is essentially the state of the atmosphere at a particular place and time. It reflects, of course, such factors as cloudiness, temperature, humidity, and wind direction. These, in turn, are the result of national, regional, and local influences. One is the continuous movement across the country of systems of high pressure, which contain good weather, and systems of low pressure which contain storms. Related to these are huge masses of cold or warm air that drift across the continent. In addition, bodies of water, mountains, deserts, and other topographic features have an impact.

Relying solely on local observations, you can make a reasonably accurate weather prediction for 12 hours or possibly longer. By taking into account information the Weather Service issues on conditions elsewhere, you can make roughly accurate estimates for 24 hours or longer. As you become experienced, you also will consider traditional weather patterns in your area, which may further increase your accuracy.

GETTING STARTED

It is essential to do some reading. A brief illustrated guide called *Weather* provides an excellent basic introduction. For a detailed discussion, consult either *Weathercasting* or *An Introduction to Meteorology*. All are listed in the Bibliography. The equipment for making observations is described below. You can obtain everything you need for under $75. An excellent source of weather instruments is Science Associates, a scientific supply house whose catalog is listed in the Bibliography. Department stores, hardware stores, and photography and hobby shops also sell such equipment. However, you can reduce the cost by making a few things yourself. In addition to instruments, acquire a sturdy, thick notebook as a permanent weather log.

MAKING OBSERVATIONS

Make two sets of observations a day, in the early morning and 12 hours later in the early evening. If you have more time, make observations every four hours. Then enter your readings in your log according to the following system:

MONTH	SKY		TEMPERATURE					HUMIDITY	
	A.M.	P.M.	A.M.	P.M.	Max.	Min.	Mean	A.M.	P.M.
1									
2									
3									
4									
5									
6									
7									
8									
9									
10									

The factors on which you will base your forecasts are cloud conditions and sky cover, humidity, barometric pressure, and wind direction. How to use these readings is discussed in the section Preparing Forecasts. The information you gather on temperature and precipitation will provide the long-term records required to define trends and patterns in your area.

Clouds, Sky Cover. A cloud consists of minute particles of water or ice suspended in air. It forms when moist air rises. As the air cools, it condenses on particles of dust as droplets. Depending on conditions, any one of three types of clouds may result: the featherlike cirrus (from Latin for "curl," "tuft"), cumulus clouds (from "accumulation" or "heap"), or stratus clouds (from "sheet" or "layer"). These occur in various combinations which are categorized by height.

High Clouds (16,000–45,000 feet):
  Cirrus. White ice clouds in wisps, patches, or narrow bands.
  Cirrocumulus. Delicately rounded clouds in groups, lines, or ripples.
  Cirrostratus. A milky-colored translucent veil that covers all or much of the sky.
Middle Clouds (6500–16,000 feet):
  Altocumulus. An extensive layer of somewhat rounded clouds in lines or waves.
  Altostratus. A gray-blue translucent veil that covers all or much of the sky.

BAROMETER		WIND		PRECIPITATION		REMARKS
A.M.	P.M.	A.M.	P.M.	A.M.	P.M.	

[ABOVE] *Cirrus clouds.*

[BELOW] *Cirrocumulus.*

[ABOVE] *Altocumulus.*

[BELOW] *Altostratus.*

Low Clouds (up to 6500 feet):

Stratus. A gray foglike cloud in layers or sheets above ground level.
Nimbostratus. A massive dark gray cloud in layers dense enough to hide the sun.
Stratocumulus. A rounded gray or bluish cloud that occurs in patches or layers.
Fog. Clouds at the surface.

Vertical Clouds (ascending from 1000 to 40,000 feet):

Cumulus: A brilliant white cloud that occurs in towers or domes and resembles cauliflowers.
Cumulonimbus. A dark, forbidding cloud in mountainous globular forms; the top may be shaped like an anvil or a plume.

To estimate the proportion of the sky covered by clouds, look above you rather than at the horizon. Record your findings in fractions or with the following symbols:

Clear, 1/10 or less   ◯
Scattered, 2/10 to 5/10   ◑
Broken, 6/10 to 9/10   ◕
Overcast, more than 9/10   ⊕

If there is precipitation, use one of these symbols instead: rain, R; snow, S; hail, H; thunderstorm, T; sleet, E; freezing rain, Z; drizzle, L.

Temperature. A satisfactory thermometer with a standard design costs $3 to $4. To determine its accuracy, place it in cracked ice or melting snow. If it doesn't measure 32 degrees, take the difference into account in measuring observations. The maximum-minimum thermometer is a more useful, more interesting, and more expensive instrument. It is known as a Six's type thermometer, for the Englishman James Six who invented it some 200 years ago. It records the maximum and minimum temperatures during a 24-hour period. Since a thermometer literally takes its own temperature, keep it in a shaded location where it is exposed to freely moving air.

A simple instrument shelter will meet these requirements. You can buy a small model, but it is easy to make one. The basic ingredients are old window shutters and plywood. Use the shutters for the sides and the plywood for the top, bottom, and roof, leaving an opening at the front. So that the sun doesn't distort the temperature inside, make a

[ABOVE] *Nimbostratus.*

[BELOW] *Stratocumulus.*

[ABOVE] *Cumulus.*

[BELOW] *Cumulonimbus.*

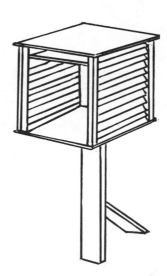

Homemade instrument shelter.

double roof from two pieces of plywood with two or three inches of air space between them. Install the shelter on a post in an open space where the air moves freely. Position it at eye level with its opening facing north so that the sun does not shine in.

Humidity. This is the amount of water vapor in the atmosphere at any time. However, the only meaningful way to measure humidity is in terms of relative humidity. This reading relates the actual amount of water vapor to the maximum amount the air could hold, which varies with temperature. For example, a relative humidity reading might be 20 per cent of maximum or it might be 90 per cent, which would be far closer to saturation and precipitation.

The instrument used to measure relative humidity is a hygrometer. One of the simplest hygrometers is called a sling psychrometer. It consists of two thermometers. One is a standard instrument which provides a "dry bulb" reading of the air temperature. The other, whose bulb is covered with a wet wick, provides a "wet bulb" reading. This is the temperature at which water starts to evaporate from the wick. Since evaporation is a cooling process, the "wet bulb" temperature always will be the lower of the two. What is crucial is how much lower. This depends on the speed of evaporation, which depends, in turn, on the amount of moisture already in the air. The higher the relative humidity, the slower evaporation will be and the higher the wet bulb reading.

To obtain a reading with a sling psychrometer, whirl the instrument on its handle for 60 seconds. If a stationary hygrometer is used, install it in your instrument shelter with your thermometer. If the temperatures drop below 32 degrees, bring the instrument inside so that the water that feeds the wick does not freeze and break its container.

Use the chart below to obtain the relative humidity. The figures across the top are dry bulb temperatures. The figures at the left represent possible differences in degrees between the wet bulb and dry bulb readings. The figure where the relevant columns cross is the relative humidity.

	30°	40°	50°	60°	70°	80°	90°	100°
1	90	92	93	94	95	96	96	97
2	79	84	87	89	90	92	92	93
3	68	76	80	84	86	87	88	90
4	58	68	74	78	81	83	85	86
6	38	52	61	68	72	75	78	80
8	18	37	49	58	64	68	71	71
10		22	37	48	55	61	65	68
12		8	26	39	48	54	59	62
14			16	30	40	47	53	57
16			5	21	33	41	47	51
18				13	26	35	41	47
20				5	19	29	36	42
22					12	23	32	37
24					6	18	26	33

Making a Hygrometer: You will need two standard thermometers, a small medicine bottle, a white tubular cotton shoelace, and a piece of plywood. Cut off a three-inch piece from the shoelace, then boil it to remove any impurities. Fasten the two thermometers side by side on the plywood with staples. Mount the medicine bottle next to the thermometer that is to serve as the "wet bulb" and fill the bottle with water. Place one end of the shoelace over the bulb and the other in the water. Fan with a piece of cardboard for 60 seconds before taking a reading.

Barometric Pressure. This also is known as air pressure or atmospheric pressure. It is the weight of the air at a particular location and time. Barometric pressure is one of the most important elements in developing a forecast. At sea level under normal conditions the air weighs 14.7 pounds per square inch. This is sufficient to support a column of mercury 30 inches high. However, barometric pressure varies with atmospheric conditions. If the pressure rises, and with it the mercury, this indicates clearing weather. If they drop, it may indicate worsening conditions.

To measure air pressure, or weigh the air, you need a barometer. A mercurial barometer is far too expensive for most amateurs. A more practical instrument is an aneroid type, which operates like a spring scale but gives "mercurial" readings. Since air pressure is the same indoors and outdoors, keep your barometer inside to protect it from corrosion. After it is installed, call the nearest Weather Service office for the current sea level pressure and set your instrument at that reading.

Wind Direction. The direction from which the wind is blowing is another key factor in preparing a forecast. A wet finger, a flag, or smoke rising from a chimney will provide the information you need, but over the long term a wind vane will be more convenient. You can buy one, or you can fashion a vane from a piece of plywood. Drill a hole vertically through the wood at a point about 60 per cent of the distance from the tail. Then mount a heavy wire in the top of a broomstick or dowel stick, position two washers at the base of the wire, and add the vane. Make certain that it swings freely and is properly balanced. This may require adding a washer or two at the nose. Finally, twist a wire around the stick to indicate true north. To find true north, find the North Star, which is only 1.6 degrees from that point.* Or use a compass and the isogonic map shown. The compass indicates magnetic north; the map provides the necessary correction to obtain true north.

* See Chapter 23, Astronomy.

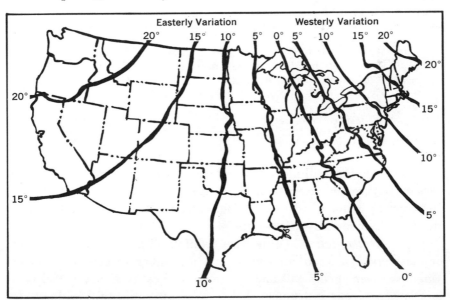

Isogonic map depicting variations from true north in compass readings.

If possible install the vane above nearby buildings. A TV antenna atop a house is an ideal mounting. In addition, an apartment house roof may have a post that can be utilized. Record wind direction as originating from one of eight standard points: N, NE, E, SE, S, SW, W, NW.

It also is interesting to know the speed of the wind. Many amateurs measure wind speed by observation, using the scale below as a guide. It is based on a scale Sir Francis Beaufort of the British Royal Navy developed in 1805 to assist sailing ships.

Wind in M.P.H.	Description of Effects	Type of Wind	Beaufort Number
Under 1	Smoke rises straight up. No perceptible motion.	Calm	0
1–3	Smoke drift shows direction. Tree leaves barely move. Wind vane shows no direction.	Calm	1
4–7	Leaves rustle slightly. Wind felt on face. Ordinary vane moved by wind.	Light	2
8–12	Leaves and twigs move. Loose paper and dust raised from ground.	Gentle	3
13–18	Small branches are moved. Dust and paper raised and driven along.	Moderate	4
19–24	Small trees sway. Large branches in motion. Dust clouds raised.	Fresh	5
25–31	Large branches move continuously. Wind begins to whistle. Umbrellas used with difficulty.	Fresh	6
32–38	Whole trees in motion. Walking difficult.	Strong	7
39–46	Tree twigs break. Walking progress slow.	Strong	8
47–54	Slight structural damage.	Gale	9
55–63	Exposed trees uprooted. Heavy structural damage.	Gale	10
64–75	Widespread damage.	Whole gale	11
Above 75	Severe damage and destruction.	Hurricane	12

An anemometer will measure wind speed with greater precision than is possible through observation, but a satisfactory instrument is costly. In recording wind speed in your log, enter the Beaufort number after the wind direction: SE-8, for example.

Precipitation. To measure rainfall, either buy a rain gauge or make one. To do so, all you need is a number 10 can, a container which is seven inches tall and about six inches in diameter. Select a location near your instrument shelter where the rain falls without obstruction. Then position the can three feet from the ground, either on a

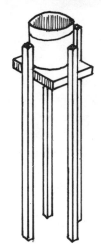

Homemade rain gauge.

stand, as in the illustration, or on a post. Measure the rainfall once every 24 hours by inserting a ruler in the can. For a more precise measurement, add a long, narrow olive jar to your equipment. Pour an inch of water into the jar, then mark its level on the outside. Calibrate the entire jar in inches, then in tenths of an inch. To measure the rain in the can, simply pour it into the jar. However, be sure to empty the jar once you have entered your data.

To measure the amount of snow accumulation, use a ruler or a yardstick. Insert the ruler at a number of locations where the snow has not drifted and has not been disturbed. Then compute and record the average depth. Meteorologists also compute the water content of a snowfall so that it may be included in their statistics on overall precipitation. The general rule is one inch of water for every ten inches of snow. For a more precise figure, melt the snow that accumulates in the rain gauge and measure the result.

PREPARING A FORECAST

Once you have made your observations, the task is to interpret them. Your daily readings should enable you to prepare a short-range forecast for 12 to 18 hours. For a more ambitious forecast, you also will need information on the weather elsewhere. One source is the latest weather map in your newspaper. Another are the reports carried on the aviation weather band that pilots use. Let's first consider local conditions.

Relative Humidity. A change in the amount of water vapor in the air may indicate a change in the weather. If the moisture increases on a fair day, for example, so does the possibility of rain or fog.

317

Sky Cover, Clouds, and Wind Direction. The proportion of sky cover is one indication of the stability of the atmosphere and the likelihood of precipitation. If the sky cover has diminished since your last observation, it is reasonable to assume that there will be no precipitation for at least another 12 hours. If it has increased, there is a growing possibility of poor weather. The types of clouds involved and the direction from which the wind is blowing provide more precise indications.

Cirrus: If the wind is steady from the northeast, east, or south, precipitation may occur within 18 hours. Under such circumstances the characteristic wisplike clouds soon are supplemented by cirrostratus, altostratus, or stratus clouds.

Cirrocumulus: If the wind is from the northeast, east, or south, precipitation may occur within 12 to 18 hours.

Cirrostratus: If the wind is from the north or northeast, precipitation is possible within 24 hours.

Altocumulus, Altostratus: With winds from the north, east, or south, precipitation is likely within 18 hours.

Nimbostratus: Precipitation is likely. If the wind is from the southwest to north, the storm will be short. Otherwise, it will be of longer duration.

Stratocumulus: Immediate precipitation is likely.

Stratus: If the wind is from the northeast to the south, there is a chance of heavy precipitation, drizzle, or an overcast condition.

Cumulus: Broken cumulus clouds with no vertical development mean fair weather. Cumulus clouds with vertical development are likely to yield showers. Cumulus clouds that fill the sky are harbingers of heavy rain.

Cumulonimbus: Immediate precipitation is likely. An electrical storm also is a possibility.

Barometric Pressure and Wind Direction. The direction from which the wind blows reflects the pattern of atmospheric pressure in a region. It also indicates the likelihood of fair or unsettled weather. West of the Rocky Mountains, for example, a wind from the south, southwest, west, or northwest is likely to bring rain. In the eastern United States, the possibility of rain exists when the wind blows from the east, northeast, south, or southeast.

When information on wind direction is combined with data on changes in atmospheric pressure, they provide a more complete picture of the weather ahead. The wind-barometer indications below were provided by the U.S. Weather Service. They apply in most sections, but there are areas where an amateur will have to modify the table in line with his experience and observations.

Wind Direction	Barometer Reduced to Sea Level	Character of Weather Indicated
SW to NW	30.10 to 30.20 and steady	Fair with slight temperature changes for 1 to 2 days.
SW to NW	30.10 to 30.20 and rising rapidly	Fair, followed within 2 days by rain.
SW to NW	30.20 and above and stationary	Continued fair, with no decided temperature change.
SW to NW	30.20 and above and falling slowly	Slowly rising temperatures and fair for 2 days.
S to SE	30.10 to 30.20 and falling slowly	Rain within 24 hours.
S to SE	30.10 to 30.20 and falling rapidly	Wind increasing in force, with rain within 12 to 24 hours.
SE to NE	30.10 to 30.20 and falling slowly	Rain in 12 to 18 hours.
SE to NE	30.10 to 30.20 and falling rapidly	Increasing wind and rain within 12 hours.
E to NE	30.10 and above and falling slowly	In summer, with light winds, rain may not fall for several days. In winter, rain within 24 hours.
E to NE	30.10 and above and falling rapidly	In summer, rain probably within 12 to 24 hours. In winter, rain or snow, with increasing winds, will often set in when the barometer begins to fall and the wind sets in from the NE.
SE to NE	30.00 or below and falling slowly	Rain will continue 1 to 2 days.
SE to NE	30.00 or below and falling rapidly	Rain, with high wind, followed within 36 hours by clearing and in winter by colder.
S to SW	30.00 or below and rising slowly	Clearing within a few hours, and fair for several days.
S to E	29.80 or below and falling rapidly	Severe storm imminent, followed, within 24 hours, by clearing, and in winter by colder.
E to N	29.80 or below and falling rapidly	Severe northeast gale and heavy precipitation; in winter, heavy snow, followed by a cold wave.
Going to W	29.80 or below and rising rapidly	Clearing and colder.

319

Weather Elsewhere. The daily weather maps and the aviation weather band provide a picture of the weather moving toward your area. In studying the maps, there are several indicators to consider. The most important are pressure systems and fronts.

Pressure Systems: The term "high" on a map indicates the location of a high pressure system and the fair weather it brings. The term "low" signifies a low pressure system or storm center. Pressure systems typically move from west to east, covering 500 miles a day during the warmer months and 700 miles a day the rest of the year. With this in mind, you can estimate roughly when a particular system will affect your area. The curved lines on a weather map are isobars, which connect points of equal pressure and define the area of a high or low.

Fronts: A front is a line along which a warm air mass and a cold air mass make contact. An advancing cold front is indicated by a heavy black line with triangular points. An advancing warm front is indicated by a line with rounded points. There also are occluded fronts, in which warm air has been overtaken and lifted by cold air, and stationary fronts which have stalled in a particular location. The arrival of a front means a change in the weather. Usually this is preceded by storm activity as cold and warm air intermingle. The approach of a front is marked by declining barometric pressure which rises again as the front passes through. By plotting changing pressures with your barometer, you can determine when this occurs.

Other Conditions: Through numbers and symbols, a map provides a picture of factors such as temperature, precipitation, and wind direction that also may affect your forecast.

Weather map.

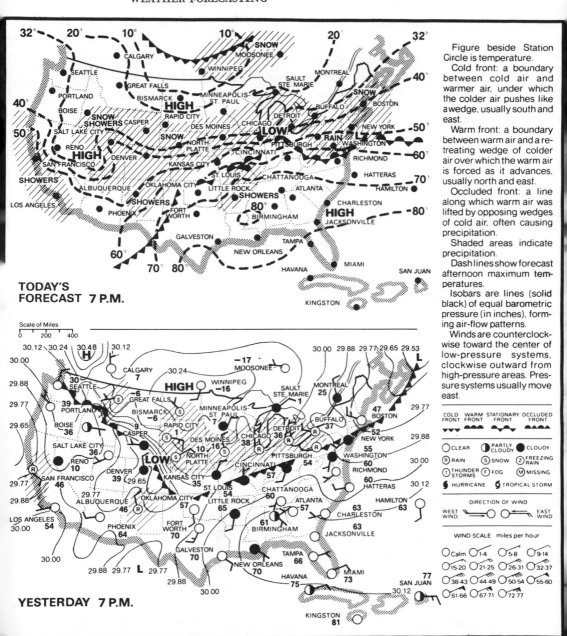

Figure beside Station Circle is temperature.

Cold front: a boundary between cold air and warmer air, under which the colder air pushes like a wedge, usually south and east.

Warm front: a boundary between warm air and a retreating wedge of colder air over which the warm air is forced as it advances, usually north and east.

Occluded front: a line along which warm air was lifted by opposing wedges of cold air, often causing precipitation.

Shaded areas indicate precipitation.

Dash lines show forecast afternoon maximum temperatures.

Isobars are lines (solid black) of equal barometric pressure (in inches), forming air-flow patterns.

Winds are counterclockwise toward the center of low-pressure systems, clockwise outward from high-pressure areas. Pressure systems usually move east.

321

ORGANIZATIONS

There are relatively few organizations of amateur meteorologists. Instead some hold membership in professional societies which have a technical orientation. A number also join the American Meteorological Society as associate members. Their membership includes a subscription to *Weatherwise,* a non-technical publication. The society's address is 45 Beacon Street, Boston, Massachusetts 02108.

BIBLIOGRAPHY

Books

Eric Sloane's Weather Library, Eric Sloane, Meredith Press, New York, 1963. Three volumes.

How About the Weather? R. M. Fisher, Harper & Row, New York, 1958.

Instant Weather Forecasting, Alan Watts, Dodd Mead & Co., New York, 1968.

Introduction to Meteorology, S. Petterssen, McGraw-Hill Book Co., New York, 1968.

1001 Questions About the Weather, Frank H. Forrester, Dodd Mead & Co., New York, 1957.

Weather, Paul E. Lehr, R. Will Burnett, Herbert S. Zim, Simon & Schuster, New York, 1957.

Weather Lore, R. Inwards, Rider, London, 1950.

Weathercasting: A Handbook of Amateur Meteorology, Charles and Ruth Laird, Prentice-Hall, Englewood Cliffs, N.J., 1955.

Weathercraft, Athelstan F. Spilhaus, Viking Press, New York, 1951. A book for young people.

Booklets and Pamphlets

Weather, Astronomy, and Meteorology, a list of U.S. Government publications, Superintendent of Documents, Washington, D.C. 20402.

Catalog

Science Associates, Box 230, Princeton, N.J. 08540.

Periodical
Weatherwise, American Meteorological Society, 45 Beacon Street, Boston, Massachusetts 02108. Bi-monthly.

Illustration credits

PAGE 48   Chandler & Price.
51   American Type Founders.
59   Eastman Kodak Company.
60   Both Honeywell.
64   Eastman Kodak Company.
65   Eastman Kodak Company.
66   Eastman Kodak Company.
93   School Products Company.
94   Norwood Loom Company.
110 (bottom)   Stanley Tools.
116   Stanley Tools.
117   Both Stanley Tools.
117   Both Stanley Tools.
118   All Stanley Tools.
130   Charles Hamilton Autographs.
131   Charles Hamilton Autographs.
140   All Smithsonian Institution.
142   Smithsonian Institution.
144   Smithsonian Institution.
150   All Smithsonian Institution.
151   Both Smithsonian Institution.
155   Smithsonian Institution.
PLATE I   *Tropical Fish Hobbyist*, photo Herbert R. Axelrod.
PLATE II   *Tropical Fish Hobbyist*, photo Herbert R. Axelrod.
PLATE III   *Tropical Fish Hobbyist*, photo Herbert R. Axelrod.
PLATE IV   *Tropical Fish Hobbyist*, photo S. Frank.
PLATE V   *Tropical Fish Hobbyist*, photo Herbert R. Axelrod.
PLATE VI   *Tropical Fish Hobbyist*, photo Herbert R. Axelrod.
196 (top)   *Tropical Fish Hobbyist*, photo Gerhard Marcuse.
(bottom)   *Tropical Fish Hobbyist*, photo Milan Chvojka.
197 (top)   Alvin Staffan, from National Audubon Society.
(bottom)   *Tropical Fish Hobbyist*, photo G. J. M. Timmerman.
203   Smithsonian Institution.
205   Smithsonian Institution.
206   All Smithsonian Institution.
207   Both Smithsonian Institution.
235   Both Smithsonian Institution.
236   Both Smithsonian Institution.
PLATES VII–XII   All Smithsonian Institution, Joel Arem.
266   Both Smithsonian Institution.
267   Both Smithsonian Institution.

ILLUSTRATION CREDIT

268   Both Smithsonian Institution.
269   Smithsonian Institution.
281   New Jersey State Museum.
282   All New Jersey State Museum.
288 (Photo)   Unitron Instrument Company.
289 (Photo)   Edmund Scientific Company.
299   American Radio Relay League.
308   Both National Oceanographic and Atmospheric Administration.
309   Both National Oceanographic and Atmospheric Administration.
311   Both National Oceanographic and Atmospheric Administration.
312   Both National Oceanographic and Atmospheric Administration.
321   National Oceanographic and Atmospheric Administration, © 1971 by The New York Times Company. Reprinted with permission.

INDEX

INDEX

A

Abbott, R. Tucker, 271
Abrasives
    how to use, 117
    types of, 113
Accessories, photographic, 62
Acidity of fish tank water, 186
Action photographs, background of,
    64
Adams, John, 132
Adjustable cameras, 58
ADS (Autograph Document Signed),
    126
Advanced cameras, 60-61
Aerator-filters of fish tanks, 185
Aesop's Fables, 90
Age, value and, of autographs, 132
Air netting, described, 220
Albert Constantine & Son, Inc., 105
Albums, stamp, 156-57
Alfred University (Alfred, N.Y.), 25
Algae, 238-39
Alkalinity of fish tank water, 186
Allied Radio, 298
ALS (Autograph Letter Signed),
    126, 129-30
Altocumulus clouds, 307, 309, 318
Altostratus clouds, 307, 309
American Craftsmen's Council, 25,
    98, 99

American Heritage (magazine), 162
American Malacological Society, 274
American Meteorological Society,
    293, 322
American Museum of Natural
    History, 217
American Numismatic Association,
    137, 146
American Philatelic Society, 158
American Radio Relay League, 297,
    301, 302
American Sea Shells (Abbott), 271
America's Money (Massey), 134
Amphibians, types of, 198-99
Amphineura, characteristics of, 265
AMsS (Autograph Manuscript
    Signed), 126
Ancient coins, 144-45
Anemometers, uses of, 316
Ants, observing, 215-16
Appearance, value and, of
    autographs, 132
Aquarium Book for Boys and Girls
    (Morgan), 184
Aquarium Club of America, 188, 199
Aquarium Stock Company, 188
Aquariums, 184-87, 193, 197
Aquatic insects, 216
Archaeology, 279-84
    finding and excavating sites,
        280-83
    See also Fossils
Arrangements, grass, 237

Art Dealers Association of America, 163

Art galleries, as source of prints and reproductions, 163

Articulated cardboard puppets, 76-77

Associated American Artists, 163

Association of Lunar and Planetary Observers, 293

Association of Variable Star Observers, 293

Associations, *see* Organizations; *and specific associations*

Astronomy, 285-94
    equipment needed for, 285-90
    sky exploration, 290-92

Attics, as sources of autograph materials, 128

Auctions
    autographs in, 129
    coins from, 137

Autograph, defined, 126

Autograph collections, 125-32
    starting, 127-28
    terminology used in, 126-27
    value of, 129-32

Autograph Document Signed (ADS), 126

Autograph Letter Signed (ALS), 126, 129-30

Autograph Manuscript Signed (AMsS), 126

Automatic cameras, 58-59

Axelrod, Herbert, 191

B

Banding of birds, 179-80

Barber, Charles E., 139

Barker, Conway, 129

Barnum, P. T., 125

Barometric pressure
    gathering information on, 314-15
    in preparation of weather forecast, 318-19

Basic Printing, Developing, and Enlarging (Eastman Kodak Co.), 70

Baskerville type face, 49

Beater-reeds, described, 98

Beating
    to catch insects, 220
    in weaving, 99

Beating instruments for paper making, 28

Binoculars, 285-86

Bio-Marine Supply Company, 192

Bird Banding Office (U.S. Fish and Wildlife Service), 179

Birds, 173-82
    counting and banding, 179-80
    identifying, 176-79
    starting study of, 174-75
    when and where to find, 175-76

Birds of North America (Robbins, Bruun, Zim), 174

Bisque method of ceramic decoration, 24

Black-and-white films, 62-63

Boat shuttles of looms, 94-95

Bodoni type face, 49

Bolts, types of, 114

Boone, Daniel, 131

Boring tools, woodworking, 111

Botany, *see* Plants

Bowls, fish, 184

Box nails, 113

Box theaters for puppets, 78, 80

Box-table theaters for marionettes, 89

Brads, 113

Braque, Georges, 164

Breeding habits
    of goldfish, 189-90
    of marine life, 194

of native fish, 195-98
Brenner, Victor D., 139
Broken bank bills, 141
Brooklyn Museum (N.Y.C.), 146
Bruun, Bertel, 174
Bryant, William Cullen, 131
Butterflies, observing, 217-19

C

Cabochons, defined, 258-59
Calcite, 253
California Federation of Mineralog-
    ical Societies, 251
Cameras
    learning use of, 63-68
    types of, 57-61
Canada, radio licensing in, 300-1
Canada, Bank of, 137
Canadian currency, collecting, 142-
    143
Cardboard prints, described, 37-38
Cardboard puppets, articulated, 76-
    77
Care
    of cameras, 61
    of coin collections, 145
    of minerals, 257
    of print collections, 165-66
    of shells, 292-93
    of stamps, 158
    of wild flowers, 233
    of woodworking hand tools, 115
Carving, see Woodcarving
Casing nails, 113-14
Caslon type face, 49
Catalogs
    of minerals, 257
    postage stamp collection, 155-56
Celebrities, autographs obtained
    from, 128

Cephalopods, characteristics of, 265-
    269
Ceramics, 17-25
    clay used for, 17-19
    decorating and firing, 23-24
    equipment for, 19-20
    organizations of and instruction
        in, 25
    techniques used in, 21-23
Ceramics: A Potter's Handbook
    (Nelson), 20
Certificates, 142
Chagall, Marc, 164
Charles T. Hamilton Galleries, Inc.,
    129
Chases for locking up, 53
Cirrocumulus clouds, 307, 308, 318
Cirrostratus clouds, 307, 318
Cirrus clouds, 307, 308, 318
Clay, Henry, 131
Clay, 17-19
Cleaning, see Care
Cleaning equipment for fish tanks,
    185
Close-up lenses, 62
Cloth beams of looms, 99
Clouds
    gathering information on, 307-
        310
    in preparation of weather
        forecast, 318
Club mosses, 239-40
Cockroaches, observing, 216
Coil method in ceramics, 21-22
Coin collections, 134-47
    care and storage of, 145
    foreign, 142-44
    sources for, 135-37
    starting, 134-35
    of U.S. currency, 138-42
Collecting Autographs and Manu-
    scripts (Hamilton), 127

Collections
    algae, 238-39
    grass, 235
    horsetail and club moss, 240
    leaf, 228-29
    lichen, 241
    mineral, 255-57
    moss and liverwort, 242
    mushroom, 244
    seed, 229
    seedling, 229-30
    slime mold, 243
    specialized, 168-69
    See also Autograph collections;
        Coin collections; Fossils;
        Insects; Minerals; Print
        collections; Sea shells;
        Stamp collections
Colonial issues of U.S. currency,
    138-39
Colonial notes, 141
Color correction filters, function of,
    62
Color films, 63
Commemorative coins, 140-41
Common signature, 131
Common weaving shuttles, 94
Condition
    of autographs, 132
    of coins, 137-38
    of stamps, 154-55
Confederate money, 142
Content of autographs, 131
Control bars on marionettes, 86-88
Controls on marionettes, 85-86
Correction filters, 62
Cosey, Joseph, 132
Costs
    of autographs, 125, 126
    of cameras, 59, 61
    of clay, 18
    of common minerals, 253
    of fishes, 188

    of floor looms, 94
    of lapidary equipment, 259
    of meteorological equipment,
        306, 310
    of papermaking equipment, 29
    of potter's wheel, 20
    of printing equipment, 47-49
    of prints and reproductions, 162,
        164
    of radio equipment, 301, 302
    of radio receivers, 297
    of "ready-warped" yarns, 97
    of telescopes, 286
    of type cases, 50
Costumes, marionette, 84-85
Cotton yarns, 97
Counting of birds, 179-80
Craftsman Wood Service Company,
    105
Crate-table theaters for marionettes,
    89
Crickets, observing, 216-17
Cropping out, defined, 68
Crocheting cotton yarns, 97
Crosscut saws, how to use, 116-17
Cullen, Countee, 125
Cumulonimbus clouds, 310, 312, 318
Cumulus clouds, 310, 312, 318
Currencies, sources of, 135-37
Currier & Ives, 164
Cutting tools
    for fossil hunting, 208-9
    for papermaking, 28
    woodworking, 111

                    D

Darkrooms, 69-70
Dealers
    autograph, 128-29
    coin, 135-36
    stamp, 152-53

Decoration
    of ceramics, 23-24
    of paper, 33
Degas, Edgar, 162
Dents of looms, 99
Development of photographs, 68-70
Diagonal lines in photography, 65
Diaphragms of cameras, 57-58
Digging for clay, 18-19
Digging tools for fossil hunting,
    208-9
Dipping vats
    for papermaking, 28
    preparing, 31
Display
    of autograph collections, 132-33
    of fossils, 212
    of minerals, 257-58
    of print collections, 165-66
Document, defined, 126
Document Signed (DS), 126
Dodging, defined, 69
Doorway theaters for puppets, 78, 80,
    82
Double sheet method of decoration,
    33
Douglas Fir Plywood Association,
    115
Dowel puppets, 76, 77
Drafts for recreating fabric patterns,
    96
Drilling, 117
Drills, woodworking, 120
Drying
    of ceramics, 23
    of paper, 33
    of wild flowers, 233
Drying press, 29-30
DS (Document Signed), 126
Durability of paper, 55
Dyes
    in papermaking, 32
    for yarns, 97-98

E

Earnings derived from photography,
    71
Earthenware, 17
Eastern Federation of Mineralogical
    Societies, 251
Eastern States Archaeological
    Federation, 283
Eastman Kodak Company, 63
Edible wild plants, 232
Einstein, Albert, 130
Em quad, defined, 50
Encyclopedia of Tropical Fishes
    (Axelrod), 191
Entomology, *see* Insects
Equipment
    for aquariums, 184-87, 193, 197
    for astronomy, 285-90
    for ceramics, 19-20
    for coin collections, 135
    for collecting insect specimens,
        220
    for fossil hunting, 208-9
    for incised printing, 40-41
    lapidary, 259
    for linoleum prints, 39
    for locking up, 53-54
    for mineral searches, 254-55
    papermaking, 28-30
    photographic, 57-68
    printing, 46-49
    for printing and developing
        photographs, 70
    radio, 297-98, 301-2
    for sea shell study, 271
    for serigraphy, 42
    for wood cuts, 39-40
    woodworking, 109-10, 113-14
    See also Tools
Essentials of Earth History (Stokes),
    208

Etching, 40
Events affecting value of autographs, 130
Excavations of sites, 281-83
Exotic Aquarium Fishes (Innes), 184
Exposure, determining needed, 68
Exposure meters, function of, 62

F

Fabric, patterns for, 95-96
Facets of gem stones, 258-59
Fasteners for woodworking, 113-14
Fastening tools for woodworking, 111
Federation of Mineralogical Societies, 251
Feeding
    of goldfish, 189
    of marine life, 194
    of native fishes, 195
    of tropical fishes, 192
Feeding guides for serigraphy, 42-43
Feldspar, 253
Fenton, Carroll, 208
Fenton, Mildred, 208
Ferns, 239-40
Field, Eugene D., 125
Field crickets, observing, 216-17
Field Guide to Rocks and Minerals, A (Pough), 251
Field Guide to the Shells of Our Atlantic and Gulf Coasts, A (Morris), 271
Field Guide to the Shells of the Pacific and Hawaii, A (Morris), 271
Film technique used in serigraphy, 43
Films (photographic), 62-63
Filters, color correction, 62

Find the Constellations (Rey), 285
Finish
    of paper, 55
    in woodcarving, 107-8
Finishing nails, 113
Firing
    of ceramics, 24
    of clay, 17-18
Fish nets, 185
Fishes, 183-200
    buying, 187-89
    equipment for, 184-86
    getting started with, 183-84
    goldfish, 190-91
    marine life and, 192-94
    native, 194-98
    tropical, 191-92
Flash guns, function of, 62
Flat-head screws, 114
Floor looms
    costs of, 94
    supply sources of, 100
Flowers, wild, 231-34
Focusing, 66
Focusing devices, 57
Foreign currencies, collecting, 142-44
Foreign stamps, sources of, 153
Forgery in autographs, 132
Fortune (magazine), 162
Fossil Book, The (Fenton), 208
Fossils, 201-12
    hunting for, 209-11
    learning about, 208
    origins of, 202-4
    preparing specimens, 211-12
    types of, 204-7
Four-harness table looms, 93
Fractional currency, 141
Frame looms, 93
Fronds of ferns, 239
Fronts, defined, 320
Fungi, 242-44
Furniture for locking up, 53

G

Gadget bags, 62
Garamond type face, 49
Garden Club of America, 227
Gardening
    with ferns, 240
    with lichens, 241
    with wild flowers, 232
Gastropods, characteristics of, 262-64
Gem Cutting (Sinkankas), 258
Gem stones, 258-59
Gem Stones and Minerals
        (Sinkankas), 258
Gibbons, Grinling, 102
Glazing of ceramics, 24
Glove puppets, 74
Glues for woodworking, 114
Goethe, Johann Wolfgang von, 73
Goldfish, 189-90
Governmental agencies, stamps
        from, 153-54
Grades of lumber, 112
Grant, Ulysses S., 129
Grasses, 234-37
Grasshoppers, observing, 217
Gravel in fish tanks, 185
Greenware method of decorating
        ceramics, 23-24
Grog clay, 19
Ground cedar club moss, 240
Ground pine club moss, 240
*Guide to the Collecting and Care of
        Original Prints, A* (Zigros-
        ser), 165

H

Habitat, defined, 175
Hale, Nathan, 131
Ham radio, *see* Radio
Hamilton, Charles, 127
Hammers, 118
Hamming, *see* Radio
Hand lenses for fossil hunting, 209
Hand tools, woodworking, 110-11,
        115-18
Hand-set types, casting, 50
Hans Wurst (German puppet char-
        acter), 73
Hardness
    of minerals, 256-57
    of water, in fish tank, 186
Hardwoods, characteristics of, 112
Harnesses of looms, 98
Harris, Doris T., 129
Haydn, Josef, 73
Head and cloth puppets, 74
Health
    of fishes, 188-89, 195
    of marine life, 194
Heaters of fish tanks, 185
Heath Company, 298
Heddles of looms, 98
Herpin, George, 148
High clouds, 307
Historical stamp collections, 149-50
History and Technology, Museum of
        (Smithsonian Institution;
        Washington, D.C.), 146
Holding tools, woodworking, 111
Home Workshops (National Safety
        Council), 121
Horizon line in photography, 65
Horizontal lines in photography, 65
Hornblende, 253
Horsetails, 239-40
Hostick, King, 129
How to Become a Radio Amateur
        (Relay League publica-
        tion), 297, 298
Humidity
    as factor in preparation of
        weather forecast, 317

Humidity (*cont.*)
    gathering information on, 313-314
Humphrey, Hubert H., 130
Hunting for Fossils (Murray), 210
Hygrometers, 313-14

I

Ichthyophthirius, treating, 189
Identification
    of birds, 176-79
    of club mosses, 240
    of ferns, 239
    of grasses, 234-36
    of minerals, 256
    of mosses and liverworts, 241-42
    of sea shells, 271-72
    of wild flowers, 321-32
Identification kits for minerals, 254-255
IGAS (International Graphic Arts
    Society), 163
Igneous rocks, 252
Illustrations, printing, 52
Imposing stones for locking up, 53
Impressions, testing of, 56
Incised prints (intaglio), 40-43
Individuals affecting value of autographs, 130
Ink, 54
    oil-based, 36
Innes, William T., 184
Insects, 213-25
    collecting specimens of, 219-23
    general characteristics of, 213-14
    observing, 214-19
Instruction
    in astronomy, 285
    in ceramics, 25
    in fossils, 208
    in gem stones, 258
    in mineralogy, 251-52
    in photography, 70
    in print making, 43
    in weather forecasting, 306
    in weaving, 92-93
    in woodcarving, 108
    in woodworking, 121
Intaglio (incised print), 40-43
International Graphic Arts Society
    (IGAS), 163
Introduction to Meteorology, An
    (Petterssen), 306
Introduction to Trees, An (Kieran),
    228
Introductory cameras, 59-60
Invertebrate fossils, 205

J

Jordan buff
    characteristics of, 18
    used in incised printing, 40-41
Jones, John Paul, 131
Junior Audubon Society, 180
Just So Stories (Kipling), 90

K

Kennedy, John F., 130
Kettle for papermaking, 28
Kieran, John, 228
Killing of insect specimens, 221-22
Kiln for ceramics, 20
Kitchin, Jim, 301
Kronovet, Milton, 129

L

Lapidary Journal, The (magazine),
    258

Laurent, Robert, 102
Leaf collections, 228-29
Leads (line spaces), 50-51
Lens opening, 67
Lenses, 62
Letter Signed (LS), 126
Letter spaces, 50
Letterpress, 47
Library of Congress, 127
Licenses, radio, 298-301
Lichens, 240-41
Life lists of birds, 178
Line gauges, 51
Line spaces (leads), 50-51
Linen yarns, 97
Linoleum prints, 38-39
Lithopinion (magazine), 162
"Little Orphan Annie" (Riley), 126
Liverworts, 241-42
Locking up in printing, 53
Longfellow, Henry Wadsworth, 131
Looms, 93-94, 98-100
Low clouds, 310
LS (Letter Signed), 126
Lumber, 111-13
Lutz, Frank, 214
Lynch, Thomas, Jr., 131

M

Maintenance, *see* Care
"Making an Electric Kiln" (University of New Hampshire publication), 20
Manually operated cameras, 59
Manuscript, defined, 126
Manuscript Signed (MsS), 126
Manuscript Society, 128
Marconi, Guglielmo, 295
Marine tanks, setting up, 193-94
Marionettes, 83-90
    controls and control bars on, 85-88

directions for making, 83-84
    theaters for, 89-90
Marking in woodworking, 116
Mason, John, 30
Masonite Corporation, 116
Massey, J. Earl, 134
Materials, *see* Equipment
Measuring in woodworking, 116
Measuring tools, woodworking, 110-11
Medals in coin collections, 141
Medieval coins, 144
Metamorphic rocks, 252
Meteorology, *see* Weather forecasting
Metropolitan Museum of Art (N.Y.C.), 146
Mica, 253
Middle clouds, 307
Midwest Federation of Mineralogical Societies, 251
Military currency, 142
Mineralogical Association of Canada, 251
Minerals, 250-60
    care, storage and display of, 257-58
    collecting, 255-57
    instruction in, 251-52
    types of, 253
    where to find, 253-54
Mints, as sources of coins, 136
Modeling of ceramics, 21
Modeling wheels, 20
Modified theaters for puppets, 82
Moisture of clay, 19
Molds (plants), 242-44
Money, *see* Coin collections
Money Museum (Chase Manhattan Bank, N.Y.C.), 146
Money Museum (National Bank of Detroit; Detroit, Mich.), 146

Monoprints, described, 37-38
Morgan, Alfred, 184
Morris, Percy A., 271
Mosaics, seed, 233
Mosses, 241-42
Moths, observing, 217-19
Mounting
    of insect specimens, 222-23
    of leaf collections, 229
    for stamp collections, 157-58
Mounts, telescope, 287
Mozart, Wolfgang Amadeus, 73
MsS (Manuscript Signed), 126
Murray, Marian, 210
Museums
    coin collections in, 146
    mineral collections in, 251
Mushrooms, 242-44
Music in puppet theater, 90

N

Nails, 113-14
National Audubon Society, 98, 177,
    179, 180, 227, 229
National Federation of Stamp Clubs,
    149, 159
National Gallery of Art (Washing-
    ton, D.C.), 164
National Oceanic and Atmospheric
    Administration (U.S.
    National Ocean Survey),
    271
National Safety Council, 119-21
National stamp collections, 149
National Wildlife Federation, 180
Native fishes, 194-98
Native wild flowers, 231
Natural clay, advantages of, 17-18
Natural dyes, 97-98
Negatives, 69-70

Nest research, 180
New Handbook of the Heavens, The
    (Bernhard), 285
Newark Museum (Newark, N.J.),
    146
Nimbostratus clouds, 310, 311, 318
Nixon, Richard M., 130
Non-adjustable cameras, 58
Non-flowering plants, 237-44
Non-stamp collections, 152
Northwest Federation of Mineralogi-
    cal Societies, 251
"Not worth a Continental," defined,
    141
Numismatist, The (magazine), 146

O

Oestreicher's (reproduction shop),
    164
Oil-based clay, 17
Oil-based printing ink, 36
Oilstones, 103-4
Old Print Center, 163
Old Print Shop, 163
Opacity of paper, 55
Orbiting Satellite Carrying Amateur
    Radio (OSCAR), 296
Organizations
    of aquarists, 188, 199
    archaeological, 283
    of astronomers, 293
    of autograph collectors, 127-28
    botanical, 227, 229
    entomological, 223
    for ham radio operators, 297,
        301, 302
    meteorological, 322
    mineralogical, 251
    numismatic, 137, 146
    ornithological, 177-80

philatelic, 149, 158-59
photographic, 71
for potters, 25
of print collectors, 163, 166
of sea shell collectors, 274
for weavers, 98, 99
for woodworkers, 121
Ornaments
fish tank, 186, 193
type face, 50
Ornithology, *see* Birds
Ornithology, Laboratory of (Cornell University), 180
OSCAR (Orbiting Satellite Carrying Amateur Radio), 296
Outer Space Photography for the Amateur (Paul), 292
Oval-head screws, 114

P

Pacher, Michael, 102
Packing
of fossil specimens, 209
of mineral specimens, 257
of shells, 272
Painting
of carved objects, 107-8
in serigraphy, 43
Paleontology, *see* Fossils
Panchromatic films, 62-63
Panicles of grass, 234
Paper
used in printing, 54-55
used for printmaking, 86
Paper bag puppets, 74
Papermaking, 26-34
equipment for, 28-30
with grass, 237
preparing pulp for, 30-31
process of, 31-33
simple, 26-27

Paper money, collecting U.S., 141-42
Paste waxing of carved objects, 107-8
Patterns
of coins, 141
fabric, 95-96
Pelecypods, characteristics of, 264-65
People-to-People Program, 152
Peter Pan, 90
Peterson, Roger Tory, 174
Petrushka (Russian puppet character), 73
Philadelphia mint, 136-37
Philately, *see* Stamp collections
Photography, 57-72
accessories needed in, 62
development and printing in, 68-70
films used in, 62-63
learning to use cameras, 63-68
outer space, 292
types of cameras used in, 57-61
Picas, defined, 51
Picking in weaving process, 99
Picasso, Pablo, 164
Pilot-type press, 47-49
Pinch pot method used in ceramics, 23
Plain weave, described, 95, 96
Plaiting with grass, 237
Planes, how to use, 117
Planers for locking up, 54
Plant fossils, 205
Plants, 226-49
botanical organizations, 227, 229
in fish tanks, 186-87, 193
grasses, 234-37
non-flowering, 237-44
trees, 228-30
wild flowers, 231-34
Plaster bats for ceramics, 19-20
Plastics used in incised printing, 40-41

"Plus X" (Eastman Kodak film), 63
Plywoods, 112
Poe, Edgar Allan, 131
Points, defined, 51
Portable power tools, 120
Portrait lenses, 62
Postage stamp collections, *see* Stamp
    collections
Postal stationery, 151
Postmarks, 151
Potato prints, 38
Potters Croft, 20
Potter's wheel, 20
Potter's Wheel Design Company, 20
Pottery, *see* Ceramics
Pough, Frederick H., 251
Power of telescopes, 287
Power tools, woodworking, 119-21
Praying mantis, observing, 219
Precipitation, gathering information
    on, 316-17
Preferred signatures, 131
Preservation of wild flowers, 233
Presses
    inking of, 55-56
    types of, 47-49
Pressure systems in meteorology, 320
Prices, *see* Costs
Print collections, 161-67
    choosing prints, 162-63
    display, storage and care of,
      165-66
    sources of, 163-64
Printmaking, 35-45
    equipment for, 35-36
    with ferns, 240
    with grass, 237
    incised, 40-41
    instruction in, 43
    with leaves, 230
    oil and water, 41-43
    relief, 36-40
Printing, 46-56

equipment for, 46-49
locking up in, 53-54
makeready in, 55-56
pulling a proof in, 52-53
stock of paper used in, 54-55
type faces in, 49-51
typesetting for, 51-52
Printing ink, 36
Prints, photographic, 69-70
Profile drafts, 96
Proofs, pulling of, 52-53
Props for puppet theaters, 80
Psychrometers, 313
Public services performed by ham
    radio operators, 30-34
Pulp
    preparing, 30-31
    storage containers for, 28
Punchinello (Italian puppet char-
    acter), 73
Puppets, 73-82
    acting with, 91
    plays for, 90
    types of, 74-82
    See also Marionettes

Q

QSL cards, 301-2
Quartz, 253
Quoins for locking up, 54

R

Radio, 295-304
    being on the air, 302-4
    equipment for, 297-98, 301-2
    obtaining a license for, 298-301
*Radio Amateur Licensing Handbook,
    The* (Kitchin), 301

Radio Amateur's License Manual, The (Relay League publication), 301
Radio Shack, 298
Rags, pulp from, 30
Range of birds, defined, 176
Rarity
  of autographs, 131-32
  of coins, 137-38
"Ready-warped" yarns, 97
Réalités (magazine), 162
Records of autograph collections, 132-33
Reflecting telescopes, 286, 289
Reflex cameras, 58, 60
Refracting telescopes, 286, 288
Regional stamp collections, 149
Reglets for locking up, 53
Regular issues of U.S. currency, 139
Regular notes, 142
Relative humidity as factor in preparation of weather forecasting, 317
Relief carving, 105
Relief prints, 36-40
Remington, Frederic, 162
Rental of prints, 164
Reproductions (art)
  display, storage and care of, 166
  sources of, 164
Research
  in astronomy, 293
  of nests, 180
  on trees, 230
Revolutionary War notes, 141
Richards, Paul C., 129
Riley, James Whitcomb, 126
Ripsaws, 116
Robbins, Chandler, 174
Rocks, types of, 252
Rocky Mountain Federation of Mineralogical Societies, 251
Rod puppets, 75-77

Roman type face, 49, 50
Roosevelt, Franklin D., 130
Round-head screws, 114
Routers, 120
"Rowing Alone" (Shaub), 37

S

Safety in woodworking, 119-21
Safety in the Woodshop (National Safety Council), 121
Sanders, 120
Sanding of carved objects, 107
Sans-serif type face, 49
Sawdust, 32
Saws
  band, 116-17
  power, 120
Scaphopoda, characteristics of, 269
Scavenger fishes, 188-89
Scenery for puppet theaters, 80, 82
Schaeffer, Jacob Christian, 30
Scholl, John, 102
Science, Museum of (Buffalo, N.Y.), 146
Scott's Standard Postage Stamp Catalogue, 155
Scouring rush horsetails, 240
Screens
  for papermaking, 28-29
  for serigraphy, 42
Screwdrivers, 119
Screws, 114
Sculpture with ceramics, 23
Sea shells, 261-76
  collecting, 270-71
  exchanging and buying, 273
  general characteristics of, 261
  identification of, 271-72
  storing, 273-74
  types of, 266-69

Sedimentary rocks, 252
Seed collections, 229
Seed mosaics, 233
Seedling collections, 229-30
Semi-automatic cameras, 58-59
Separate control bars for marionettes, 86
Serif type face, 49
Serigraphy (silk screen printing), 41-43
Sgraffito, defined, 23
Shadow puppets, 81-82
Shadow theaters, 82-83
Sharpening of woodcarving tools, 103-4
Shaub, Paul, 37
Shedding in weaving process, 99
Sheets of paper, making, 32
Shells, *see* Sea shells
Short-wave listeners (SWL), 297
Shutter speed, 67-68
Shutters of cameras, 58
Shuttles, weaving, 94
Sierra Club, 180
Signatures
    common, 130
    defined, 126
    preferred, 131
Sieving, defined, 220
Silk screen printing (serigraphy), 41-43
Single control bars for marionettes, 86
Sinkankas, John, 258
Sinnock, John R., 139
Six, James, 310
Six-string marionettes, 84, 86, 88
Six's type thermometer, 310
Sizes
    of autographs, 127
    of lumber, 113
    of nails, 114
    of type faces, 49-50

Sizing in papermaking, 31
Sky exploration, 290-92
Sky and Telescope (magazine), 287
Sky cover, as factor in weather forecasting, 318
Skylight filters, 62
Slab method used in ceramics, 22-23
Slime molds, 243
Slip clay, 19
Slipstones, 104
Slugs, defined, 50
Society for Philatelic Americans, 158-59
Softwoods, advantages of, 111-12
Solar observation, 292
Sound effects in puppetry, 90-91
Specialized collections, 168-69
Speed rating of films, 63
Spikes of grass, 234
Spore prints of mushrooms, 244
Squeegees for serigraphy, 43
Stage curtains for puppet theaters, 80-81
Stage lighting for puppet theaters, 81, 83
Stamp collections, 148-60
    catalogs for, 155-56
    sources of, 152-54
    storage of, 156-58
    types of, 149-52
Stampings, described, 37
Stanley Tools, 116
Star Gazers Exchange, 287
Starke, Tom, 27n
State issues of U.S. currency, 138-39
Stationary power tools, 120
Steichen, Edward, 79
Step-by-step Ceramics (Jofsted), 20
Stick puppets, 76
Stokes, William Lee, 208
Stoneware, 18
Stones, gem, 258-59

Storage
of autograph collections, 132-33
of coin collections, 145
of fossils, 212
of insect specimens, 222-23
of marionettes, 88
of minerals, 257-58
of negatives and photographic
prints, 90
of print collections, 165-66
of sea shells, 273-74
of stamp collections, 156-58
of woodcarving tools, 104
of woodworking tools, 115
Stoss, Veit, 102
Strainers for papermaking, 28
Stratocumulus clouds, 310, 311, 318
Stratus clouds, 310, 318
Subject selection in photography,
63-66
SWL (short-wave listeners), 297
Synthetic fibers used in weaving, 97

T

Table looms, 93
Tanks, fish, 184-87, 193, 197
Techniques
for collecting insect specimens,
220
of fossil hunting, 210-11
for incised printing, 41
for linoleum prints, 39
for serigraphy, 43
for making ceramics, 21-23
for sharpening woodcarving
tools, 104
for wood cuts, 40
woodcarving, 105-8
Telephoto lenses, 62
Telescopes, 286-90

Temperature
gathering information on,
310-13
of water, in fish tanks, 190, 192,
194
Terra cotta, 17-18, 40-41
Terrarium, building a, 232-33
Texas Federation of Mineralogical
Societies, 251
Thackeray, William M., 132
Theaters
marionette, 89-90
puppet, 77-81, 82-83
Thirds, rule of, in photography, 64
35-millimeter type cameras, 58, 60
Threading drafts, 96
Threading hooks, 95
Three-dimensional carving, 105-6
Three-string marionettes, 83-84, 86
Tokens in coin collections, 141
Tools
for fossil hunting, 208-9
for making ceramics, 20
for mineral searches, 254
papermaking, 28
woodcarving, 103-4
woodworking, 110-11, 115-21
Traditional theaters for puppets, 79
Transfer of designs, 36
Transfer prints, 36-37
Treadling drafts, 96
Trees, 228-30
"Tri X" (Eastman Kodak film), 63
Tripods, function of, 62
Tropical fishes, 191-92
True north, finding, 315-16
Tusche and glue technique, 43
Twill weave, 95-96
Two-string marionettes, 83
Tympans, installing, 55
Type cases, 50
Type faces, 49-51
Typesetting, 51-52

U

United States, radio licensing in, 300-1
United States Assay Office, 136, 137
United States currency, collecting, 138-42
United States stamps, sources of, 153
Universal Autograph Collector's Club, 127, 129

V

Value
    of autograph collections, 129-32
    of stamps, 154-55
Van Nostrand's Standard Catalog of Shells, 273
Vats, papermaking, 28
Vegetable fibers, pulp from, 30-31
Vertebrate fossils, 204-5
Vertical clouds, 310
Vertical lines in photography, 65

W

W1AW (Relay League radio station), 301
Walter R. Benjamin Autographs, 129
Warping boards for weaving, 95
Washington, George, 131
Water for fish tanks, 186, 190, 192-95
Water-based printing ink, 36
Watermarks for decorating paper, 33
Wave lengths assigned to ham radio operators, 296
Weather (Lehr), 306
Weather forecasting, 305-23
    instruction in, 306
    making observations for, 306-17
    organizations, 322
    preparing a forecast, 317-21
Weather map, 321
Weathercasting (C. & R. Laird), 300
Weatherwise (magazine), 322
Weaving, 92-101
    fabric patterns for, 95-96
    with grass, 237
    looms for, 93-94, 98-100
    projects for, 96-97
    supply sources for, 99-100
Webster, Daniel, 131
Wedging, 19, 21
Weight of paper, 55
Weinman, A. A., 139
Western Pine Association, 116
Whittling, *see* Woodcarving
Wide-angle lenses, 62
Wild flowers, 231-34
Wind direction
    as factor in preparing a weather forecast, 318-19
    gathering information on, 315-16
Winnie the Pooh (Milne), 90
Winter twig collections, 229
Wood cuts, 39-40
Wood for woodcarving, 105
Woodcarving, 102-8
    techniques for, 105-8
    tools for, 103-4
Woodcraft Supply Corp., 105
Woodworking, 109-22
    equipment for, 109-10, 113-14
    lumber used for, 111-13
    projects and plans for, 115-16
    tools for, 110-11, 115-21
Wooden box theaters for marionettes, 89-90
Wool yarns, 97
Word spaces, 50
Workbench, woodworking, 109-10

World Radio Laboratories, 298
Wren, Denise, 20
Wren, Rosemary, 20

Young Men's Christian Association
    (YMCA), 70, 93, 285

Y

Yarns, 100
Yeoman, Richard, 134

Z

Zim, Herbert, 174
Zorach, William, 102

Alvin Schwartz has written many books on many subjects for families and for young people. He has written on games and folklore, on crafts, travel and nature, on fatherhood, on museums, universities and labor unions, and on urban problems, politics and public opinion.

Mr. Schwartz has been writing books for a decade. For many years he has also taught part-time at Rutgers University. Earlier he was a newspaper reporter. He holds an M.S. degree in journalism from Northwestern University and an A.B. degree in the social sciences from Colby College.

He lives in Princeton, New Jersey, with his wife Barbara, who illustrated this book, their four children, and two cats.